JESSIE KRESA is ODB
One Dirty B*@#!

**JESSIE KRESA
& KENNY CASANOVA**

PUBLISHING INFO:

Authors – Jessie Kresa & Kenny Casanova
Editor – Jamie Hemmings
Publishing – WOHW Publishers
Cover Design – Scott McGregor
Cover Photo – Mary-Kate Anthony

WARNING:

© All rights reserved. No part of this book may be reproduced or transmitted in any form or by any means whatsoever without express written permission from the author, except in the case of brief quotations embodied in critical articles and reviews. Please refer all pertinent questions to the author. Failure to do so could result in a head injury from a flask.

All people in this publication were very important people in ODB's life at one time or another. Therefore, we have tried to best recreate events, locations and conversations from ODB's memories of them, but in some cases, minor details have changed due to the effects of many years of steel chair shots to the head. In order to maintain anonymity, ODB has also changed the names of a few individuals, places, identifying characteristics, and details - such as physical properties, occupations and locations. Although the authors have made every effort to ensure that the information in this book was correct at press time, the authors and/or publishers do not assume and hereby disclaim any liability to any party for any loss, damage, or disruption caused by errors or omissions, whether such errors or omissions result from negligence, accident, or any other cause.

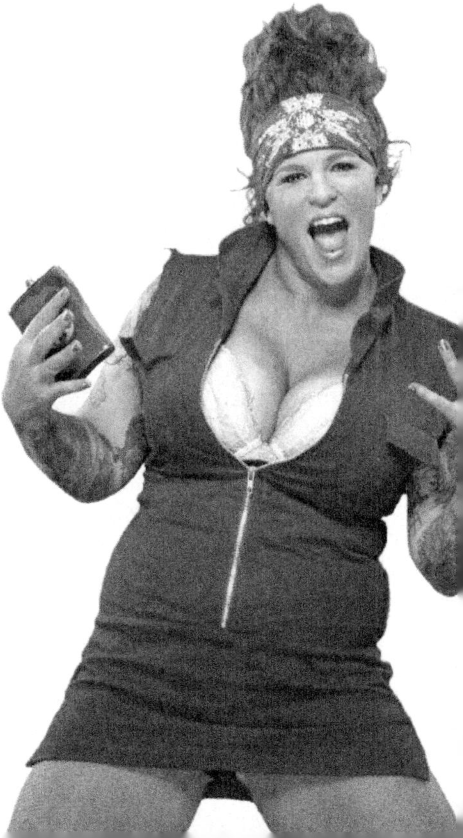

Printed in the USA
ISBN: 978-1-941356-16-6

Jessie Kresa is... ODB: One Dirty Bitch!
Copyright © 2022 by Walking on Hot Waffles Publishers
in conjunction with Kenny Casanova & WOHW.com

TABLE OF CONTENTS

LETTER FROM A LEGEND	2
CHAPTER ZERO	3
CHAPTER 1 – Kid Stuff	10
CHAPTER 2 – College	48
CHAPTER 3 – Early Wrestling Days	67
CHAPTER 4 – TNA Wrestling in 2002	90
CHAPTER 5 – Ohio Valley	134
CHAPTER 6 – TNA Contract	152
CHAPTER 7 – Knockout Champion	168
CHAPTER 8 – Hogan & Bischoff's Impact	202
CHAPTER 9 – Work Husband	219
CHAPTER 10 – Fishing For a Future	226
CHAPTER 11 – Boy Bands & Family Recipes	235
CHAPTER 12 – One Dirty Bartender	243
CHAPTER 13 – The Food Truck	255
CHAPTER 14 – The Sausage Party	263
CHAPTER 15 – Burnt Ends	276
FINAL NOTE TO FANS	295
CREDITS	297

LETTER FROM A LEGEND

Hey Kenny, how are things going?

The other day, ODB was asking me about my book writing endeavors and about the possibility of doing a book project, and I thought you might be a good guy for her to talk to. I told her we worked together on the coloring book (Cactus Jack & The Beanstalk), and the Vader and Kamala stories and that you did a great job on all of them. I also think you could do a great job with her book project if you wanted to take it on. I really believe she has a very interesting story to tell.

Of all the wrestlers I have met, she is one with a life well-lived without making to the big one. Al Snow used to always tell me that whenever he was asked which women were ready for the WWE roster when they were looking to bring in new female talent, he would always say "ODB" without hesitation. However, every time they would tell him that she was "not what WWE was currently looking for." She didn't give up though. She kept doing her own thing and made quite a career for herself despite all that.

I think she really could have been great in WWE if they had just given her a chance. I do think, however, that if you give her a chance, it could be a great read.

Thanks and let me know what you think!
Mick Foley

>>> What do I think?

How does one say "no" to The Hardcore Legend? ~ Kenny

CHAPTER ZERO

It was New Year's Eve. It had already been two hours, but the ride wasn't over yet for what was to be one of my biggest appearances to date.

Once I had heard the news on the promotion's plans for me, it didn't matter how far, how long, or what kind of travel conditions I was going to have to deal with. It didn't matter to me if the road to get there was the shits. I was going to weather the storm to get there no matter what.

Drive. Drive. DRIVE!

I had already held the Total Nonstop Action Wrestling (TNA) Knockout title twice before what was now going to be my third time as "the female face of the company." Even though it is all a work, ask any wrestler what a belt means and they will say the same thing: it means everything. It really does mean something to a wrestler to get that championship title strapped around your waist. It means the company believes in you and the company is banking on you.

It means you've finally won the race.

Being the TNA Knockout champion for a third time meant there was no fluke, there was no mistake about it. For me, the third time was going to be the absolute charm, for sure. Holding the gold three times was going to put all eyes on me more than ever before, and I knew it. This meant more opportunities. More offers elsewhere. More money.

There was still another hour left to get there first on that last pay-per-view (PPV) of the year, so my drive continued.

Drive!

The trip to get there was going fine at first for what I had hoped would just be an easy night, or as they say in pro wrestling, "just another day at the office." I was in full "keep on trucking" mode with my cruise control on. I could see the light at the end of the tunnel as they say. I even daydreamed. I pictured the gold again back in my hands, and the onlooking crowd of thousands cheering me on, and then all of a sudden... there was a massive bump.

What in the hell was that?

I stopped autopilot.

Hitting something that hard should have turned on at least a proverbial warning light for me if not a real one, but it didn't. I ignored it.

Yes, something seemed definitely off, but I wasn't going to let it bother me. I never let stuff get to me. Once you start to worry, it slows you down and sometimes stops you altogether from achieving what you want to do. I always drove hard, and worried about stuff later. Therefore, I ignored that stiff bump and kept on going.

I was determined to reach the finish line.

Over the years, I must confess, it was always tough for me to ever take a second to slow down. I was different.

The ODB (One Dirty Bitch) character I had created for myself had a reputation for being tough. ODB didn't show up to a show in a fancy, freshly-washed red corvette. She was more the dented beat-up Jeep-type.

ODB didn't worry about her hair being out of place. She didn't care about a broken nail, or wasn't going to let something lame like smudged makeup slow her down.

ODB was different than the others.

She was a tough cookie in a cookie cutter world.

I can't tell you how many times I pushed harder than I really wanted to because I had to live up to the reputation I was trying to build, and not because that was what I really wanted to do. I had created a measuring stick for myself that was a mile high. However, in looking back at it today, I would do it all over again. I wouldn't change a thing.

Therefore, after hitting that loud bump, it didn't matter to me if I had totally lost a wheel or not, I was going to make it to my destination. I was going to make it crawling on all fours or driving on a rim if I had to.

I wasn't concerned with being the picture-perfect Mercedes or the Corvette in order to get where I needed to go. I was more like the mail truck with neither rain, nor sleet, nor snow stopping me to deliver.

No matter what, I knew I wasn't going to let one horrible bump and the possibility of a broken headlight let me or the TNA fans down.

So, of course, I didn't stop. That wasn't the ODB way.

As I continued on my journey to become a three-time champion in the company that made me who I am today, I

ignored the fact that I was riding with a slight body tilt and the probability that my alignment was now way off.
    Something didn't feel right, that was for sure. And what I didn't know at the time was that something actually was not right.
    Houston, we have a problem.
    I had already hit all kinds of bumps that night, and at some point later on, I would learn that I had developed a slow leak.
    I was losing air.
    For a fleeting moment, I think that the horrible thought of the leak had entered my mind and that the worst might have happened after I hit that hard bump. My drive was off. I felt like my balance was off or like I was moving along lopsided, but as quickly as that distraction popped into my head, I popped it out. I just rolled down my mental window and tossed that shit to the side of the road.
    I had to.
    The show must go on. I will worry about problems later.
    So, I just kept on going.
    As a wrestler, we all learn that we will have moments when you have to pull out all the stops at all costs. You don't worry about the outcome. You don't look for potential damage. You don't see the future. You don't worry about anything. You live for the now. You live in the moment.
    I was in one of those moments. I was on my way to win the gold with blinders on. There would be no stops along the way. There would be no detours. It was going to happen.
    There was still a good distance to go, and the road to get there was a tough one. I continued to hit every bump hard. The idea of doing any real harm was not even a possibility. My speedometer was set on full speed. I hit the gas hard.
    The end was near, so I remained focused. My time was finally coming.
    I had to keep on pushing, and push I did towards what for me was uncharted waters. I pushed it so hard that, eventually, there was no question about it. Something was wrong.
    Bump… Bump… BUMP!

Ouch. That last hit was hard. I had yet another red flag that something under the hood wasn't right, but I would worry about that later on down the road.

My attitude: something wasn't right, but the hell if I cared.

The second hard jolt wasn't going to stop me any more than the first one I felt that night, so of course, I ignored it just like the last one.

I was determined. Peddle to the metal.

My directions for *New Year's Knockout Eve* was to give the fans an awesome experience that they would not forget for our last event of the year...and that was just what I was going to do. I was moving at 100 and nothing was going to slow me down from making that happen.

At the show, everything was "rush-rush-rush" like it always was. For those of you who don't know, wrestling is always "hurry up and wait" like that. That tone builds the whole time you are on the road until the moment you walk into the building. Then you are rushing to get ready for your match, even if you are the last act of the night. It doesn't matter. "Hurry up and wait" is how things work everywhere in this crazy business. That is why I didn't realize the leak at the time I thought it happened, nor did I think to look for it after the show was over to be safe.

I was a triple busy camper that night to say the least. I won a tournament where I wrestled three times and, in three days, I was set to become a three-time champion.

I was psyched, but there was no time to celebrate that night after my third match. When I walked back into the dressing room, my girls were speaking to me, but I barely heard them. Wrestlers came up to me and congratulated me. Even though I hadn't officially won the title yet, but that night set things up for my new run. I thanked all of my well-wishers but I was quickly being swept up for interviews and an obligatory after party appearance.

It all happened so fast, but when it was all said and done, I made my way to my hotel room and crashed hard. I was out like a light. I finally went to sleep that night after quite a journey, and I slept like a soon-to-be three-time champion.

It wasn't until the next morning that I would finally have a moment to breathe. I felt like I had been hit by a truck.

CHAPTER ZERO

I woke up.
I was stiff.
My arms were sore.
My shoulders popped and cracked as I sat up on the cheap bed. I couldn't tell what was creaking more, my body or the cheap mattress.
I yawned and stretched.
I need coffee.
I took a moment to slow down and finally give myself some much needed "me-time" before rushing off to the next town as the next TNA Knockout Champion.
I looked around the room. Clothes were thrown around much like my body had been the night before. I tilted my neck and heard another slight crack.
Off to the corner, I saw an empty end table where I would soon lay my championship belt. That made everything worth it.
I pictured it sitting there, just as it actually had in the past. That familiar image gave me chills.
I reached down and held up the invisible title to an audience of no one and smiled. I looked at it like a little kid again, feeling accomplished, before setting the belt I didn't have yet back down on the table.
"I gotta take a piss," I said to the invisible fans.
I headed to the bathroom.
I turned the hot water on in the shower all the way. "Shaaahhh..." The sound of the water emulated the reaction I was going to get from all of my adoring fans only a few days from then after winning the title on *TNA Impact!*
As I envisioned what the pop would sound like, I stretched my arms again and heard my own bones pop.
I took off my shirt to get ready to soak off sleep for the new day and turned to the mirror to see what a three-time champion actually would look like.
When I looked back at my own reflection, I made eye contact to start. Then like a lot of guys I meet, my eyes shifted elsewhere down to my trademark double D's. Only this time when that happened and it was me doing the looking, I realized that something was wrong.
That is when I saw the damage that I had done.
Living in the moment truly had a price.

Yes, I essentially had the gold, but in achieving that soon-to-come accolade (and the championship strap that went along with it) something happened.

I looked down and learned that I had been driving hard all night on a different kind of flat tire.

I put my hand under my deflated boob. There was absolutely nothing in the casing at all.

I squeezed it. It was an empty bag.

"Oh boy," I said looking at a double D and an A- at best.

That shit looked malnourished.

Yes, you read that right. The leak was on my body not in my car! Some of you naturally are going to have to reread that whole last section, I bet! Gotcha! Go on, go back and read through it, I can wait!

(Waiting…)

It's funny though. I didn't freak out. I didn't lose my shit. ODB couldn't do any of that, after all.

Getting a "flat tire" didn't matter. Nothing mattered then. The fact of the matter was, I had made it to the end. Some would argue that I had made it further than most women ever would in this sport – and I was proud.

I beat three names on television, and I was ready for my big championship match in three days. At the first live show of 2010, I would work the main event, and there, there I would become a three-time champion!

However, the reality on January 1st was that I didn't know what condition I was going to be in for the first show on the new calendar year.

I only have three days to fix the flat?

The real damage I ignored last night was staring me right back in the face.

The spotlight was on me, but I had a headlight out.

Now, how in the hell am I going to wrestle a match on live TV with wrestling fans who criticize your every move – with only one tit?

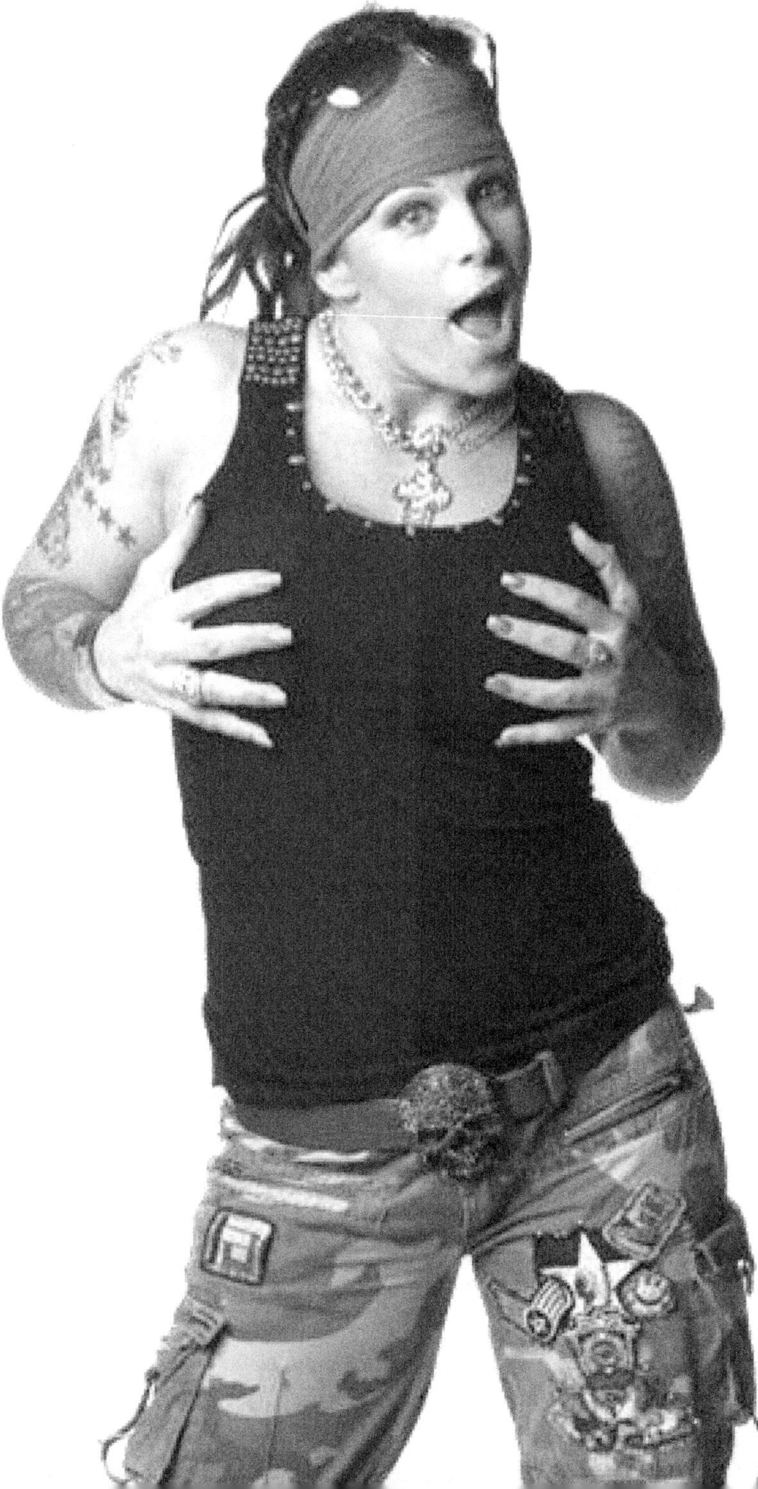

CHAPTER 1 - KID STUFF

My parents have a weird history. They don't have a funny story of a blind date or meet up like from an online dating website or something. Their first date didn't happen at a coffee shop. It didn't include a sensual candle-lit dinner with all the trimmings. They didn't go somewhere nice where they could chat and talk about how they liked long walks on the beach. My parent's first experience together was at a show.

It wasn't the movies, though, either. They sat down in a packed arena with a few thousand screaming, bloodthirsty fans at an American Wrestling Association (AWA) television taping event.

Romantic, huh? I mean, what could really be more romantic than watching Dick the Bruiser, anyhow?

Fast forward through the movies, and the dinners, and all the good stuff. Some years after an impressive courtship's first night of googly eyes and gorilla press slams, a baby was born in Maple Grove, Minnesota.

One Dirty Baby, to be exact.

I come from a tight-knit family that very much believed "a family that plays together stays together."

My mom and dad are still married today, and they still live in the very same house I was raised in. We are all still very close. We did everything together back then and still do, including my brother who is three years older than me.

I guess you could say we were traditional and had family values. However, I wouldn't say that back then we looked like one of those '50s families like you would see on *Leave it to Beaver*. My earliest memories looked more like The Griswolds.

The family ideal was always there. We were always going on Chevy Chase-like vacation trips whenever we could. We would pack up in our Ram Charger with sleeping bags and beef jerky, grab grandma, and just go rough it in the real world.

Yes, we were CAMPERS.

CHAPTER 1 – Kid Stuff

Every year, we would make our 26-hour Mecca, our religious journey, to the Shangri-La for all campers. We would hit the road and head out to Camp Fort Wilderness in Disney World.

The hours were long and, in hindsight, trained me to be a wrestler. We played all kinds of road trip games to pass the time. We would play a strange version of *Name That Tune* using the radio. We would play I Spy. We came up with all kinds of contests, too. My brother, in fact, would even go on to become the undisputed champion of "the silent but deadly fart game" that he alone created, but nobody wanted to win that game. (Nobody wanted to play it either, besides him.) I still have memories of trying to unroll the window before my face turned green.

We would find attractions along the way. One year we stopped in Nashville and stayed at the Grand Ole Opry. That was when I saw my very first concert: *The Oak Ridge Boys, front row baby!*

When we finally got to our final destination after more hours of traveling than any of us wanted, we would get out of the vehicle. We would stretch our stiff legs, then prepare ourselves for the stiff backs we would endure over the next two weeks, as we set up our tents. Our initial days at Camp Fort Wilderness might have been stiff, but it was stiff heaven.

Eventually, we would switch to "glamping" every year. For those of you unfamiliar with the term, "glamping" means riding in a hot-air balloon, climbing a mountain, or gallivanting through the desert, all while having a glamorous campsite as your refuge at the end of the day.

But our original campground destination, was 100 acres of nothing but trees, RVs, porta-potties, and rustic cabins. There was a beach. There were hiking trails. There were mud pits and *Tarzan* swings.

There was a big lodge with arcade games and a canteen snack bar where we would buy popsicles. Since it was a Disney establishment, sometimes furry mascot characters like Chip and Dale would come out to greet the campers and maybe play ping-pong with you. We would go do that while my parents would escape, and hit up Davy Crockett's Tavern for a pitcher of beer.

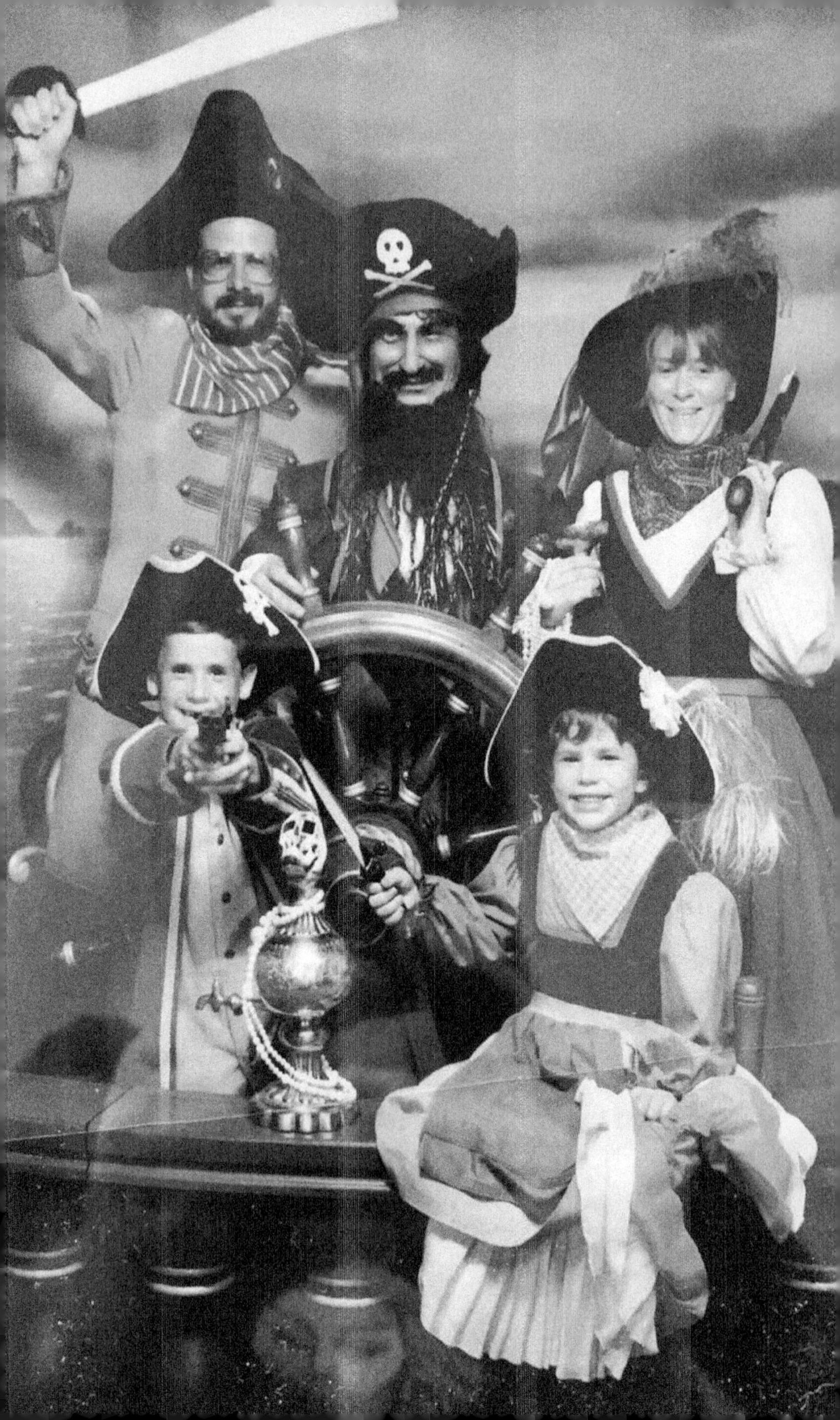

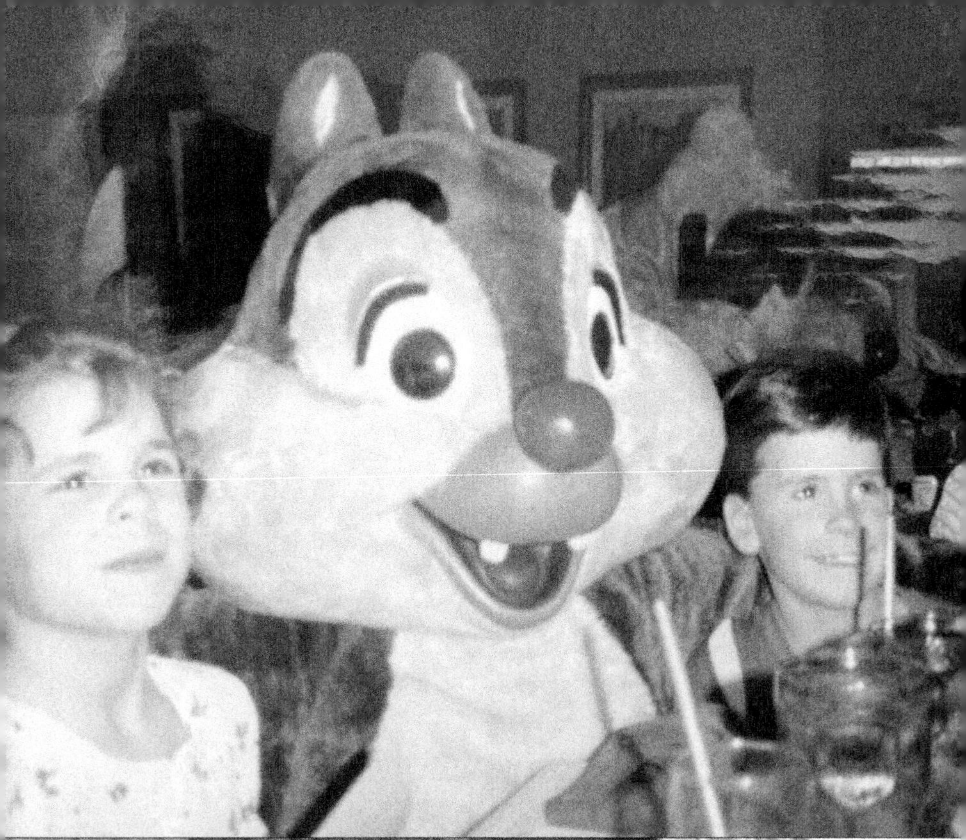

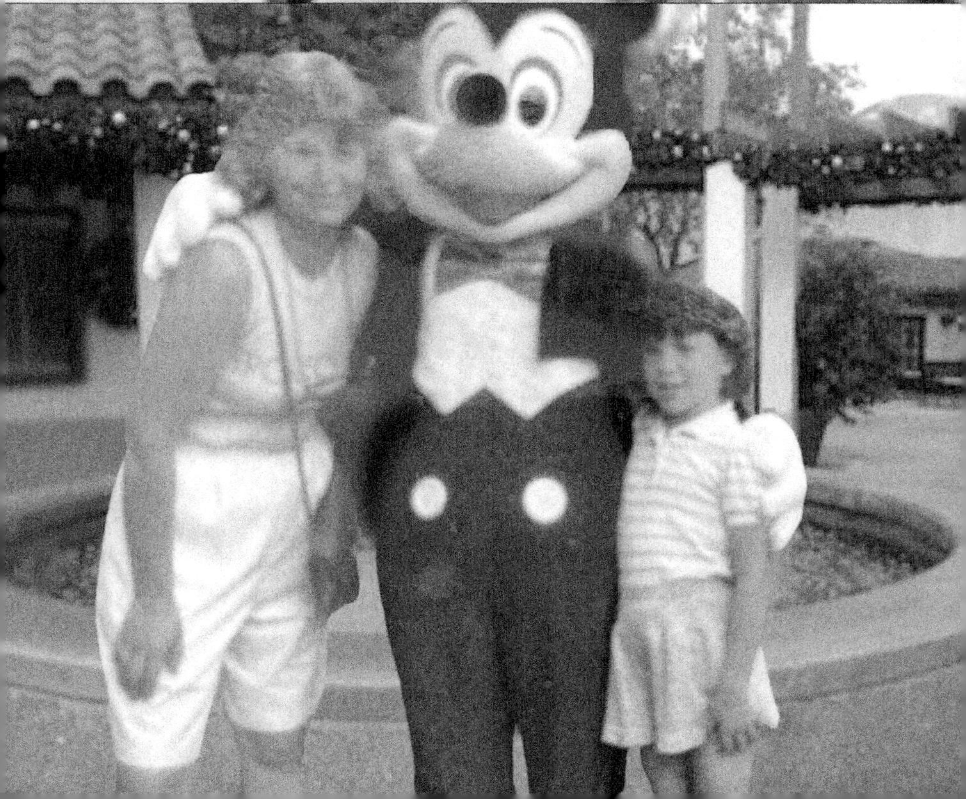

BLUE STAR
MEMORIAL HIGHWAY
A tribute to the Armed Forces
that have defended the
United States of America

CHAPTER 1 – Kid Stuff

Inhale. It's funny how a smell can take you back.
I can still smell the burnt wood of a campfire and the salty smell of hotdogs. There were cookouts every day and orange flickers every evening under the starry sky. There were movie nights lying on beach blankets on the dewy grass, and sing-a-long hikes in the woods.

The fun never stopped there while we were at the camp, and we didn't let it stop either after we left.

During the year, my parents tried their hardest to recreate the Camp Wilderness life at home. We would set up the tent and have sleepovers in the backyard, while my parents would have friends over to the garage to drink. Their friends' kids would run out back and we would have a good old time. We would make s'mores with our residential campfires, play horseshoes, or do anything to fulfill our love of being outside, which I inherited from my family.

In fact, as kids, we never outgrew it. We still get together and do two Disney World trips a year as a family with our parents all these years later! I still have "the call of the wild" in me because of our camping gene. Even today, I still sometimes feel a sudden urge to walk in the woods, or ride on a golf cart and drink a six-pack whenever I see that the terrain allows.

When my family wasn't playing, we were working. You need to work so you can pay to play later. Free play didn't exist, because even roughing it costs money. Does that make sense? Because of this, that is all I knew. I grew up always busy. Like the rest of my family, I was always "working for the weekend," as Loverboy used to say.

My dad worked for the railroad and by watching him, I learned a lot about the importance of having a great work ethic. When you were doing your job, you had to give it your all because you never knew if that job and that lifestyle would go away. When my dad lost his job, he didn't just allow us to collect unemployment or welfare or something. He went and took all these random jobs and worked doing little gigs at airlines. Sitting on your ass was not an option for him, or the rest of us either.

My mom worked in whatever hospitality job she could find. She worked in grocery stores and restaurants. Work ethic was everything to them and became everything to me.

My parents taught me at a young age that whatever life throws at you, you have to be ready. You never cry victim. You never say "poor me." You figure out a way to fix the situation you are in because there is always a way to fix it.

As a side note, one fortunate thing for us as a "glamping" family was that my dad eventually found a job for Northwest Airlines. That meant no more driving hours and hours to rough it at "The Happiest Place on Earth." We all got to fly there for free!

HOME

We worked hard and it paid off. We lived in a nice suburban home that my parents built from the ground up. Our house was one of the original ones in that establishment. We lived somewhat comfortably, middle-class, as they say.

My parents trusted the neighborhood, and we didn't really have a curfew. We didn't have to worry about stuff like that back then. We didn't think about Michael Myers coming to hack us up, or Peter the Pedophile coming to throw us in his white van and haul us away. We just rode our bikes everywhere, and with NO HELMETS. This was before any of the fucked-up concerns we see on the news today.

Swoosh!!!

A lawn dart flew up in the air and came down deep into the soil on our front lawn.

Nobody died.

My parents threw big parties almost every weekend. A lot of their friends would come over, bring food, and get drunk. There was a lot of drinking and enjoying each other. My grandma would come over, too, and she was not a voice of reason. She could party with the best of them! She would drink beer – a lot of beer and act like she was at Miami Spring Break.

These parties weren't exclusively for adults, however. Kids would come too and we all had our own area.

I had a lot of childhood friends around the hood, and many of them are ones I still keep in touch with still to this very day. At these parties, I hung around with the homies.

There were three girls in particular next door that I played with named the Strombergs: Tracy, Stephanie, and Valerie. The sisters were about the same age range as me, so I hung out with all of them for the most part, some more than others at different times. See, I would be friends with one and switch with others depending on who was being cool and who was being a bitch.

I was kind of a tomboy, could you guess?

In the summer, we played stuff that involved riding our bikes like big elaborate Hollywood chase scenes. We were cops and robbers a lot, or sometimes treasure hunters escaping from monsters. We built forts in the woods a lot.

Winters were cool, literally. I wasn't into ice fishing, but we always found a reason to stay right outside, bundled up. I remember building ice forts and loving them so much, I would practically move into them for the season. I would make a snow bed and just chill there and read books.

SATURDAY MORNINGS

As a kid, I rolled out of bed at the break of dawn. I stepped out of the room carefully with the precision of a surgeon, walking barefoot on the carpet trying to avoid any creaks in the floor.

I needed to claim my rightful spot in front of the old television set in the living room.

I threw my favorite throw pillow off the couch and onto the floor. Then, I ran to the kitchen for fuel.

We ate a lot of meatloaf and goulash as kids, as well as anything that my parents could quickly whip up from the Crock-Pot. One of those was a tater tot hot dish that was absolutely my favorite. When that was in the fridge, I might have to have a little sample. After that, I would push the leftovers off to the side and reach for the milk.

Mmmm.
Breakfast of champions.
Yummy.

The Kresa household did a lot of cereal. I lived off of Cap'n Crunch Berries and Fruity Pebbles in the bowl, as well as Life cereal if I was trying to be healthy.

18   Jessie Kresa is... ODB: One Dirty Bitch!

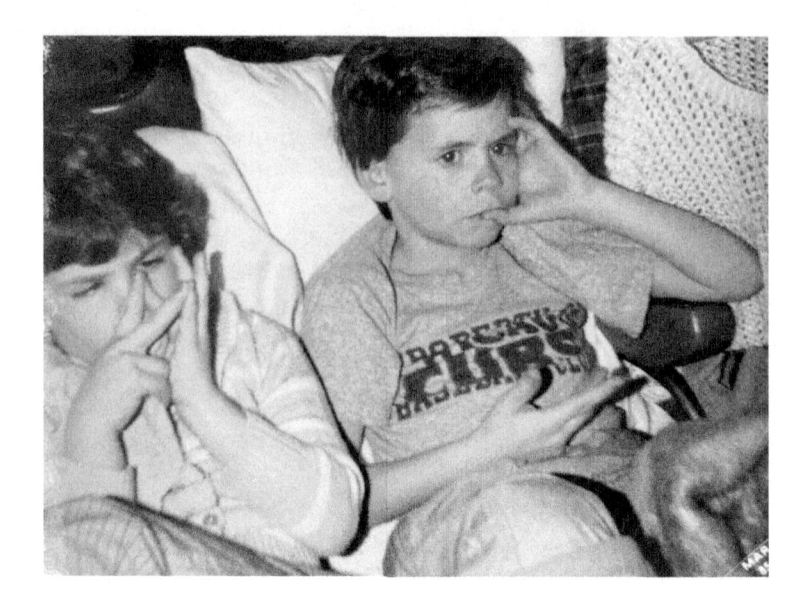

Eating my cereal on weekends was part of the routine. I would just sit there and veg out watching my cartoons. I was a big *Woody Woodpecker* fan, as well as a mark for all the Hanna-Barbera stuff you would see on a Saturday morning. That meant *Scooby Doo, Captain Caveman, The Blue Falcon,* and *Jabber Jaw.*

One fateful Saturday morning full of cartoons, I saw a commercial that blew my mind.

Oh my God. They are going to meet?!

They were advertising this one big crossover where *The Jetsons* went back in time to meet *The Flintstones*. The Jetsons were supposed to be going on a 25th-century vacation to relax in the future, but at the last second, Astro flipped a switch and they ended up in the past. That blew my mind because it was awesome! This would be like the equivalent of a World Championship Wrestling (WCW) meets the WWF super card back then.

Speaking of wrestling and Saturday mornings, yes, they were also synonymous. I came from a wrestling town, so yes, wrestling was always on the TV in our house.

The prime of our wrestling fandom was in the mid-'80s, meaning I had the Ultimate Warrior, Jake the Snake, and Rowdy Roddy Piper gracing my screen after the cartoons went off the air.

Being a weirdo at heart, my love of Hulkamania eventually dwindled. I was a huge fan at a young age, don't get me wrong, but that soon transformed. Eventually, I learned to hate the good guys and cheer for the villains.

I think this stemmed from the fact that I got sick of the same "Superman" Hulk Hogan persona they were feeding us for a number of years, as many diehards did in those days. WWF was pushing him down our throats and many fans eventually wanted something else. (Sorry, Hulkster!) Therefore, in protest, I became anti-Hogan for a time and anyone who seemed to align with him.

So I routed for the bad guys. So what?

I guess I am just a heel at heart!

My brother and I had the big rubber LJN action figures of most of our favorite wrestlers. We would make them fight each other during the show. The Hulkster doll had the most paint missing from him because he took the hardest poundings every Saturday morning.

Come Sunday nights, if there was a PPV, we would watch those too!

We would get pizza and watch the TV in the basement with a bunch of our friends. We would start off with the action figures, but then stuff would get more amped up as the night went on. Eventually, my brother would attack me and try to do moves on me. I was tough though. I would give it right back to him – kicking and biting, and head-butting him in the nose. Once the ice had been broken though, his friends would see the violence and want in on the brutality. Then, they would try to beat me up. As tough as I was, it was very difficult to take on a handful of boys a few years older than me.

Eventually, my dad would hear all the screaming and do a run in.

"What the hell is going on down here?" he would say, running down the stairs. He would take one look and see me in the figure-four leglock, or some bullshit one of my brother's friends saw on TV. However, unlike a normal parent, he would laugh and join in on the carnage.

The good part was he always sided with me.

"Now you boys are going to get it!"

He would jump into the pile of kids looking like Andre the Giant in a battle royal. They would loosen their focus on me and immediately jump to the new big threat. But nine times out of ten, their advances were of no use. My dad would hold his hand high in the air before making an example of one of the kids.

"No! It's the iron claw," my brother would yell, as my dad grabbed one of his friends by the stomach and squeezed him like Baron von Raschke.

"Uggghhh!" Billy would scream, half selling the move, and half screaming in actual pain.

Outside, we played kickball and whiffle ball a lot. Whiffle-mania got so epic that eventually, my dad built a ball diamond out back to hold tournaments. I would be lying, however, if I were to say that wrestling matches didn't also

OF MIGHT
SUMMERSLAM
VENICE BEACH
CALIFORNIA
SUPERSTARS
FRI., DEC

often break out on the green in the middle of a game. I guess you could call that cross training, no?

One time, I remember someone sliding into second base, and one of their legs was in the air. Being the opportunist that I was, I slapped the figure-four on them as quickly as possible. Everyone laughed except the player taking the move. They instead sold it like Ricky Morton, because, yes, that shit really did hurt!

Sometimes we would actually go to the Met Center to see the wrestling shows live. We were smart. We would get the cheap nosebleed seats and watch the audience on the floor. We would observe the sea of humanity until we identified a spot where nobody seemed to be sitting before making our plan. Then, when nobody was looking, we would strike. Maybe during an entrance of a big name, or at the end of the match when people were distracted, we would run down to the lower level and claim the more expensive, more illustrious, golden ringside seats as our own.

Once we were settled down there by the ring, it didn't matter if someone showed up late. We would just play musical chairs with the empty spots until we had great seats that were also unclaimed. It always worked out for us.

I liked when we would find some over near the tunnel to the locker room.

During the match, I would often be distracted by what was going on behind me rather than the spotlight in front of us. I would turn around constantly, trying to catch a glimpse of anyone standing by the curtain backstage. Whenever I did, I would hold up my "Hulk Sucks!!!" sign to let them know what I thought about their front man.

One time while watching the back, I saw one of my favorites, "Ravishing" Rick Rude come out and sit in a chair off by himself. He was watching the show from the back, I guess, but figured nobody would see him if he came out for a little better view. He sat there all incognito with a sweatshirt on with the hood pulled up over his head. He watched a few matches, I think, and nobody was really the wiser. Nobody, except for me, that is.

I tried throughout those matches to get his attention, and it finally worked. When the Ravishing one saw me, he laughed. He acknowledged my sign with a nod that he agreed, then he even gave me the thumbs up. I don't know if he was supposed to do that or not, but he became my absolute favorite after that.

That memory never left me, and it was cool that he took the time to put a little girl over who wasn't a cookie-cutter fan like the rest of them.

The WWF was not the only show in town. Fortunately for me, my dad grew up with a lot of the Minnesota boys as a kid. From time to time, he would meet up with them before shows when the AWA was over at the armory.

One of my dad's good friends was an AWA referee. Around 1988, I remember the ref sneaking us in to meet Jumpin' Jim Brunzell and Curt Hennig before the big show. On that same show, the referee snuck backstage to the other side of the dressing rooms where the heels were. We weren't in there for long, but we did get to meet Barry Darsow (see right). It was cool because he put me over like Rick Rude did. We both had mullets, and we were both sporting practically the same pair of loud Zubaz. Remember those ugly things? They were like MC Hammer pants before MC Hammer. "You've got great taste in fashion, kid!" Darsow said.

FASHION

I liked to be a slob. Even for special events, you were lucky to get me in a ripped T-shirt and dirty jeans.

I don't know how many times I fought trying to look lady-like for one of my birthday parties. I always politely declined to do so, and *sometimes as loudly as I could*. Because of my passionate objection to the idea of wearing a dress, my parents never really pushed me to do so, and usually just skirted the issue.

I don't know how old I was when I decided to finally let my mother play dress-up with me for my birthday. I think come 10 years old though, or so, I decided to give in and wear my first dress at that year's obligatory birthday party.

I didn't like the whole girly thing. I watched wrestling on TV. I had *A-Team* action figures. I rode everywhere on my bike. I used to flip over rocks in the woods and go bug hunting with my brother. So, when my parents wanted me to dress up and look nice for a big gathering like my birthday party was supposed to be, it just wasn't me.

At this particular event, however, my mom begged me to wear a dress, so I did.

I waited in the house for my dress debut. I looked out of the blinds in the house and watched as all kinds of friends and family showed up and circled around to the backyard.

My father lined up a few folding tables and had a nice blue canopy set up where the guests could lay out their presents. My extended family from far away even showed up with tons of boxes, all for me!

I watched, one by one, as they all brought their offerings to me placing giant brightly wrapped gifts on the table. I felt like baby Jesus about to be presented with frankincense and myrrh from the three wise men, but there was nothing I could do about it. Despite my curiosity, I fought my impulses and stayed in the house.

I was a kid and therefore I was super excited. I wondered what was in each one of those boxes with my name on it, but at the same time, I stayed put. I was too embarrassed to walk out and be seen wearing a dress. It felt like I was wearing a clown costume or something.

This just isn't me.

Finally, my mother pushed me out of the nest. As I walked down the bluestone to where everyone was waiting, it felt like you could hear a pin drop. All of the people were shocked to see me all made up.

Hell, I was shocked, too.

"Oh my God, Jess," one said. "You look beautiful."

"Wow, you polish up nicely."

They all commented on how nice I looked, and I will admit, the attention did boost my ego a little.

For this birthday, my dad pulled out all the punches. He wanted me to love it, and he wanted the guests to have a night they wouldn't forget. Apparently, he looked far and wide for the finest quality entertainment to appease the masses on my special day.

He booked a girl in a *Strawberry Shortcake* costume who walked around the party. She was kind of acting as a clown would do, but without the comedy. She let her costume get her over and posed for pictures. She talked to us and sprayed us all with strawberry perfume. It was really something.

We ate some food and had a good old time before the main event. Then, it was on.

Yay! Present time!

I opened some gifts up like a savage, throwing gift-wrap this way and that. My friends and family knew me, and therefore I got some cool things. I got LEGOS. I got *He-Man* action figures and a number of other things that you wouldn't normally think of when buying presents for a 10-year-old girl.

If you were to look around at the first 10 boxes or so that I opened, one would think the accumulated pile of presents must have been for a boy.

I, of course, loved it all.

However, one particular gift I got that day for my birthday stuck out as extremely special. As I tore open the paper and ripped opened the box, behold, there was an invaluable treasure sitting before me.

I held it close to my heart.

"Yes! Oh yes!"

"What did you get sweetheart?" my mom asked as I tossed the packaging over my shoulder.

I held up a bright green shirt with a familiar face on it to the circle of faces around me.

Before anyone could see what it was, I started to disrobe in front of the whole party. All bets were off.

"Jess?"

My grandmother laughed hard, as I pulled off a lace over shirt. I threw that shit right into the bushes.

"What are you doing?" they laughed.

"What do you have there?" my mother said, not scolding me, realizing how happy I was with my gift.

"Look," I said, holding the shirt up again. "It's Mr.T!"
That's right. Mr. effing T in the house!
My dad laughed, "Mr.T?!"
"Yes, it's not funny. One day I am going to marry him!" I declared. Someone got me a sweet-ass Mr.T t-shirt that was as wonderful as it was fantastic. I couldn't put that sucker on fast enough. To me, that was a fashion game changer. Adding that to my wardrobe felt like the best thing in the whole world.

In all of 10 seconds, I was modeling that life-changing apparel like I was a princess on a red carpet.

I must say, the story that I was telling with my ensemble was one of boldness and originality. The brutal clash of Mr.T's scary mug and the pretty dress that stuck out underneath it was riveting.

It was a fashion statement. I don't know what the statement actually was, but it must have been one for somebody, at least somewhere.

I bowed and curtsied. My guests laughed and applauded. I finally felt like *Cinderella* at the ball.

What a novel gift!

After my special day, I wore the hell out of that shirt, too. It was perfect for everything. It was perfect for playing. It was perfect for school. It was perfect for church. (Hell yeah!)

It was also great for bike riding. My bike was a pink Huffy with a banana seat and a circus horn. It was very little girly-looking, and that was something that often bothered me. But once I broke out that shirt, Mr.T fixed everything.

Wearing that shirt, I looked less like a baby who just got her training wheels off making her way to a tea party and more like a warrior. When riding my bike sporting an intimidating, mohawked black man on my torso, I looked more intimidating. I mean, come on. Duh?!

The angry image adorned to my torso was unique. It was a statement. That photo was not one of just any old fighter. I was wearing the same face who kicked the legendary Rocky Balboa's ass in *Rocky III*.

Wearing Clubber Lang gave me power. That shirt indescribably let me beat up the streets just like my brother.

I looked up to my brother. He was strong. My brother drove a red BMX bike like it was nobody's business. I secretly wanted to be like him in every single way.

Even though he seemed rough, he was still pretty cool. He knew I liked his bike. Sometimes, my brother would tie a jump rope to the back of his bike, hand me a handle, and sit me on a skateboard behind him. Then, he would ride hard and pull my ass through the neighborhood.

The wind hit my face. My hair flew behind me.

The sensation was liking eating a Peppermint Pattie on the top of an icy mountain of badassery at the start of an avalanche.

It was the absolute best!

I was jealous of his wheels.

I will admit it. When he wasn't around, I would sometimes take his bike out for a joyride when he wasn't looking. I know, I know, I was risking the potential revenge of a camel clutch from him if he caught me, but it was worth it.

The coast is clear!

I jumped up high on his bike, wearing my shirt and hearing the *A-Team* theme playing in my mind. My feet just barely reached the pedals, but I stood upwards and pushed hard. I was off. I darted out to the fields and found the most dirt and mud that I could. I went off jumps with his bike and everything.

Freedom.

So, I never got into any trouble as a kid. I was "Daddy's little girl" after all. I guess when I did come close, my parents would fight over who had to discipline me and who would be good cop or bad cop. I think my dad was good at making my mom play the role of the bad guy. I was smart though, and knew the deal. I was a little worker even way back then. All I had to do to get out of trouble was to put on a little smile and I could get away with anything.

HALLOWEEN

On Halloween, we fully took part in the tradition of TRICK or treat. Back then, you could get away with more craziness on this holiday than anyone could probably pull of today in this generation. Back then, it was expected and the cops were never called. What would never would fly today was just harmless fun. (I think today, if anyone tried to ever pull the shit that we did back then, people would be afraid that someone would come out and shoot you.)

Come Halloween night, we would go out and get as much candy as we could. Then, when it got too late, we would evaluate who was a stingy bastard and put them on our shit list.

Now, as you know, a good piece of shit is always complimented with a good piece of toilet paper so we did just that.

I would hang out with my brothers' friends until just the right time and then go toilet paper houses as a courtesy to all. That's right. If you gave pennies to the trick-or-treaters in my neighborhood, you risked waking up to sheets and sheets of toilet tissue all over your car, the branches on your trees, and even the front of your house.

It was so fun that eventually the Halloween TP Bandits took to avenge people everywhere, and would toilet paper houses all throughout the year.

We would make a plan, sneak out at night, and paper whoever needed reform. It was pretty easy for us to get away with it too, because there were no real curfews. We lived in a nice suburban area.

I remember that there were two hot guys a few years older than me. Eric and Jeff Fannen were brothers, and I had a crush on them. One night, I broke out and TP'ed the hell out of their house, all alone. I don't know if I was marking my territory, or what I was doing.

The next morning there were streams and streams of toilet paper all over their front yard.

I think my parents got a call from their parents. I heard my mother pick up the phone and after pleasantries, I identified an unsatisfactory shift in her tone.

"Wait, who GOMBA?" she asked. (That was my nickname.) "Oh no, we saw her into bed last night. She wouldn't do that, anyhow!"

It was cool that my mother had my back, but honestly, I am not sure she even suspected me.

After that, I always wondered if the brothers knew it was me. So, every time they drove by my place, I would run and hide.

That didn't stop the shenanigans, however.

Soon after that, I went to TP someone's house, but found I was all out of toilet paper. I did what any TP Bandit would do in that situation, I raided the fridge for a dozen eggs.

The next morning, I actually felt bad. I rode the pink Huffy by the house I'd egged to learn that my neighbors were having a hell of a time trying to clean the egg goo off of their siding. It was so bad that eventually they had to re-side their house!

Nobody back then believed it was me.

I guess after all these years later I am coming clean after they couldn't make their siding come clean!

DANCING

Growing up, my brother and me weren't just partners in crime. We were also partners in dance.

That's right. ODB started as a dancer.

The dance stuff was a big part of life for us back then. We took all kinds of dance lessons week after week, learning little foundation steps that built up to choreographed numbers that ultimately end-gamed at these giant pageants.

We took tap, jazz, ballroom, and ballet. We would train for months and months like clockwork until we had banged out an entire routine. Then, we would pimp ourselves out with that routine to anywhere and everywhere that had a contest. Our goal was to win trophies and ribbons all over the country.

I don't exactly know how to explain what this circuit was like if you haven't lived it. The closest thing I can liken it to is to say I was in a dance-oriented cult from probably four-years-old to 15.

"Wait, a dance cult?!" you might say.

Yes, this was actually a thing. A cult is defined as a group of people holding excessive devotion and admiration for a particular thing. That was us.

The competitions we were preparing for had a number of other dance-a-maniacs there with us, day in and day out. It really looked like some *Honey Boo Boo* shit.

Our dance studio where all the sinister acts went down was called The Northland School of Dance. Basically, every class looked like a scene out of *Flashdance*, only with kids as the lead.

The dreaded dance dojo was in a strip mall next to a pizza place and a barber shop. When we would pull up to park, we could see right into the place through the big open windows.

There were long stretch rails and mirrors everywhere so that you could monitor your form. We all wore animal print leotards and neon leg warmers. It was the epitome of dance in the '80s.

1-2-3-4… 1-2-3-4!

As you stepped into the training facility, some kids would be there a little bit early putting on gear or stretching on a mat. The class before ours would just be finishing up. A boom box with additional output speakers sat on a wooden shelf on the wall. Maybe Debbie Gibson, or Tiffany was playing; whatever white bread popcorn bullshit song was popular.

CHAPTER 1 – Kid Stuff

This was my life as a kid, but I loved it.

In hindsight, however, the training for these contests was kind of brutal on a young girl though, I must say. I wasn't the ideal model dancer as far as the other idyllic dancers were concerned. I was athletic and a little big-boned for my age, but by no means a fatty. Yet, because of the different blueprints I was made from, I was constantly being told that I had to lose weight.

The kids were pretty good. They didn't say anything to my face. They knew if they did, they would suffer the effects of a Boston crab, perhaps. The heat came from the instructors, and I had one dance coach in particular who was like a female Sgt. Slaughter.

"Listen up, Jess," Miss Slaughter would say, leaning over my 10-year-old frame. "Do you want to be a success in dance? Do you REALLY want to make it?"

"Yes," I would say, hesitantly, just hoping, praying that she would get away from me and move on to another student.

"What was that?" she would ask, again.

"Yes, ma'am," I would say, a little louder. "I really do."

"Well then," she would say, pinching my chubby cheeks. "You really need to lay off all of the frozen pizzas and ice cream."

In what I can only call a passive aggressive diss, she would actually pinch my cheeks and make me feel like shit. It was horrible, I tell you, for a 10-year old to have to endure.

During class, if Miss Slaughter would see me struggle with a move, she would repeat her mantra of the day and once again say that if I really wanted it I "needed to lay off the frozen pizzas and ice cream."

That wasn't all, however. Then, on top of all the insults and fat shaming, Miss Slaughter would weigh us once a week like we were professional boxers or something. It didn't matter that I was only 10 years old and not even slightly overweight! All of us maggots were getting on that scale.

On a weigh in day, we would all file into the place with our dance parents, who acted like Hollywood child actor parents, mind you. Our parents would enter the studio then move over to the back of the room to mingle with the other moms. Then the dancers would pile together and head over to the scale.

On the walls were posters of pink princess ballerinas with inspirational quotes.

"Any kind of dancing is better than no dancing at all."

"Life is better when you dance."

"Dance is the joy of movement and the heart of life."

"Don't try to dance better than anyone else. Only try to dance better than yourself."

On each of those posters there was a picture perfect dancer with 3.6 percent body fat or less smiling and setting the tone for the entire world to look at.

And then, we would all be off to the Slaughter.

"Okay, girls. Now, kick off your shoes," our evil Cruella de Vil dance coach said.

Like the mindless, trained sheep followers that we were, we all lined up like cattle. We ironically walked passed all of those uplifting posters, just to be let down.

One by one, we walked up to an ominous prison scale in the corner of the room. We all waited patiently to be insulted.

One by one, we stripped off any extra layers that could equate extra poundage and tossed them against the wall. Then, we each took a deep breath and a step closer to front of the line.

When it was finally my turn, I would take another deep breath, but then exhale as much as possible. I would blow every last ounce of air out of my lungs because I truly believed that the oxygen in my lungs carried weight.

You do what you have to do, right?

I remember on this one particular flash weighing session, I immediately knew I was doomed. I had eaten so much bad shit during the week that there was no way I was going to pass.

I had put a number of things into my gut over the last few days; french fries, chocolate thingies, string cheese and a number of goodies that would be perceived as "baddies." I felt like all of that food was still in there, and no amount of shitting before my turn was going to help. So, I waddled up to meet my demise.

I felt guilt. I felt sorrow. I felt fear as I waited my turn, about to step up on the evil pad of doom. I waited there for the drill sergeant to look at the results and mark it on her little clipboard.

This was a demeaning thing to put little girls through, right? Think about it. What does a 10-year-old kid want? Do they want awards, or do they want tasty treats? Put a blue-ribbon dance award next to a chocolate chip cookie and the girl will go for that cookie every time.

I took off my pink Jane Fonda leggings hoping to shed the last few ounces of weight that I could. I continued to jettison unneeded layers as I awaited my pending turn. I took off my necklace and bracelet and dropped them on my pile of excess clothing, and even spit out my gum.

As I stood there in that studio, all lined up with the others for the weigh in, I felt my breakfast inside me. It was a big filthy lump of goo. I knew damn well that I had two bowls of cereal (maybe three) that very morning during my Saturday morning cartoon binge, along with all the other chow I ate during the week.

Please, God. Please.

Now, I don't know if I wanted to make weight, or if I was more worried that the other kids would *see that I didn't make weight*. I pictured hearing the worst, then having to walk passed all my peers who would shake their heads, knowing that I ate way too much ice cream to be a real dancer.

I sat there in the line petrified.

Suck it up, Jess!

I decided to take my brother's advice, the only person I had confided in to about my fear of weigh-in day. I decided to think good thoughts, because if you pictured good stuff happening, *good stuff can happen.*

"Winners don't picture themselves losing," my brother said.

I decided to think good stuff. I daydreamed about getting off of that scale after making weight and going on to become the best dancer in the world, with gold cups, confetti, and money flying through the air all around me.

Then, I saw I was next and instantly my dreams turned to nightmares.

I pictured my turn coming up, and me stepping on the scale and then the scale groaning "Ouch!" and telling me to get off. I pictured the whole class laughing and me being the ridicule of the entire class.

"Okay, Jess," Coach Slaughter bellowed. "Jessica. It's your turn."

When it was finally my moment to hop on the scale, I walked slowly like the cow going to the butcher table. I had removed my shoes, hair ties, and even disposed of my chewing gum hoping to shed any extra weight as possible to meet my goal. I was as ready as I was ever going to be.

I took a deep breath, then forced it out. While I was frightened, I didn't succumb to my fears. I knew that I didn't have that ballerina look, but it didn't matter. I was determined to make things happen whether I had bigger legs than my dance mates or not.

My weight is not going to hold me back.

As I stepped up for my impending doom, my smart aleck side kicked in. I looked all around me for a life hack on how to survive the moment.

Then, a voice sounded in my head. A wise man once said, "Win if you can, lose if you must, but always cheat."

In a moment of clarity, I looked down and strategically stepped on the white part of the scale, the base. Instead of standing fully on the measuring pad, I rested the ball of my foot on the frame in hopes that it would register less weight and work in my favor.

"Very good, Jess," Miss Slaughter said, writing some numbers on her chart.

It worked! I made weight!

I knew I cheated, but didn't care. I didn't cheat to win. I more or less was only cheating my way out of having to do a walk of shame. In my mind, I only cheated my way out of being looked at as little Miss Piggy as I walked by the other dancers, as a failure.

After that day, I added frame-standing to my move-set every time there was a weigh-in at the studio. I would step up to the scale, get up on one toe on the frame, then get down my magic number. This move, of course, was very graceful and it opened the door for me to enjoy far more cheeseburgers during the week than without it.

Basically, the dancers' weight never mattered anyhow. Even though some elements of dance were cosmetic like wrestling is, there weren't weight classes as you would see in wrestling. Nobody ever disqualified anyone from participating due to a couple of extra pounds. The focus on weighing was more of a scare tactic to get us to stay fit and, in turn, do a better job on the dance floor. It was good for us, and it was also good for them, financially. Later in life, I would see that dance had an awful lot of parallels to the wrestling world. Just like in wrestling training camps, if students were disqualified for any reason, there would be no income, right? That is why, in the end, you would overlook some things.

After weigh-ins on some Saturday afternoons, all fatties would be scolded and all the skinny minis would be praised for their dedication. Slaughter would pick out one of the skinniest students and put them over for apparently not eating during the week.

"Examine the famine, ladies."

Everyone would look and marvel and long to be that model student. After that, we would all be directed to stand in a new line, this time in the back of the room.

When class started, we took our places. We stood around and waited with mirrors all around us. It looked like the end of that Bruce Lee flick, except for the fact that everyone was wearing flower print unitards.

Next, the instructor walked in front of us all and turned on the stereo that sat on a shelf. She waited until the right part of the music kicked in, and nodded her head. Then, like the true master that she was, she modeled a routine that was so complex that I almost always felt I would shit my pants.

It didn't seem possible. The choreography she displayed was always so perfect, so beautiful, of course, that I didn't think anyone in the room could ever do it right.

After the steps, she broke it down. She took time with us and showed each of us how to get the steps right. In hindsight, I must admit, the teaching part was always very good. The instructors were all very patient and very understanding during instruction.

After the steps had been isolated and broken down, it was our turn. She would hit the music and then wait to watch us – selecting a few to watch individually. She would then observe other students taking turns mimicking her, one at a time, out of the lines.

There was some anxiety here, as I recall, as well. I remember watching all of this knowing I was soon to follow. I watched as each dancer approached the front and nodded. Then, they spun, got up on the tip of their toes, did a demi plié, and finally leapt into the air like a pixie, completing a full-body spin – knowing I was next.

Oh my God. I hope I can do that?!

I was sweating bullets when my turn to "tiptoe through the tulips" finally came – almost as badly as I was when I was waiting to tip the scales.

My heart skipped a beat again when the instructor finally called my name.

"Jessica," she said. She waited, cleared her throat and called my name again. "Um, Jessica?"

"Yes ma'am." I hesitated took a deep breath.

"You are up."

I nodded.

I went for it.

Maybe I was not perceived as a graceful swan on a lake by everyone there. Maybe they looked at me as being more like a bull in a china shop. I don't know. But whenever it was my turn, I sucked it up and went for it. I was actually pretty athletic and strong, due to playing sports with my brother and while I didn't have the frame of a classically-built dancer, my athleticism definitely helped.

I pulled all of that one crazy sequence off without missing a beat! I hit all the steps on time.

Yes! I did it!

The positive thinking thing did work to some degree, I think. After I hit all my spots, I felt like I should hear the roar of a standing-room-only audience after my performance. When I turned around, nobody said anything however, but the instructor smiled and nodded in approval.

That one day, I beat a number of obstacles, and I was on cloud nine. I learned during that lesson something much more important than any dance step or sequence. I learned that being positive was how I needed to move forward.

To me, the underdog of the class, I realized that not letting stuff get to me more and more was key. Even though I was still pretty shy at this point in my life, I stayed positive and didn't let fear take me out.

I took my nervousness, and I used it as fuel. Any fear I had only increased my courage to find success. Nobody was going to stop me.

PAGEANTS

I remember sometimes on Saturdays, we would pull into White Castle's drive-thru and get a little something to eat and then head over to dance for pageant practice. My brother and I would have lots of practices, three times a week at the studio. If we could get there early, we could start with our warmups and work on some stuff by ourselves before class.

"Okay, class," one of the coaches would say. "I hope you have been working on your stretches at home."

When Miss Slaughter and the gang weren't concerned with weighing us in on a particular week, they were more worried about our flexibility. Sometimes we had these stretch evaluation days where they would test how bendy we could be.

The worst was when they would test our splits.

"Okay, class," one of the instructors would say. "Turn to your right, do the right split."

The whole class would drop low like they were in a club, sporting their Apple Bottom jeans. Then the instructors would walk around and inspect the space between our booties and the floor.

Anyone who wasn't down all the way or was down but struggling – they became the victims. Like bloodthirsty sharks, they would smell out the weak and the less bendy. On occasion, they would actually get out a ruler and measure the inches between your taint and the ground. Sometimes when they didn't like what they saw, they would actually come by and push you down by the shoulders.

Collective groan.

I mean, yeah, some of the skinny minis could do picture perfect splits. Some of them could set up two chairs and put a leg on each of them and go even lower than a regular split like Rob F'N Van Dam. But that wasn't me. Whenever I got pushed to the floor, that shit hurt!

I would look over to my brother. He would laugh at my pain, and he would laugh because he could do a split better than me – even with him being built differently, if you know what I mean. He would bust my balls every chance he got.

After the split tests and the drills were done on ballet day, everyone would start on one side of the room. Then they would get up on all their toes, three across, and run the length of the room in time.

Now I should point out that we didn't have to dance to classical music all of the time. The music part was actually fun. The coaches would pick popular songs off the charts for us to perform to. We loved this. That's one of the reasons why we could endure the crazy training stuff. None of us wanted to dance to "Beethoven's 5th" or do splits to the "Nutcracker Suite." Our routines to the music we heard on the radio made it all worth it in the end, no matter how cult-like the process had been.

We created routines to songs by everyone from AC/DC to Madonna and Debbie Gibson. We did choreographed numbers to stuff like MARRS "Pump up the Volume," and even Run-D.M.C. The music was great and the costumes we wore were even better. One summer we did Prince's "Batdance" and half of us would dress like Batman and the other half of us would be the Joker.

Another year we did *Grease's* "Summer Nights" as a routine. For this performance, they picked half the class to dress as Sandy and the other half to be Danny. Since there were more girls than boys in the class, however, I was typecasted. I was always picked to be the fucking guy. (That sucked!)

The drill sergeants put you in the front of the group if you were better. In most of the routines, I was in the front. However, in ballet where grace was prevalent, I was always in the back. (I have to admit for those, a lot of the time I would just goof around.)

"Go home and work on your plié."

I never did.

By the time the dance recitals came at the end of training, we had already had a lot of fun so that was the frosting on the cake, so to speak. The pageants were fun. I had fun and my parents continued to pay for our lessons until it wasn't fun anymore.

When my brother and I were really on top of our game, we competed in groups of 15 kids or so. I was always in the main group for my age, while there were some other less talented groups. We also competed in duo partner competitions.

As teenagers, my brother and I continued to take lessons during the week and practiced our routines every weekend. Once we had our own routines down, we would take our show to the road. We would seek out dance competitions across the nation. Then, we would travel hours to strut our stuff on their dance floors.

We had a lot of fun on these competition journeys. We would go to Vegas, or Florida, or Chicago – any damn place that was hundreds of miles away and had a contest running. It didn't matter how far away it was.

We knew what the judges wanted, and we gave it to them a few times a month. In return, the judges gave us back hundreds of trophies and ribbons. In the end, we had a whole room in the house dedicated to our winnings.

Those days were building blocks to what would eventually lead up to my wrestling chops. I was shy growing up, but dancing every weekend gave me practice on a stage with tons of strangers watching you.

I never fit the mold. I was never the cookie cutter dancer, but this built character. While it may have held me back a little in dance, the discipline and the competitions were teaching me other lessons that I would need later on in life.

Every weekend, we dedicated our lives to the craft. We were putting on the miles for these cramped road trips to hotels everywhere, cramming kids into our Ram Charger truck.

After the trip was over, the parents liked it. They would get together and they would drink beer by the hotel pool. Us kids would swim or play on the elevators. I remember also playing ding dong ditch in the middle of the night waking up random people. We were crazy.

One thing I did learn about myself during these days was that I don't like elevators. I don't know if it is because I am claustrophobic, or what, but I learned I felt more comfortable using the stairs so I did just that – and even still do so to this day whenever I can.

Now as far as the competitions themselves were concerned, they were always in a hotel convention room. When you would go in, there usually were a few hundred people in the audience there watching and a table off to the one side in the front with four big dance judges.

We always bedazzled the hell out of our costumes. Bling-bling to the max! Everything was sparkly. There were sequins and rhinestones everywhere and we all had big hair. We all wore pink rollers overnight, the night before the event so that we would have the picture perfect *Annie* hair. We also caked on the blue eye shadow.

There was always an emcee that introduced us. We would perform our dance and then hear feedback from the judges. Then, we would often head out to the hallway and get feedback again from one of our instructors if they had made it there on the trip with us.

As a side hustle, there were always videos of performances available to order so that parents could "bring home a memory" for a price. If your team won a trophy, you would only get one video that the studio could display. However, for another nominal fee, you could also purchase and exact duplicate of your group's trophy so that you could display your hard work at home. We won a lot of competitions. We won some big trophies, and my parents always brought home a trophy we could keep.

In later years, we had loaded the trophy case at our dance school. On top of that, my brother became the star of the studio. He became a very good dancer, despite the fact that he didn't turn out gay as some might have thought. He just trained hard and took it seriously, and people began to notice.

He was on the news a lot in our town. He won a lot of competitions, and then he went on talk shows to talk about what happened. They loved him.

Eventually, he saw that there was a local search for dancers who would perform for the *1992 Super Bowl Halftime Show* at The Metro Dome. The press release hit every news station, directing all dancers to head over to the state fair for tryouts.

My brother tried out and nailed it, of course. He was chosen to be one of the five main dancers with none other than Gloria Estefan.

The day before the Super Bowl, he showed up for practice at the dome for the big routine. He had spent hundreds on his costume and was ready, dressed to impress. Gloria, however, was a giant let down.

"Where is Gloria?"

"She's not here," one of the organizers explained. "She will be here tomorrow though!"

That wasn't good enough for me, however. I watched from the sideline as my brother practiced all the steps out with her double.

What a total douche.

Come the big game, we watched, but were even more excited for halftime, of course. We were all backstage before that, but Gloria wouldn't come out because she was a diva.

The dancers made their way out to the field and everything came off without a hitch, but Gloria was admittedly kind of the shits.

It went without surprise to hear the next day that Gloria's performance was voted the worst Super Bowl halftime show of all time.

SPORTS

Usually, we had most of the summer off from dancing so we would then do what more normal kids would do – play sports in the down time.

Sometime during middle school, I took Tee-ball and that led to softball. Eventually over the summer when I got a little older, I would travel with our fast pitch league – Osseo Orioles. Now, I played outfield, but I wasn't just a dot on the green. Whenever a ball came my way, even the easy ones, I made my catches as over-the-top dramatic as I could. I would do a forward roll, or a dive – anything to make the save look as epic as possible. Maybe this showmanship was my first taste at performing in an athletic sense, and a move that was getting me ready for wrestling down the road.

I was a catcher too, but when playing centerfield, I would make it a point to dive every game just to show off! I wanted to be known.

We went to championship games, and often made it to the finals.

Now, while I did pretty well on the field, that wasn't exactly the case for all of my sports endeavors. When I joined my gymnastic team, I thought that my dance background would make me a sure-win for that category and lead to some good success.

In the end, I just sucked ass at it.

I mean, I liked to be busy with sports, but gymnastics was not my thing. You know how cats always land on their feet? I don't know what animal I was on the gymnastic mat, but I do know this much; I wasn't a cat.

Whenever I did a gymnastic meet at other high schools, I had to dumb down everything or end up looking dumb. For all of my floor routines, I couldn't even flip, so most everything ended into a very low-rent round-off cartwheel. I mean, yeah, dancing helped, but I was kind of a joke in that realm.

In Maple Grove, Minnesota, the winter seemed to last longer than the summer. That being said, I started playing hockey in high school in junior year. Unlike gymnastics, I was very into that sport and did pretty well at it!

Back in 1994, the thing that drew me to it was that I was able to be on the first ever women's hockey team for our school.

When it was first announced that they were going to have a girls' team, I wanted to make history. I wanted to go down as being in the very first group, and perhaps be looked at as one of the best ever. There was one thing that stood in my way, however. I didn't know how to skate.

I mean, I could skate, but just barely, and not at all what was needed to play hockey with skill-wise. All hope wasn't lost, however. My dad was supportive. He always was of us kids. He said, "You know, Jess, if you are going to go out for hockey, you need to know how to REALLY skate. Let's make it happen."

We had a pond out in our backyard which helped a lot. So, what we did to prepare me for tryouts was we borrowed my uncle's gear and I picked up some used skates at the Salvation Army, then I was thrown out onto the ice.

I'll never forget that first day when I forgot to take my skate guards off and fell face first my first time. There were some guys around watching too, laughing, which made it even worse. When I finally got up and moving, it seemed I got the hang of it. I was moving pretty well when I realized that I didn't know how to stop.

That's why I became a goalie.

Once we had our game plan, we were ready to go. Besides the pond, we had other ideas on how to help me in my hockey training right in our backyard. We took the measurements of how big the net would be and decided to confine me to an area of the same size.

So, to make a long story short, my dad tied me up to the fence and threw pucks at me.

We did this for some time until I got good at it.

I made the team. I went on to be the MVP the first year, and captain in my senior year. Stealing a page from my baseball career, even if it was an easy goal to save, I made my goalie catches dramatic.

The guys on the boys' hockey club team all thought girls' hockey was a joke. But we proved them wrong.

We ended up being very good.

COMING OUT OF THE SHELL

I went to Osseo Senior High in Osseo, Minnesota. We had a big graduating class of 900. I never had like a real part-time job in school which was cool because it let me do all the after school stuff and participate in whatever sports I wanted to. My parents thought it was important for me to focus on high school and whatever was going on there. That meant I was at school a lot, even when school wasn't going on.

By my junior and senior year, all of my extracurricular endeavors started to take their toll on me and the shyness in me started to subside. Playing sports made me more social, more confident. I started coming out of my shell more and more.

I was actually a pretty regular member of the Osseo High Drama Club. I was never selected to be a main lead for a role, but I had dancing experience, so I ended up being in a lot of the high school plays. I learned a ton about performing and how it is important to do everything big from that club.

I was also in the school choir. I had to sing in front of teacher a lot, which I hope she got a bonus for. I sang at all the recitals in which my parents had to come and witness the train wreck live and in person. I mean, there is just no way, NO WAY… that they could've have enjoyed that shit! I saw a VHS of one of these concerts recently. Back then, I thought my singing voice was great. But after playing it back to me, I realized that I sounded like a dying walrus!

One time, I remember singing Bette Midler's "The Rose." The lights were bright on the stage, but I squinted the best I could to see what my parents thought. I could have sworn they had a flask on them too, and were passing it discreetly to the other moms to help them make it through the night.

Despite the bad singing, I never got into trouble at school. I just hung out with jocks who played sports a lot. We went to some parties, but they were pretty much all tame. There was no real drinking on my behalf until college.

As much as you might like to think it, I didn't have a high school sweetheart, or anything. I did go to the prom with a kid named Nate Leelah. But when I say "went to the prom" that is pretty much all that happened. We just went to prom. We didn't date. No kiss.

I wasn't the best communicator at this time and he was likely as shy as I was. I told my parents at the last second that a bunch of us were going camping after the big dance. My parents didn't like it, but it was all very G-rated in the end. There was no drinking and certainly no sex. It was the furthest thing from a John Hughes movie that it could be.

CHAPTER 1 – Kid Stuff

Towards the very end of my time in high school, I was always well liked. I was not a drinker, or a partier, but ended up being popular, nonetheless to some degree.

I wasn't raised to be a partier, despite all the parties I saw my parents throw. It was always "do as I say, not as I do" and followed that golden rule. I was a good girl. When I saw other girls at school doing adult-like stuff, I would say, "Oh my God. I can't do that," and I just didn't participate.

"Just say no," I thought. Right?

I remember one time, I was riding in the passenger side of one of my best friend's ride and we started by checking out the guys by the park, but they were all scrubs, and "I didn't want no scrub" as the song goes.

Some of them wanted our numbers. "No."
Some of them wanted to meet us. "No."
Some of them wanted some of our time. "No."

They were all unappealing, and the girl who was driving thought it was all too funny. I wasn't really interested in any of the boys we saw, and for good reason. They were all scrubs, and they were all pretty lame. She could see that I was bored with the whole scene, so she tried to make it interesting.

"Hey, girl," she said. "Want to make things fun?"
"Sure," I said.
"Open the glove compartment."
I shrugged and obliged.

When I did I saw something shiny and metal gleam out from underneath some paperwork. It was not a gun. This was not a gangster rap video, and I was not about to pull a drive-by on the scrubs. This was Minnesota. The worst that things were going to get was some underage drinking.

After fishing around in the open drawer under the dashboard, I revealed some kind of container. It was a flask, and I pulled it out.

"There it is, girl," she said, laughing. "Vodka. Take a sip."

I replied to her the same way I had to all of the scrubs hitting on us by the park.

"No!"

At this time, I was still pretty innocent. Who would have known then that a flask would become a big part of my life?!

I guess I was a late bloomer, so to speak, and probably too shy back then to act on any of the taboo pleasures of life.

Being a chick was weird, especially for someone like me – *the future ODB.*

I don't want to say I was bipolar, or had split personalities, or anything like that. Maybe I was just a hormonal mess. I don't know. I think it was fair to say I was still discovering who I was, and who I wanted to be. I was teetering on both sides of the fence, personality-wise. I wanted to be known, and I loved attention. However, I still also had this shy girl personality in me that double-checked everything I did.

Coming of age.

The shy girl in me liked boys, but never said anything to them. Around other girls, I was pretty open, but also sneaky on how to go about changing in the locker room. It was a different time. Nobody talked about stuff like this back then, and I didn't quite understand sexuality and stuff like that. Once I realized there was the potential for gay girls in the locker room, I particularly didn't want to show off my stuff. Cautious of sending any wrong messages, I decided to always leave the packaging on the meat.

If I had to change, I would first fake having to go in a stall to pee or something. But since I had my shirt hanging over my shoulder anyhow, I would just quick change next to the toilet. It made sense to me, anyhow.

I always covered up. I always wore boxers and tank tops underneath anything we wore.

Also, after practice, I didn't jump in the big open jail showers with the rest of the girls. I would rather go home stinky and shower at home than flash boobies with them. Shy Jess never ever took the risk of walking around in the group shower, looking for some help washing my back.

That would just be weird.

Today, however? It's "please pass the loofah."

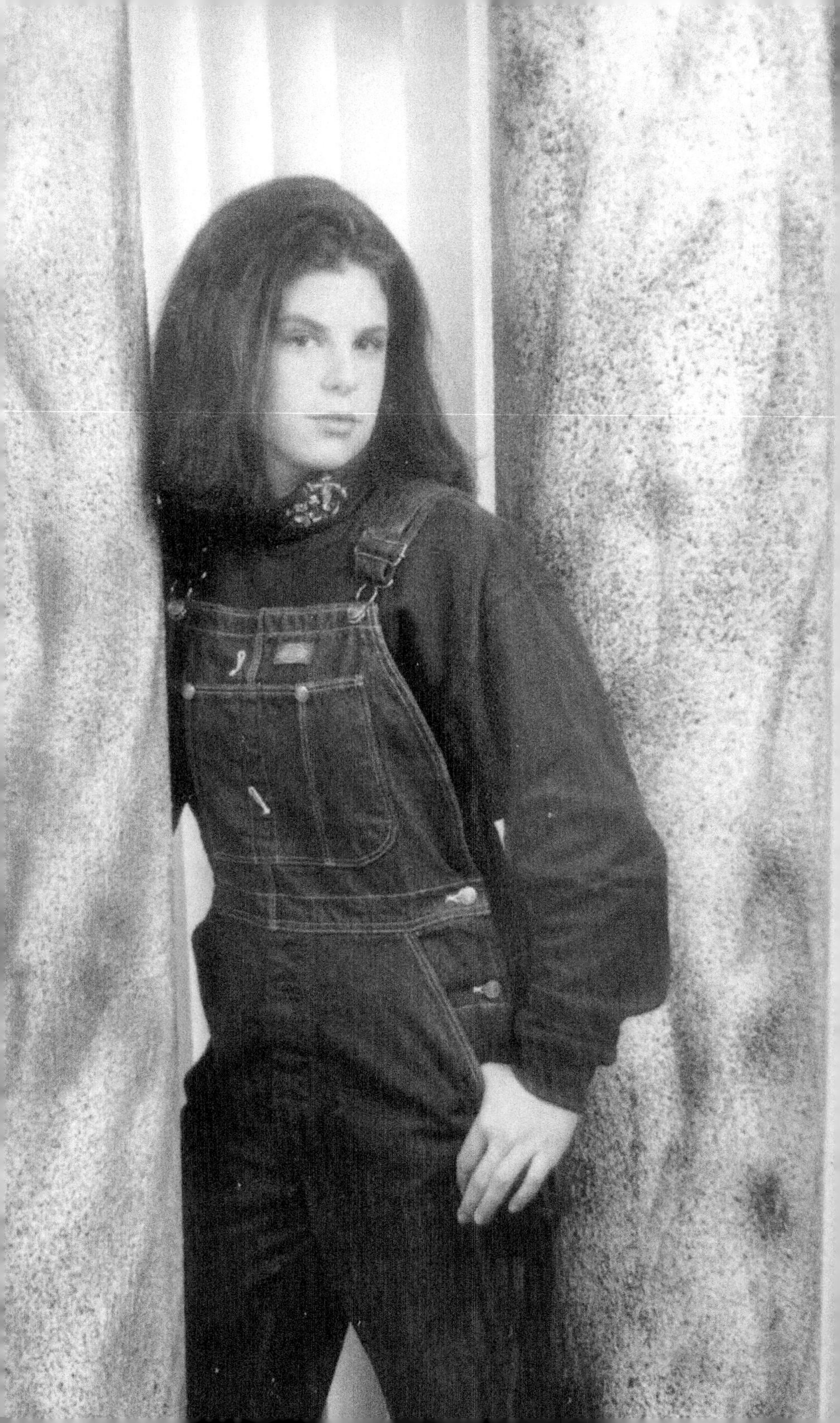

CHAPTER 2 - COLLEGE

After high school, I enrolled in Saint Cloud State University Minnesota, which was about 45 minutes to an hour away from home. It was a safe distance away from everything that I knew was good, but that isn't what made up my mind to go there. I think the overall draw for me was the intrigue of why this school was voted "one of the biggest party schools in America."

I was soon to find out why.

I didn't have to work during my college days to get by. Just like in high school, my parents wanted me to focus on the actual work at school. They figured that work would come soon enough after my studies. Therefore, they saved all they could for my brother and me and paid for it all out of pocket.

Once I got to college, I realized that I was free. Not having parents breathing down my neck meant I could do whatever I wanted. It also didn't take long to learn that in college, the professors were not at all like high school teachers. They didn't give a shit. That meant that I could learn what I wanted, or opt to attend when I wanted.

Adult life is awesome!

There were still some rules I had to adhere to, however. Living at a dorm on campus meant you did what the other campus residents did. For this school, that meant you migrated to wherever the parties were. Monday was beer pong at Mitchell Hall. Wednesday night was a party at Stearns aka the "Hockey House." Friday night was a party at Stateview aka "the Pink Taco" house.

I was a quick learner. Determined to live the college life to its fullest, my dorm soon voted me "the most likely to go to jail."

For my short-lived experience at Saint Cloud, I again played hockey, but the school didn't have a women's division. For this shot, I was on a club ice hockey team called the St. Cloud Huskies, and no it was not because the other girls looked like dogs! Hockey was still a big passion of mine and I enjoyed playing during my time away from the classroom. For my actual classes, I officially majored in Liberal Arts (a glorified 13th grade) and minored in Party Performance Arts. You see, when I wasn't studying, I was immersing myself into partying so hard that every week, I was teetering on the verge of expulsion.

I think my independent studies there at St. Cloud is where ODB was first developed. Being away from my parents, my new home was every frat house and hockey house I could find. Unlike my dry days at high school (aka the quiet before the storm), "drinking all you can drink" became a great means of independent study for me, and I was getting good at it with all the time and research I was putting into that area.

With that being said, it was no surprise that I was eventually kicked out of college for bad grades. There was just too much partying and too many liquid lunches outside the school cafeteria in between.

Not wanting to leave all my beloved new dear friends (and drinking buddies) in St. Cloud, I begged my parents to stay. My parents were supportive and did want me to get an education, so they said I had to go over and enroll in the technical school there instead.

At St. Cloud Technical Community College (SCTCC), I majored in advertising. I continued to play hockey with the Huskies and also pursued my independent studies. I went there for about two semesters and did a little bit better than my first time around at the university.

At the end of the second semester, I was doing better. I learned the value of moderation and kept my ears open. One day, I wandered into SCTCC career services, and saw a big job opportunity poster with a giant mouse on it. Being a Disney girl at heart from all of my days training on location at their campgrounds, I made an appointment to find out more from the on-campus guidance counselor.

We polished my resume. We got together a good cover letter (impressive for a university dropout like me, if I must say so myself.) Then, I collected letters of recommendation. Once I had all of these things, we put a package together, mailed it out, and waited. This time and effort paid off.

One day when I checked my mail cubby at the dorm, I reached in and I pulled out a handful of spam out as usual, and dragged the pile across a counter to the end so I could check it out. I dropped a number of in-house party flyers printed on colored paper into the recycle bin at my feet, which was a pretty regular practice at this point. I continued to do this until I came across an actual envelope. To my surprise, it was addressed to me and had a very familiar signature on the return address label.

Oh shit! I have a letter from Mr. Walt Disney himself!

Yes, before me was something very different. My heart dropped. I tore that envelope open like a savage. I skimmed it and soon realized it was not, in fact, a rejection form letter. I was one step closer to being offered an opportunity of a lifetime at just 19 years old. The company that I was born and bred to love was considering me for the internship!

One of my dreams had always been to work there. I remember during our camping trips that we would always finish up with treks over to Disney World. As a little girl, my eyes always opened wide as I approached the iconic Magic Castle that was featured in the opening credits of all of the Disney movies I loved. Just like the song said, I felt my dreams were about to come true:

When you wish upon a star
Makes no difference who you are
Anything your heart desires
Will come to you

If your heart is in your dream
No request is too extreme
When you wish upon a star
As dreamers do

Fate is kind
She brings to those who love
The sweet fulfillment of
Their secret longing

Like a bolt out of the blue
Fate steps in and sees you through
When you wish upon a star
Your dreams come true

I specifically remember saying to my parents as kid that I was going to work at Disney one day. I remember getting off the teacups and going right up to my mom laughing. She asked if I had fun, and I nodded then told her that one day I would be running the rides for other girls like me to have fun on.

There was one more formality. *The interview.*

My interview was all set to take place at school. For this, I decided not to wear my infamous "*A-Team* featuring Mr. T" T-shirt, but rather pulled out all the stops. I dressed to the nines and made a real attempt to look as professional as I could.

There were two people there conducting the interview; a younger man and a woman. They asked all kinds of questions. I kayfabed everything and anything that could have made me look like a party girl.

I did, however, tell them all about our family trips. I didn't pull back any punches there. I just rolled with all of the good stuff my family had done for me in the name of Disney.

I watched them listen. I watched their faces as I told story after story. They smiled. They wanted to hear more. I was the epitome of what the company wanted to make out of young people: a dreamer, a believer, a storyteller of happy memories. They nodded as I shared with them my fond anecdotes of camping under the stars, magical journeys of fun... just everything.

I got the job.

I'm going to Disney!

DISNEY WORLD

My ride was an '86 Chevy Beretta. This was my first car, and it was a hand-me-down from my mom. (The first car I would actually buy myself some years later was a Scottsdale baby blue pickup.)

In 1998, I was off to be an intern for six months. I packed my hockey bags up in St. Cloud, Minnesota, and I headed down south to sunny Florida!

Walt Disney World is, of course, known as a magical place where dreams come true. To make dreams become a reality, they created a Walt Disney World College Program that let certain scholars receive a behind-the-scenes look at the magic in the making. (Feel free to insert your own Ric Flair Space Mountain joke HERE. Wooooo!)

Disney World has been recruiting students as interns for more than 30 years, and while not every intern story comes with a "happily ever after" ending, most do. I was banking on the latter as the fulfillment of a longtime dream.

When I arrived, a number of us got on a bus heading to an orientation facility on location at Disney World. We took our seats. We were all so excited to be there. We looked out the windows with our eyes wide open, taking in all the visions from the road.

I knew it was going to be an experience to work with all the great people behind the fence. I dreamed eventually they would hire me to work on the shows at the park. While I had no idea where I would fall, I wanted to be part of it all. I was determined to work for Disney somewhere down the road, even though I knew the work was going to be hard.

I am not going to fuck this up.

I had already heard the details and I was cool with it. I had been informed that students should "not go there to make money." With a starting intern wage of about $5.90/hour, saving summer earnings is difficult. Any money we made would easily be consumed. I was used to not making any money, however. That is how it went at college for me. I knew that this experience was all about going there to learn and make contacts.

Once we got off the busses, about a hundred of us or so were corralled into a large building. Inside, it looked like a conference room, not unlike the ones I had spent many hours in at hotels hosting dance competitions. There was a little podium in the front of lines and lines of chairs. There was a laptop stand. There was a PowerPoint screen.

The first person welcomed us, then called up a former intern to speak. She had majored in business management at college, completed her internship and then got a job with Disney as a campus representative for the internship program.

She talked about what we could come to expect. She described her season working as a food and beverage hostess at the EPCOT Disney park. She talked about her positive experience with it all and also stressed the importance of "finding contacts in the departments related to your career goals."

Disney is massive. It is such a large company with all kinds of attractions that there are very specific career opportunities available in all kinds of areas. Everything from horticulture to theater to animation, she encouraged all of us to "find your passion and start your career there."

Come lunchtime, they moved us into another room where trays were waiting for us with sandwiches and apples. I sat at a table and talked to a few of the others like me. I learned that plenty of participants were there without the actual lifelong dream of working for Disney, but rather to "take advantage of the opportunity." Some were there to work, some wanted to play, and others just wanted to learn what they could in Florida.

As far as living accommodations went, I was stationed at a big apartment complex that was provided by Disney. It was the same for everyone in that we all were assigned roommates from all over the world. "It's a small world after all!" Actually, it was more like MTV's *The Real World*. There were six of us in a three-bedroom apartment that was already totally furnished, set up in a very *Melrose Place*-type area.

In 1998, I opened up Animal Kingdom. Then my first official position was a greeter there. You know, kind of like the greeters you encounter at Walmart. My job was to set a tone for each guest, and help out when needed. From this initial station of my internship, I learned the Disney way of working. The work ethic was "while you are working – you are always on." This is a very valuable mindset to have and one I still have today. Phoning stuff in sucks.

That is not the only motto they drilled into us. We had classes once a week in where I learned soft skills and generally "how to be professional," so to speak. Unlike college the first time around, I never missed a class.

Now don't get me wrong. I didn't just convert my ways to little Miss suit and tie. I still had the party life in me and that wasn't dying anytime soon. I just started to realize when to flip the switch. For instance, I had these two real straight-laced Mormon roommates from Utah. They ended up being pretty wild by the end of our first internship stay, and it is quite possible that I may have had a part in that. Along with another roommate from the Dominican Republic, I started to bring my hommies out to our own version of "Pleasure Island" after work was over.

Pleasure Island was bumping! It's not there anymore, probably because of the level of partying that it incited, but picture like a downtown Disney late night scene that had a bunch of dance clubs. Pleasure Island would have been rated quite a bit higher than the G-rating a lot of Disney's flicks often carried, that is for sure.

For one thing, I was not 21 yet – but that never stopped me before. I had a fake ID at 19, and it worked out in Florida just fine, with me using it there probably just as much as I had back in Minnesota. I used it so much that eventually it got taken away right on a Disney property. They didn't call my bosses or anything, they just took it and said, "Okay, you just need to go!" After that happened, we just had to run the pregame and drink beforehand. A lot of the clubs would let you in, you just couldn't order alcoholic beverages. So, we would just team up with some of the 21-year-olds who would get stuff for us. All was well.

After I came home from Disney from my first round, I tried the whole college thing again. Realizing that I just wasn't a traditional learner, I again knew my school career was running out fast.

It was the shits.

I lasted only a few months.

I stuck around in school wallowing in my classes just long enough to apply again to Disney.

I found my way back to Orlando.

My second time around at "The Greatest Place on Earth," I was no longer an intern. I was now an official employee! I also ended up working at their rival theme park, Universal Studios where I opened Islands of Adventure.

Eventually, I got my dream position at the Magic Kingdom. My dream job, you see, was to be a skipper driving the boats. Essentially, without wearing the fuzzy furry gimmick, I got to be a personality.

As "goofy" as I was (pardon the pun,) I was never assigned to be a character like Minnie Mouse or Donald Duck. I couldn't have even if I wanted to. I was too small to fit into the costumes, as they had very specific body types that they adhered to for casting out those roles.

As an official Jungle Cruise Tour Guide, I was basically a ship's captain with a mic. The boat ride sat about 20 people comfortably looking for all the insight I could bring to the strange surroundings we were sailing through. The ride would bring us down a river into a tropical rainforest complete with everything you could think of in such a setting. It was loaded with animatronic robots along the way with a real live headhunter at the very end. It was my job to point out the scenes and offer a little finesse. My choice of fluff was sarcastic to say the very least, and I pretty much buried everything along the way. The people loved it.

This experience was invaluable to me, because, while I had no problem performing, it was the first real improv/public speaking that I ever got to do. I also was able to develop a little more of my sense of humor. By writing little canned lines that I could use and working on my own on-mic character, I got pretty good at being witty on the spot. This position definitely further helped to get me more out of my shell.

I took my creativity liberty seriously. As time went on with this position, I learned what worked and what didn't. I also had written something like 30 pages of jokes for when the boat would get stuck, because we had a lot of technical difficulties. Being able to default to my pre-written stuff around certain topics, while also having to be able to cut a promo on the spot, was really cool stuff for me.

So again, I never played any furry characters because being only 5'4" was "not the right size," but I got to create and play my own character. One of my roommates eventually did get to play Pluto, but by the time that happened, the magic for me getting to play that type of role had kind of gone away.

I remember running late one time going to Magic Kingdom after a night of hard partying, and putting myself into the position of having to get dressed there. There is kind of an underground behind the scenes there where cast members could go and get dressed for the day, take a break from the heat, and eat in a special furry cafeteria. When I showed up there to get dressed, a bunch of guys were walking around with their heads off. The whole scene was surreal, kind of like seeing a clown smoking a cigarette. The whole thing kind of creeped out the little kid in me, and I never went back in there again.

I worked on a number of different jobs along the way and became a Jack, or should I say Jill, of all trades. I was at Islands of Adventures at Universal Studios. Sometimes I was a greeter, sometimes I worked on the mechanical side of things. I also worked on a ride that I think was called Dragon Challenge or Dueling Dragons at the time – something like that. One time Courtney Cox and David Arquette came through on my ride! I also seated the Dixie Chicks on it as well. Pretty cool for a young kid to bump elbows with celebs, aye?

If you did your job, everything was just fine. Disney World was a world of good little workers. However, they squashed everything that fell out of line immediately. If you were playing Mickey Mouse, you could not take pictures backstage half in gimmick with your buddies. There was to be no sharing the secrets, no showing the magic, and absolutely no bad stuff in costume. One kid took a picture of a number of his coworkers getting ready and flipping the bird at the camera. He posted it up near the lockers and mysteriously enough, everyone in the picture, one by one, disappeared. Some say they were fired. Some say they were killed alongside Bambi's parents in a giant midnight forest fire purge filled with heels and bad employee rejects. At Disney, there is absolutely no breaking kayfabe… or else!

I did my time. I was there for about three years. The fringe benefits made it hard to leave. All we had to do was show our card and we would get free admission to all of the parks and we also got half-off for food. My favorite food was the big turkey legs like the Vikings used to eat until I found out it was actually emu meat and almost barfed.

By the time I had my 21st birthday in downtown Orlando, that was about the end for me. I was aging out of Disney when I could legitimately attend any bar crawl that I wanted to, and also get into any club with a real ID this time.

Even though I liked to drink and unwind at night after working all day, the big bars weren't my scene. I was more of a hole-in-the-wall bar person who would pre-game to save money, but load the jukebox with Spice Girls and "Mmmm Bop" by Hanson, despite the potential alienation of whatever bar folk frequented the joint I was sitting in.

Eventually, I had enough of Disney. Just before taping out, I was assigned this new female roommate from Minnesota. Even though she was from my neck of the woods, she was far crazier than I was. I could only take so much of her shit. I could drink and party with the best of them, but this chick was way into drugs. She started bringing coke and ecstasy back to the apartment, and would use the shit right out in the open with no shame like it was fucking Woodstock or something.

I had to get the fuck out of there. I called my dad, and he was totally cool with me packing up and picking up where I left off back home. Therefore, I decided to move back to Minnesota with my parents, and never talked to the booger sugar chick again.

Since I already had a car, my dad flew down and took the road trip back with me.

CRABS

I moved back home late in 2000. I was tough enough to leave my comfort zone and go back home. My parents and I figured I should either go back to school in Minnesota, or get a job. Not wanting to look like a failure Disney School Dropout, I decided to do both.

This time around, I went back to school for the third time at a junior college. Also, I got a job that made me very familiar with crabs.

Oh boy. You sure are nasty for thinking what you were thinking.

No, I got a job working at the world-famous Joe's Crab Shack.

For those of you unfamiliar with Joe's, the place is ridiculous. It is like the Disney World of seafood. There are personalities. There is dancing. And there was actually something Disney didn't provide; good money and tips.

At Joe's Crab Shack, I was a server. A lot of what I learned at Disney came into play. Using personality and offering positive, good service helped me do very well for myself in the gratuity category. My brother worked there, too. When we were both working at the same time, the shack was shaking in 15 minutes. We would get up and start dancing to songs like "Macarena" and "Cotton Eye Joe."

A cool group of us became close. We would all go out drinking every night after work to unwind. If it was too late to hit up a dive bar, sometimes we would go to my brother's house. There we would drink, watch TV and I would wrestle everyone.

TOUGH ENOUGH 2000

On one particular day, after making almost nothing in tips because it was raining out and there were just a bunch of cheap bastards coming into Joe's, I went home to relax and watch wrestling.

I'm sitting there watching the action and then all of a sudden there is a weird opportunity/reality show mentioned called *Tough Enough*. I wasn't all that familiar with it, but I watched intently and it looked cool. Afterword, Jim Ross and Jerry Lawler said that all you had to do was send in your VHS video and you could apply to become a WWF wrestler.

Oh shit! A talent search?

Now, I have lots of experience in contests and competitions. Hell, I have been all over the country competing for various different titles for dance alone and won quite a few of them. Even though I didn't have any formal pro wrestling experience, I did have amateur wrestling experience. My

CHAPTER 2 – College

brothers used to beat the shit out of me, and I quite often returned the favor. I also knew how to do the figure four leglock from my baseball days.

After doing the math, I decided that this was the life for me.

I talked to my brother who is a bit of a techie nerd. He got his VHS camcorder out and we started talking about what we should do to get me noticed. At this point, I wasn't all that sure about what to do. I knew I could work in some of the attitude that I had built up at Disney as the tour boat guide. But I needed to be even more over the top. I found a couple of promos that were just God awful. Since I was a big fan of heels, my promos talked about how I was going to kick the ass of the babyface and take their titles from them. But it all seemed so weak now.

It was actually my brother who came up with my gimmick name "ODB." I hadn't really even thought of the Wu-Tang Clan's member One Dirty Bastard at that time. When he came up with the name ODB, he just had a number of funny catchphrases to go along with it. It was endless material for me, so I was sold.

We redid the promos and I finally came up with one that I liked. The next day, I put the tape in a bubble wrap envelope and mailed it out to Stamford.

A few weeks later, after looking in the mailbox every day and hoping that I would be receiving something from the WWE, my dream finally came true. There was no letter, but there was a call.

I got a call saying I had been selected along with 250 other people to go to New York City for the *Tough Enough* tryouts. The tryouts were held at a place right in Times Square. You may recall if you have been watching WWE for a long time that some of *the Tough Enough* episodes were filmed right at the then WWF New York restaurant.

Along with the other 249 contestants, I had to fly myself in on my own dime. Looking back, that was a good financial decision on the WWE's part. There were a number of other people that I am sure would probably just be eliminated on sight alone, if not smell. Once I got up to the front of the line, I told a woman wearing a WWE badge what my name was. She went through a list and found me and checked me in.

We walked into the restaurant. Down some stairs revealed a huge television screen setup, almost Titantron like, taking up almost the entire wall. In front of it was a wrestling ring and a few judge tables. There was even an audience booked to watch and respond as the tapings for the competition went on.

It turned out that this whole concentrated effort was a tag team one. The tryout was for a television show that both WWE and MTV were putting on together. That meant we didn't just have to impress the WWE with our potential for professional wrestling. There were also officials from MTV productions there evaluating us for reality TV. I guess one could argue that this meant we had both fake and real going on at the same time.

I remember being a bit starstruck as I saw some promos being shot right in front of us, being added into the crowd as an extra at first. I remember Mick Foley standing there and interviewing Al Snow. I also saw Tazz and Jacqueline Moore.

There was a house guy in charge of us kids. His name was Big John. We were grouped together and each given some time on the microphone to be evaluated. When my team came up, I felt the hair stand up on the back of my neck and my heart started to pound.

This is my moment.

I swallowed hard and broke out into a sweat.

They called up our group, and we all just stood there looking like a bunch of newbies. Out of nowhere we heard a siren sound, and I knew what that meant. It was Tazz.

Tazz walked out exactly like his wrestling entrance. He had the towel on his head and everything. When he made his way over to our line, he came right up to us like a drill sergeant.

"So you think you got what it takes?" he asked.

"Sir, yes sir."

"You think you can be a wrestler?"

He got into each of our faces and cut a promo on us attacking everything about us he could to put us down. Eventually, he and some others called out names off of a clipboard. The person would then get inside of the ring and be asked to do a number of things.

They would have them run the ropes and get blown up, have them do a ton of different cardio exercises and get blown up, and then get a hold of the microphone and cut a promo – you guessed it – while they were blown up.

When they called me up for my spot to shine, they had me do all the same type of things and a little type of shuffle at the end. Yes, I was blown up, but I didn't let that bother me. I was not going to let that bother me. It was already in my head that life is about overcoming the obstacles that stand in your way, and this was just another obstacle for me to get by.

When it was time for me to cut a promo, I did just that. I called myself ODB just as planned, and the audience loved it. I flexed my muscles and posed just as I did practicing with my brother. Everybody laughed including the judges, and they all liked it.

All in all, it turned out to be a really good tryout. I stuck out as being different, and I was pretty sure of myself when it was over.

Most of my fellow competitors before me looked like wrestling fans, not wrestlers. There were a lot of cocky, fat, out-of-shape assholes. I was miles ahead of the majority of them. I knew this and so did the judges.

After my performance, I sat back down. They had filmed me and my turn was over. I didn't expect to be called again up to the stage again any time soon, but I was.

Over the loud speakers, they called ODB back up to the judges along with a few other names. We were the ones that the WWE judges had hand-selected. I was elated to learn that I had made it to the top 25!

We were dismissed for the day. I walked around New York City trying to take everything in, but my mind wandered at the possibilities. The same thing happened that night when I went back to hotel room. I knew I should probably get some sleep to be fresh for the second round of auditions, but I couldn't help it.

Am I going to be the next WWE Superstar?

The next day, I did even more for the WWE judges. Again, they seemed very into me and everything went very well. I was still kicking around after everybody else had been sent home. My name was on the shortlist, and I was jazzed. There was only one step left, it seemed. I needed to win over MTV.

I got all psyched up for my interview with the reality show people. A member from their production team brought me back to a much smaller room. There, they had a number of different tables set up to crank out the interviews with the 25 different people being brought back in by the WWE as favorites.

The woman from MTV who interviewed me had an assistant with her. He was a skinny little turd. He probably was not much more than a year or so out of being an intern himself for the company. They both sat me down and were pleasant, but immediately I was getting a bad vibe.

I don't think I fit into whatever storyline they have in mind!

"Do you have a boyfriend?" the MTV official asked.
"Um, no?"
"Do you like girls?" the skinny intern asked.
"Um…"
They both leaned in and looked at me.

I realized right off the bat what they wanted. They wanted ratings. They wanted diversity. They wanted me to be a lesbian.

Kayfabe my love of softball.

Now, I am not against the idea of what Dusty Rhodes once said, "never let the truth stand in the way of a good story." However, just because I was muscular and a little rough around the edges, I was not going to pretend that I was gay to get a gig. I refused to be gay for pay on a reality show, no matter how scripted they apparently were.

You can quote this section of the book for any magazine or any wrestling newsletter or website that deems it appropriate: *"ODB loves the cock. End of story."*

I didn't mind playing some kind of character or whatever for a role in wrestling, but I wasn't about to pretend that I was something I was not in real life for a fake music channel. Fuck MTV. Not at that capacity, not ever.

Sure, I could have probably faked gayness and gotten the gig. I thought about it for about five seconds. I could just wink at the female producer and even maybe slap her ass.

Then, confetti and streamers would fall. Then, another siren would go off and Tazz would grab my hand and shake it and say, "You did! You finally did it!" Then, someone from MTV would come running out and hand me my big gay golden ticket to the *Tough Enough* chocolate factory.

Do I fake it?

I could have fame and fortune. I could have wrestling. I could have everything I ever wanted, but at what cost?

At that moment, I could also picture the ramifications of faking my sexuality. My parents would be watching *Tough Enough,* and all of a sudden I would do some gay shit on TV that the director wanted that just wasn't me. I could just see my parents drop everything and look at each other and say, "what in the actual fuck?!"

If I pretended to be something that I was not, that would just be fucked up. Reality television was believed to be real. Depicting a lesbian on TV would be perceived by most who knew me that either I was living a lie in the real world, or lying on television. Either way, I would be come off as lying bastard in general, so I decided that I wasn't going to do it.

"Do you like girls?" the skinny intern repeated his question.

"Yes," I said. "But I don't bang them, if that is what you mean. Strictly dickly, here."

A few of the WWE officials were there. They were off to the side, and they laughed at my honesty.

The MTV intern dude checked something off on his clipboard then thanked me before shouting, "Next!"

I looked different, but wasn't different enough. The rest of the audition crawled by, and I wasn't being looked at anymore. It was obvious. They pushed me over to a few more people at tables, but it went nowhere. I was eventually showed back out of the room and into the restaurant where I sat and watched some old WWE PPV on the big screen.

Nobody came for me. Maybe an hour later, it was even more obvious.

Don't call us, we will call you.

Eventually, I got up ready to do the walk of shame. There was to be no medal or trophy at this competition. I wasn't even going to get the dreaded participation award. Before I left implicitly being told I probably wasn't getting the role, I was surprised. I found myself being stopped by somebody on my way out the door.

I could recognize that mustache anywhere.

It is Al Snow!

"Hey Jessica, right? I just wanted you to know that WWE really liked you. I mean we really, really liked you a lot."

"Thanks," I said. "I thought that was the case. But let me guess, MTV did not?"

"You might be right but I am not positive."

No poker face for me. I must have shown my cards right there on my face.

"It isn't over though," he said trying to keep me encouraged. "Now, anything can happen in professional wrestling, right?"

I turned and saw that another person had joined our conversation. Mick Foley jumped right into our circle.

"We, as in WWE, we do want to take your number down," he said, "in the event that something else could become of this, for you that is."

"Yes, yes," I said. "Please do."

I knew they already had my number, but figured this was Mick's way of saying maybe we can still do something for you here. That was super nice of him and Al to do. In hindsight, I now know that despite MTV's opinion, they saw something in me for wrestling, and they didn't want me to give up hope.

"Absolutely," Al Snow said. "Like maybe WWE might have something else for you. If not, we can at least put you in the right direction if you are interested."

"Definitely. Thank you very much," I said jotting my information down for them both, with Al Snow returning the favor.

Bittersweet. I went home that day somewhat sad and somewhat distracted, but I knew that I did stand out enough to make two big names in wrestling catch up with me to lift my spirits and let me network. I knew that was a plus. I got my taste, and because of their kindness, I wasn't ready to give up.

In hindsight, I'm glad I didn't get it. If I played into the casting agents' bullshit whims, who knows where MTV would have put me? I may have been forced to shift my dreams into some other kind of ridiculousness. Maybe I would have become some weird reality star for them, rather than what I really wanted to do.

Maybe there would have been a show called, *ODB: 17 and Pregnant on the Jersey Shore.*

Who knows?

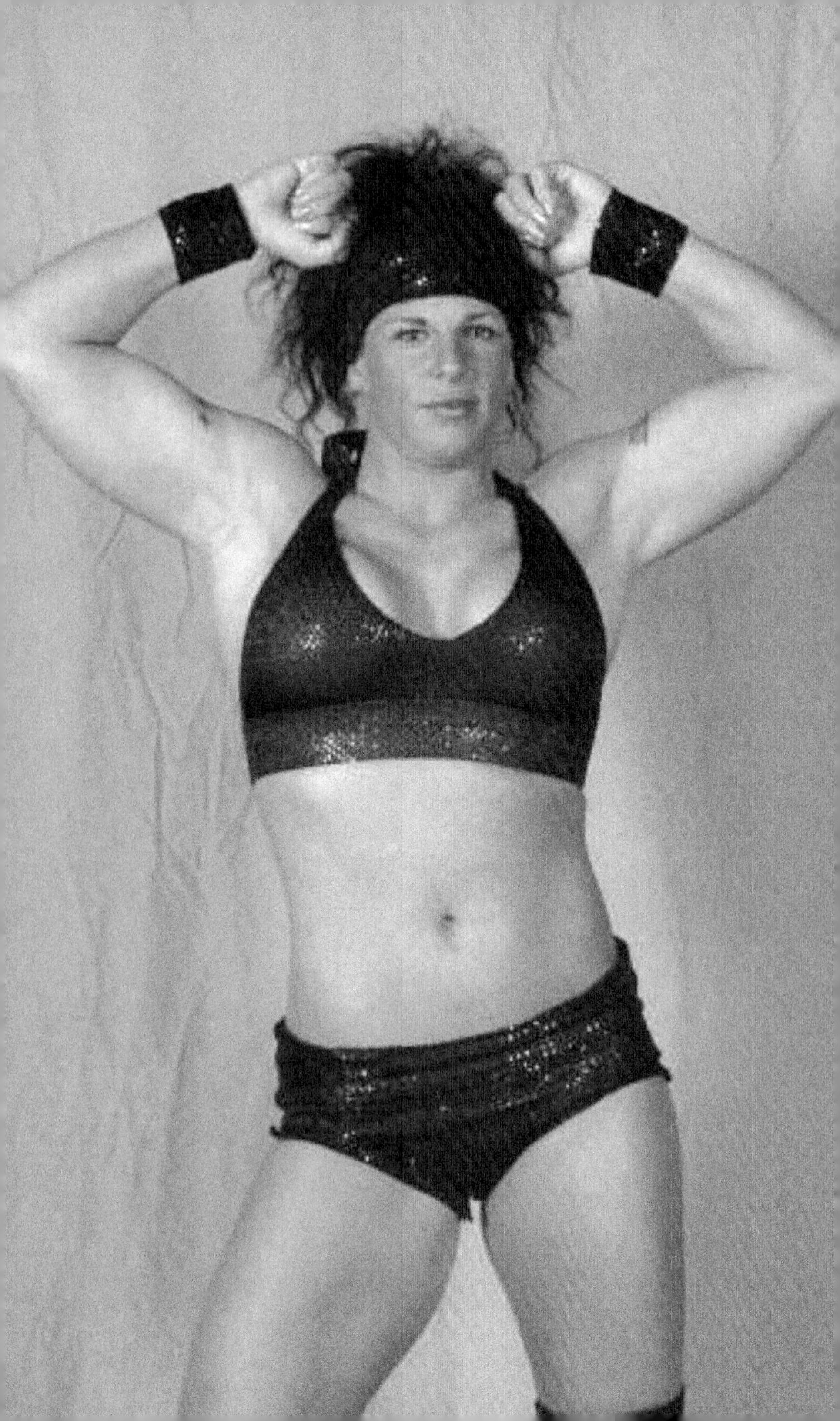

CHAPTER 3 – EARLY WRESTLING DAYS

I went back to living at home with my parents when I had made the commitment in my mind that I was ready to take up training for professional wrestling. Not long after the *Tough Enough* tryouts, I found myself on the computer staring at an internet search page. I typed in two words: *wrestling training*.

I was fortunate. Gone were the days where breaking into the business was a next-to-impossible feat. Wrestling was huge on TV with the whole Attitude Era. It was really hitting the mainstream pop culture. At this point in the wrestling business, promoters were opening shops all over the country. They were trying to capitalize off of wrestling's success with the nWo, The Rock, and Stone Cold Steve Austin touting "You too could be the next WWE Superstar."

There were no longer any secrets. Wrestling training wasn't being hidden. The cat was out of the bag, and people were doing anything for a buck.

There were more training schools to pick from than ever before. Everyone and their mom apparently wanted to own a ring, run shows, and set up training camps – and were doing so. At around the turn of the century, research was showing me that wrestling schools were popping up everywhere regardless of their head trainer's experience or contributions to the industry.

In 2001, I finally made my selection, and honestly, location played a major factor in it. I went to train with a guy by the name of Eddie Sharkey.

Now, when I showed up to the first day of the rest of my life, I was in for a surprise. This place didn't look anything like you would maybe see on TV with the production they did for *Tough Enough*, or what the NXT facilities look like today. It also didn't look anything like its pictures did on the internet. Basically, I opened the door and peeked in to see a beat-up ring in a warehouse that had a leaky ceiling with orange buckets spotlighting each of the holes.

I had seen *Rocky*, however, and I wasn't going to look a gift horse in the mouth. The good thing about finding this holy wrestling sanctuary was that it was only 20 minutes away from St. Louis Park, MN.

Because of that, I was positive. I thanked God, said a little prayer for my well-being, and moved forward, all the while side-stepping a container of scummy rain water in the entrance.

I am in wrestling heaven.

The very first time I stepped foot into Eddie Sharkey's wrestling gym, I got the grand tour. Beyond all the buckets, the place was kind of like a big storage unit with metal walls sporting some light rusting around the beams.

Aside from the facility, I noticed right away that it was sticky in there. I guess it got hot in there fast with guys running all around, but fortunately, the gym had a big garage door on one side so that the muggy, thick air could be easily alleviated. One good yank and the stank was gone. Opening that hatch was like taking one of the walls down, and raising the door inversely would cool the place down quickly.

In the back corner, there was a little dispatcher-like office with a phone to facilitate the business end of things. There was a bathroom too in the other corner for the other kind of business, unisex of course. Unisex, of course, meant the bathroom was shady-looking with all the guys who were using it, however. I opened the door and saw just as I had expected. They apparently pissed on the floor like all guys do and the toilet seat looked diseased. I would imagine if a girl sat on it wrong, she probably could get pregnant or, at the very least, some kind of STD.

Eh, I can probably just hold it.

Speaking of girls, I looked around that first days and took inventory on their clientele. Class was already in session and I was the only chick there. There was nothing fancy at all to speak of, but it was wrestling... so I was ready to go!

"This is perfect. I am in."

After paying my $2000, I started working as hard as I could. The regular classes were Mondays, Wednesdays, and Fridays for their instructed training schedule. It would start at 4pm, and I would stay pretty late.

Midwest Pro Wrestling's (MPW) Arik Cannon was a big name in the indy scene in and around Minnesota at the time. He had connections to International Wrestling Association (IWA) Mid-South and would later do a lot with guys like Mike Quackenbush over at Chikara, as well as tour with Dragon Gate in Japan. He was in my class, as well as another guy you probably know even more.

Shawn Daivari was there and ready to go!

Much like me, Shawn had gotten his first taste of wrestling and wanted more. On October 19, 1998, a very young Shawn bought a ticket to a live taping of WCW's *Nitro*. At some point, Mike Tenay went out into the audience to talk to some of the fans and get their reactions to stuff going on between the Horsemen and the New World Order (nWo) factions. The angle had Eric Bischoff finally getting his ass kicked by Ric Flair the week before, and fans were solicited to help put over the story. Tenay, crowded by a number of fans, eventually put a mic in front of Daivari's face and he said, "I think Eric Bischoff got what he deserves. Ric Flair is a 13-time world champ, and he deserves to be full time on Monday *Nitro*. And Hogan? Bischoff just needs to let him go."

We hit it off and Daivari became my new dance partner to a different kind of dance. We trained quite a bit together, and I still appreciate all he did for me early on.

While training, we would often hear Sharkey shout some comments from outside of the ring. Yes, sometimes, he would pretend to be interested. He would come out of his little office and would sit on a lawn chair to watch us bump. For the most part, however, we knew the deal. The inmates were running the asylum. Sharkey was cool and all. He was a nice guy, but really, he just wanted our money. Sharkey was ready to throw us to the sharks when we were done.

To stand out as being different and not just some girl in a man's world, I went there a lot and played off my participation with *Tough Enough*. I milked the shit out of that for everything it was worth. Talk about "flogging a dead horse," I even wore a *Tough Enough* shirt to train whenever I could to try to earn street cred with all of the male students.

Within a month or two, I was networking, just like I learned to do at Disney. I was keeping my ears open and inviting myself to go along on any road trip that I could. Sharkey always said that you should bring your gear with you everywhere you go, so that is exactly what I did. I decided to always keep my ears open and actively work on jumping in cars with whomever to see if I could get booked.

While we were training, I saw that the students around us started to drop like flies. Only a few of us took it seriously. Everybody else was content with just staying on the local independent scene and did not want to branch out. So eventually at some point, it was just Daivari and me.

Daivari caught a break early on and worked a show with Adnan Al-Kaissie. The good "Sheik" took a liking to him and helped him out a lot, even taking him out to dinner early on to just talk ring psychology. He also stressed that the best way to learn to be a pro wrestler was by being in the ring – no matter how shitty the show was. Shawn Daivari took the advice to heart and did just that, pushing me to do the same.

On my first few attempts looking for work, I realized that there were a lot of chores that needed to be done at any show, so I figured I would offer to do these things to get my foot in the door. When it came right down to it, I was totally happy to "pay my dues" anyhow, but also thought it would be a good thing to mention in order to help me get a gig actually wrestling. Eventually, someone took the bait. I ended up working for a smaller promotion called MPW by promising to help set up for the show with the eventual possibility of someday being looked at to have a match on the card. While they didn't have a big production with lights and a fancy ring, they ran pretty regularly. I was totally shooting for quantity over quality.

I was on Cloud 9.

The promoters for this group were real characters in their own likes. We called them "Shifty & Sherriff" because one guy seemed on the up-and-up and the other looked like a criminal. Rather than renting a hall to do business like most promotions did, MPW was set to run regular shows at a bar called "First Avenue."

After four months of setting up the ring and putting up chairs at First Avenue for Shifty and Sherriff, they decided to give me something back for my hard work and dedication. They finally booked me for my first match.

Come August of 2001, I rolled up to a new venue for MPW. This stellar event was taking place at 2200 4th Street in Minneapolis at a lovely venue called Grumpy's Bar. Grumpy's was a tiny little dive bar with barely enough room to drink, let alone set up a wrestling ring. It was one of those deals where you couldn't even jump off the top rope because the ceiling was so low that you would hit your head if you did.

    Anyhow, this was my *WrestleMania*. I invited all my friends and filled the place with everyone and anyone I knew. For the big little event, I was booked to work with a girl named Mystique Ladon. She was a local who never really made it, but a decent enough kid to work with, either way.

    For our actual match, it was the most basic shit you would ever see. I did the whole Memphis "hip toss, arm drag, bodyslam" thing and tore down the house – in at least my own mind. Eh, it was good enough to pass, however, and I had finally proved myself to the promoters. After that, they started to use me more and more.

    I was finally in!

    Because there weren't a lot of girls around to pick from, I was mostly working with Daivari in intergender attractions. It made sense. We trained a lot together, so we had time to get our shtick together. Working intergender matches correctly was an art form, and we got better and better at it. We had to work hard to make it believable. The moves had to make sense and the selling needed to be there. If a guy was fighting with a girl for real, the spots had to make sense or nobody would buy it.

    We wanted to make it as real as possible so we practiced a lot of extra hours for our matches. We came up with some cool original spots at the warehouse that we could plug in or take out of any match. Daivari and I fine-tuned and polished everything. For both being green, we did a decent job putting our stuff together; I think so anyway. This made us both look even better to promoters who thought maybe we were making the best of things and just calling it in the ring.

    For the bar shows, we specifically played off of all the stereotypes we could, be it gender or race, we knew that the crowd watching us was more of a gathering of drunks than one of wrestling fans. This pushing buttons was the Memphis way. Knowing our crowd worked. We gave them just what they wanted from a chick in the ring and a young guy with darker skin than theirs. Because of this, we would get some of the biggest pops of the night.

    After we really polished our act, we took the show on the road. I worked with Daivari on a whole lot of gigs all around our region after that. We were basically the same size which made things a little more believable for the audience, and we came up with our own storylines. A little bit of mic work here and there was all we needed, if any, to get over what we were selling. (I believe that another lost art form these days is that you should always tell a friggin' story!)

Daivari had a great mind for wrestling and how to tell a tale in the ring. He really was one creative motherfucker! He would say, "Listen to me. Follow me," and I did just that, and I am glad I took his direction. He played it great. He was not afraid to work a girl, and vice versa. We had chemistry and used it. Because of this, we were getting noticed.

Here and there, however, shit happens. A few times, I had the wind knocked out of me, but I never sold it. Mistakes happen. Unless there was a real reason to, my motto was to stay quiet. I learned that day one from my training.

Even though Sharkey was a shark himself, he did teach me a lot. He taught me to be quiet, shake everyone's hand, and to always hide your wallet. (In the end, one of the main people I hid my wallet from was Sharkey!)

Sharkey was the one who taught me locker room etiquette and the importance of not sweating the little things. He always said to be polite and quiet as to keep away from heat with both the wrestlers and the promoters. He said not to call someone out on getting stiffed unless it was intentional, but when you had to – give them a receipt eventually after a few hard shots to get them to lighten up.

One time I was at a show somewhere and BANG! Daivari nailed me hard in the chin.

Oh shit!

He was off with his calculations. He hit me so hard with a European uppercut it transported me to Ireland.

Lucky charms. I saw yellow stars and blue diamonds.

I didn't have the pink hearts to tell him he messed up. I didn't say anything. I didn't want to ever do or scare Daivari into handling me all "prim and proper" and fragile-like because I was a girl. If he started taking it easy with me, that would make our matches suck. I certainly didn't want that.

Daivari played it cool. He didn't say anything, even though he must have known he potatoed me. I mean, he hit me so hard it had to have hurt his hand.

CHAPTER 3 – Early Wrestling Days

In the same match, he did it again, so I did what I was taught to do in training. I gave Daivari my first receipt. Yep. I kicked him square in the green clovers.
"Even," I said.
He knew he fucked up. We laughed between groans.

KEN ANDERSON

Eventually, Ed Sharkey started to run shows using talent from his own camp. This was a normal formula on the independents and still is to this very day. You get a number of students signed up and dangle spots on your show under their noses to keep them around. Then, you get both the money from them at the school, and to use them as free talent on your shows. In the end, however, this money-saving practice has cranked out a lot of shitty cheap "talent."

Another promotion called American Championship Wrestling (ACW) out of Wisconsin had ties with Sharkey back then. In an effort to better their shows, they initiated a bit of a talent exchange with Sharkey at this time. So we would use some of their guys, and they would use some of ours. It was a win-win for both of us, maybe with Sharkey getting the better end of the talent exchange, I don't know.

A group of us would go to Green Bay, and promoter Jason Jerry returned the favor exchanging talent by sending in Ken Anderson and a few others quite regularly for a while, maybe twice a month. The same thing started to happen with a core group of guys traveling to Milwaukee to work Mid American for Carmine DeSpirito, and to Chicago (where I met guys like CM Punk, Colt Cabana, and Austin Aires.)

Sharkey took to a liking to Ken Anderson and decided to book a lot of things around him in our area. Anderson was a natural entertainer. During high school in Green Bay, he was a swimmer and competed in track and field, and also announced for their basketball games. There, someone dared him to make the announcing funnier, all old school, saying each surname twice. He did just that. As we know today, that stunt followed him into wrestling where he would be known as, "Mr. Anderson… Anderson."

By the time I met Anderson, he had a couple of years on me. He had already been trained by Eric Hammers and Mike Mercury in Wisconsin. In 2001, I think he had about 20 matches under his belt before he got a break. He was booked as enhancement talent for *WWE Jakked*, where he had his first match on television was losing to Essa Rios.

One weekend, Anderson came down with his whole crew to Minnesota to spend a weekend working for Sharkey. I took one look at him and was like, *"Oh, yeah."*

It was weird. He wasn't really my type. I wasn't typically into his style, but there was something about him.

He was a nice guy. He was handsome. He quickly became my first serious boyfriend.

I guess you could call it love at first sight.

I knew the expression, "don't shit where you eat." I knew dating someone you work with is a risk. It is an emotional risk to you and it is also a risk to the company you work for. Therefore, it is also a risk to your career.

Love can be complicated. Mixing love and work makes it even more complicated because you are involving coworkers, your boss, and even your livelihood.

I knew all of this, but I was still ready to take the risk. I was like a hungry fish who knew what a worm on a fish hook looked like, but was willing to go for it anyhow. It made no sense and I knew all of this at the same time.

So why did I fall for Anderson?

According to a recent study, 39% of workers say they have dated a work colleague at some point in their career, and 30% of those people went on to marry the coworker. I would venture to say this number is probably even higher in the wrestling business. While the actual time in the ring pitted against each other might not look like much, it is the outside of the ring action that pits us together even more. Wrestlers work more hours together than arguably most other professions because of all the time we are isolated on the road from the real world.

The only people we see day in and day out are typically other wrestlers. It's not easy to find connections with other people off the road because you don't have time to grow with them. There is no time to learn who they are and appreciate them and let your relationship grow together, because you are never around. The people wrestlers spend time with are other wrestlers. They understand us the best because they are the same as we are. They are the only ones who can really understand.

It's no wonder that sometimes the locker room looks like a human zoo – a breeding ground for romantic entanglements. These are our people.

Anderson was the perfect package for me then. He spoke my language. He drove on my road. He was everything that complimented me at that time.

So, after only about a month after meeting, we realized we didn't want to be apart, so he packed his bags and moved to Minnesota. We immediately found ourselves copying keys at the local hardware shop. For those of you keeping track, yes, in about a month we were moving in together. I mean, seriously, though, our first real date was to U-Haul.

So big deal. We ended up living together right away. It wasn't bad at all. Seeing how he had a few years in the game more than I did, he ended up helping me quite a lot with wrestling, bills, and just life in general.

Once we moved in together, Anderson also became a personal trainer at the local Bally's Fitness Center. That was cool because I also got a free gym trainer and gym membership out of the deal.

I was still working my regular job at the Crab Shack, so we were doing well enough to easily pay the bills. It also helped that we started to get booked a lot and were on the road all the time, bringing in some supplemental income from indy bookings.

I would drive with Anderson and Daivari even when I wasn't booked, but they would always put me over. Soon after that I would get booked by association, following the golden rule that was "always bring your shit with you."

See, while Anderson and I were dating, Daivari was there so much that he practically moved in, and we all lived together. Daivari and Anderson became the best of friends around this time and their friendship brought them both to the next level, as well as it did with me. Anderson also looked after Daivari as he did with me and took him under his wing the best he could. Nobody would fuck with you if they had to deal with Anderson in doing so.

The exception to this rule was maybe Austin Aries. Daivari's first impression of Austin Aries was that he was a total dick to him, but Daivari decided to handle it without Anderson. His plan was to kill him with kindness. Daivari said that, one time, he had to drive 300 miles with Aries who got all fucked up on Mike's Hard Lemonade. Daivari played it cool and pulled over every 20 minutes so he could puke. Aries appreciated that and after that he lightened up. So eventually, Aries grew on Daivari and vice versa apparently. He says today that while Aries "is still in fact a dick" he gets it now, and Aries just "marches to the beat of his own drum."

Anderson and I were together two years. We mostly worked Minnesota and Chicago, but we also went to IWA for Ian Rotten where paydays were just brutal. Working at shitty shows like that only made us grow closer.

You see, IWA shows went on until two in the morning. There, Angelina Love and I would wrestle our hardest. We would put on some great matches for the crowd, and then at the end of the night we would look to get paid.

"Where the fuck is Ian?" I would ask Angelina.

"Hell, if I knew, girl. He hasn't paid me either."

We would see him way down the hall and go after him, and he would run off and still manage to get away.

It was obvious that on more than one occasion, he would do everything he could to avoid us. He just didn't want to pay and hoped we would just give up.

Ian Rotten eventually created an extra layer of confusion when it came time for the pay window. He had this guy named Dave Prazak who was his lackey. His bitch. If I would finally catch up with Rotten and get him in the corner, he would just direct me to Prazak.

Then, I would seek out that little turdburglar who would ultimately say, "Settle down. Now you want gas money? That wasn't part of the deal to my understanding."

This is when having Anderson really paid off. He came to our defense and set those guys straight so we didn't have to walk out of there with just a "hotdog and a handshake."

Having a big debt collector dude around was great, and made me love him all the more.

CHAPTER 3 – Early Wrestling Days

STEEL DOMAIN WRESTLING
★ ★ ★ PRESENTS ★ ★ ★

YEAR END SLAM II
★ LIVE PRO ★
WRESTLING

DEC. 28 ★ 7:30PM
WEST ST. PAUL ARMORY
1346 S. ROBERT

★ ★ ★ 7 MATCHES INCLUDING ★ ★ ★

LENNY LANE vs. ADRIAN LYNCH
SDW HEAVYWEIGHT TITLE

Magnus vs. Zappa, Aries vs. Bambino
Burns vs. Anderson, ODB vs. Miss Natural
Tony DeNucci Returns and More!!

WATCH SDW TV SATURDAYS 2PM KSTC CH. 45
Tickets at the Door $15 & $5 for Kids
SDW IS FAMILY ENTERTAINMENT
CALL 651-306-2231
www.sdwrestling.com

Jessie Kresa is... ODB: One Dirty Bitch!

STEEL DOMAIN

They weren't all bad, however. Early on, I got booked for a number of shows for a promoter who was much better to deal with than Rotten. This promoter was named Ed Hellier and he ran a promotion called Steel Domain Wrestling (SDW) out of Minnesota. While they were smaller and not widely-known internationally, they were consistent and were one of the Midwest's oldest and most successful independent wrestling promotions around at that time.

They say that you can't get better unless you work with people who are better than you are. The catch-22 is that if you are new, promoters don't often want to waste good talent on rookies – so green guys work with other green guys. Fortunately for me at Steel Domain, this was not the case. Maybe one of the reasons for this is that traditionally around this time, there was a bit of a shortage for women wrestlers so getting any girl to work for a promotion was always a plus to fill out the card.

After getting booked there, I had no idea that I would be working with Sherri Martel so early on in my career.

Now, Sherri was just great. I had, of course, seen her as a kid. I thought she was just awesome. There was only one problem I could see with this booking; I was afraid to work with Scary Sherri. She was actually scary to me!

I had heard a story about her. I guess one time, while she was managing Macho Man Randy Savage, they were booked for a number of matches against Dusty Rhodes. During that black and yellow polka dotted run with "The Common Man," Dusty also had a manager named Sweet Sapphire. Sapphire was as green as grass. I had heard that there were a number of mixed tag team matches pitting Savage and Sherri versus "The American Dream" and his partner, Sweet Sapphire.

Now, Sensational Sherri was a legitimate badass and not someone to be messed with. This rookie Sapphire was blowing spots left and right, and Sherri quickly got fed up and was ready to hand Sweet Sapphire her sweet ass. The straw that broke the camel's back apparently was that Sapphire only had one pair of tights, and didn't do a great job of cleaning them. That's right, she went to the "Vader School of Dry Cleaning" to do all her ring gear laundry.

A few weeks in on this run, and Sherri had had enough of Sapphire's stank ass. Before the show, Sapphire arrived... and her opponent was there waiting – *drunk*.

Sherri literally stripped Sapphire down in front of Macho and Dusty, who couldn't believe their eyes.

"You are going to take a shower whether you like it or not!" Sherri belted, throwing Sapphire into the shower and scrubbing her back, prison style. "You nasty smelly bitch!"

"Helllppp!!!" Sapphire screamed.

Macho and Dusty shrugged. "Above our pay grade" was the general consensus. Nobody wanted to get in on that, even if it potentially involved two naked soaped up chicks.

I had heard of this "vet versus a rookie" story, and it was definitely in my mind when I showed up to the casino for my first match with Sherri that day. I made damn sure to take two showers that day, and scrubbed my ass extra hard with a raspberry loofah.

Anyhow, I was booked with Sherri for a number of dates at the Redwing Minnesota Casino. For the whole weekend, she was working with me, and we knew that some of the same faces in the hotel might see more than one show. With that in mind, we came up with a little story arc for our matches. The idea was that she would go over on me a handful of times, then towards the end, the babyface would finally prevail. It followed the classic southern style where the good guys would get their asses kicked until the very end when revenge would be exacted.

On the final day, I was booked to win. I was excited that I was going to get a clean victory over such a big name, and even though it was a work, it was a good bragging right and one that could have helped me elevate my career a little.

When I showed up to the conference room where the match was set to take place, the promoter (Ed Hellier) came up to me with a bad look on his face.

"I'm afraid there are going to have to be some changes tonight," he said.

"Oh, no," I said, knowing immediately that I was not going to be going over on Sherri anymore. I had figured that she had changed her mind, and that was it. I knew I was not supposed to say anything, but I was disappointed and I was really looking forward to the payoff of the series I was promised.

"It looks like you know what's up, but it's probably not what you think," he said. "Come with me."

Ed led me out to the lot where the ring truck was. Sherri was in the back asleep. She was motionless and there was vomit all over the place. She looked dead.

"Oh boy," I said.

Ed Hellier as the promoter of Steel Domain Wrestling had to make a judgment call that night and did. "So, as you can see, obviously we are not putting you over on her – or even against her. She is too messed up."

So, I got to work with my arch nemesis again for the 300th time – Daivari the Great.

While that sucked, Ed did make good, however. Soon after that, he created a women's belt despite the fact that he didn't have a real division as there was not enough female talent to pull from.

He made me the first women's champion of SDW.

That wasn't my last encounter with Scary Sherri. A number of indy promotions near us started to bring in Sherri a bunch around this time because she was local, even though it was starting to become a bad time in her life.

In 2002, I was still just passed my first solid year in wrestling, and I was tapped to work with Sherri again at a promotion in Milwaukee. At this particular show, CM Punk was booked to be her manager. We were all set to wrestle in an indoor volleyball arena that had sand and everything. When we got there, we read the card. Anderson praised CM Punk, but Daivari pulled me off to the side.

"You have worked with Sherri before and know the deal," he said. "But look out for that Punk. He can be a stiff little bastard."

I nodded and made a mental note of it. Daivari didn't bullshit and always had my back. He still does today.

I remember that there was a big locker room in the back all set up for all the boys, but just like I was coming to learn from most promotions, there were no real provisions made for the girls. We were an afterthought.

I went exploring. I wheeled in my bag over the cement floors that were peppered with the beach sand that everyone's feet had tracked into the back area. When I looked for a place to get ready, I was sent back to change in a broom closet. I shook my head, but I knew the deal.

When I opened the door, I saw a familiar face in her underwear who didn't even attempt to cover up.

"Oh, hey," Sherri said. "ODB right?"

She remembered me from working some for Ed at Steel Domain. Still being relatively green, you never really knew if a name was going to remember you, so it felt good that she did.

Sherri shook my hand then went back over to her shelf where all her shit was crammed next to some bottles of floor stripper. She dug through her bag and rather than to reveal some kind of tights or something, she pulled out a bottle of vodka.

I watched her thinking getting hammered before a match was probably not a good practice to engage in, seeing how we were just about to get in the ring with each other and handle each other's bodies.

Someone could end up with a broken neck, or something.

Sherri saw my wheels turning. She watched me watching her, and I must have set off a red flag or something. I guess I probably looked like a deer in headlights or something.

"How rude of me," she said. Then she took the bottle away from her lips, and slid it across the shelf towards me. "Would you like some?"

Fuck it.

I figured if she was going to be drunk out there with me, I may as well do the same.

"Sure," I said. "Breakfast of champions."

So, there I was, drinking in a janitor's closet with Sensational Sherri.

It was truly sensational.

We had a three-way match that night, and surprisingly, nothing went wrong. I just went in there and I listened to her, despite the fact that I was tipsy as fuck. Hell, if The Sandman could do it, so could I.

Now again, we had to wrestle in an indoor volleyball arena that night, so there was sand all over the floor outside the ring. No matter how much you wiped your feet like Razor Ramon making an entrance, the sand got on the canvas and gave me hooker knees.

Besides that, everything went well, until CM Punk, her manager, bodyslammed me as hard as he could onto the sand. I decided not to be the polite girl that the promoter wanted and broke the silent rule because it felt like I landed on fucking cement!

"*You dick!*" I said to the future Mr. Cult of Personality. I didn't give a flying shit who he was.

Soon after that, however, we all started getting booked more and more in Steel Domain, as well as Chicago. We started hanging out more and more with CM Punk and Colt Cabana whenever we would see them on these shows, so we had to get along, right?

Daivari had admitted that Punk had been a dick to him on their first few encounters. Knowing it was inevitable that he would have to work with him again in the future, Daivari was smart and decided to squash whatever heat there might be, on his own with him. He recognized that Punk carried himself like a star and figured that someday, he very well could be, so there was no better time to fix problems than the present.

Daivari asked to have a word with Punk before a show, and they both went outside into the lot. Daivari was very open, he told me, in attempts to see what the issue was, without being accusatory or off-putting. I guess when Punk first saw Daivari a few months back, he looked into him and went to his website. There Punk figured that Daivari was a jabroni, because he had a website before he even wrestled in his first match. He felt that was a dick move, but also realized that Daivari was brand new and likely didn't know better than to put himself over when he had accomplished absolutely nothing.

They shook hands and all was cool. They squashed all that easily, probably in part due to Daivari aligning himself with Anderson, who was also cool with Punk. A big part of wrestling, I was coming to learn, was not what you did in the ring, but rather all the stuff that happened outside of it.

ON THE ROAD

Anderson and Daivari were always outspoken and funny on the road.

Whenever we were on the road, one of the things we did on our time off was train. When we got into town early before a show, we would check into the hotel, then find the local gym. That was the life, so I took to it.

When I started hitting the road with those guys, I was already lean and muscular from school athletics. Anderson was a trainer, and he helped me get to the next level. I was a big fan of *American Gladiators*, and one day we were watching it and told him, "See that? That is what I want to look like," and he knew how to make it happen.

"It will take a lot of work and a strict diet," he said. "Think you can do it?"

"I know I can."

I wanted to see how far my body could go. I wasn't sure about having a full-fledged six-pack, but figured that muscles and wrestling should go hand in hand. After all, it is a cosmetic sport.

I thought to myself, you know, girls are not really jacked like this, but maybe getting bigger could help push my wrestling career, so that is what I decided to do.

Once I started to excel at it, I had to make a decision. Did I want to be a fitness-type muscular girl, or, did I want to be a monster? Because there weren't a lot of women like Chyna or Nicole Bass in the business, I decided to go almost to that level, but not quite to the Frankenstein-with-lipstick degree.

That is when I started training for a fitness-competition style body alongside my wrestling schedule.

I knew it was a lot of work and knew it would all go away when I started eating like shit again, but I didn't care. On top of the training, of course, the diet was strict. I had to eat right. This consisted of eating every two hours for four months like clockwork. I mostly ate only chicken and brown rice, tuna, protein shakes, egg whites, and oatmeal.

And, yes, I cut out all alcohol.

The name of the one fitness competition I finally registered for was The Minnesota North Star. There were only four people in my category. In the end, I took second. The judges said I was "actually too muscular."

The person who won was not nearly as ripped and jacked as I was, and, yes, ODB could have easily kicked her ass if we were in a ring and not on a stage. Just sayin'.

As I mentioned before on the wrestling side of things, while on the road, we would check into the hotel and then find the local gym.

Anderson was a beast and an excellent trainer. When I was training with the boys, I was training like the boys. I was leaner and muscular from my training and didn't have the fake boobs yet.

I didn't go all out for looking pretty at the gym. I didn't get dressed up and put makeup on. That was all fake bullshit and I didn't have time for any of that. I was there for one thing and one thing only, and that was to build muscle and train. (Even though I didn't have time for the nonsense, I will say this, the boys found time to pretty themselves up, even more than I did and were always looking in the mirrors at themselves.) I also had a bit of a deeper voice probably from my college days. I wouldn't say I was at the level of a Nina Blackwood, or a Tone Loc or something – just a little deeper due to all the excessive partying I did at the time. So, if you add all these variables up and sometimes if you looked quick at the big muscles, I guess I could get mistaken for a guy.

You see, sometimes on the road when we would pull up to a new gym, I would see what we now call a "Karen." She would move very quietly, but make no mistake about it, her movement was very calculated.

I would get out the car with Anderson and Daivari, maybe eating something small, like a scoop of dry protein powder or whatever. I would see the local Karen and think nothing of her, but what happened next started to happen so much that eventually I could predict it.

Our theory was Karen would run ahead of us to talk shit. "Hey girls," she would say to whomever might listen in the gym. "See that person over there by the car?"

"Yeah," someone would reply.

"Don't let him fool you. That's a guy."

"Huh?"

"Yes," she would say. "I heard his manly voice in the lot, talking to the other two. I bet he is dressed up like a girl so he can catch a glimpse."

"Wait, what?!"

"Probably does it so he can go in the locker room and check out the ladies while they are changing."

"Are you kidding me?"

"Heard him talk with my own ears," she would say, pulling her Vera Bradley bag back over her shoulder.

"Warning," she would say as she entered the women's dressing area. "There is a guy coming in here in a minute, dressed as a girl."

I could just picture the bitches scramble.

Then, of course, I would walk into the club clueless of Karen and check in at the front desk. When I was done, I would find my way to the girl's locker room, set down my bag, and go about my business. The other girls had already run for cover. Some hid in the shower stalls, other ran to the bathrooms, and others quickly pulled on their clothing and cowered in the corners learing at me. This of course was a different time when people were less "accepting" of others.

That motherfucker did it again.

Believe it or not, this happened a lot. I don't know if it was jealousy, or what, but apparently Karen had heat with me.

"Okay, um," a female employee would say walking up to me into the ghost town. "We need you to help us get something straightened out."

One time after having enough of that bullshit again and again, I finally gave up. Without arguing, I just dropped my pants to end all question of my gender and just change for my workout. I swung my girl parts in faces for all to see.

"That work for you, babe?"

In doing so, I killed two birds with one stone. The questioning employee looked down and saw what I was and was not packing.

"Sorry ma'am," she said blushing, leaving the scene with her tail tucked between her legs after seeing that I didn't have anything tucked between mine.

"And you should be," I said, having some fun with it myself and pulling on my gym shorts. Honestly, I didn't care, but it was bullshit.

Because of whatever scene that the employee made returning back to work, it was obvious to my workout partners what had happened again. I would then find Daivari almost dying from laughter somewhere in the corner of the gym. Boy, he had a sick sense of humor. If I didn't know better, I would have to wonder if Daivari was in cahoots with Karen, and he was working me somehow.

Daivari is actually a convicted known ribber. He was responsible for an ongoing bad rib that he liked to pull on me whenever we went to the airport.

It was so lame! Before a flight, we would check our bags and head over to TSA for security screening. Anderson and Daivari would just walk right through the metal alarm and there was never any problem. However, nine times out of ten when I went through, no matter how carefully I checked my stuff, it would always go off.

Daivari (or one of those assholes) would always plant something on me. And I know it wasn't Karen.

Never a dull moment, I tell you.

88 Jessie Kresa is... ODB: One Dirty Bitch!

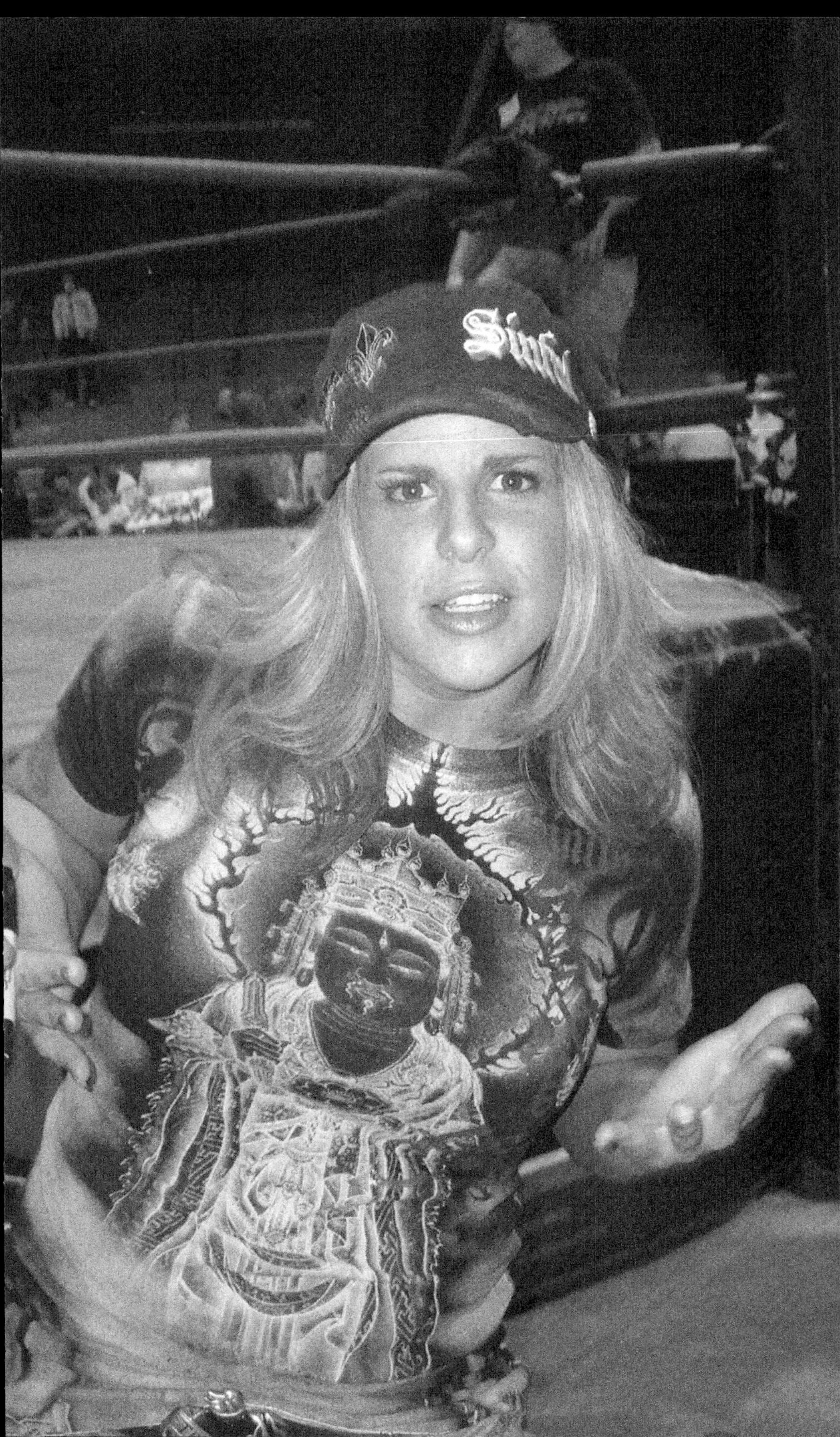

CHAPTER 4 - TNA WRESTLING IN 2002

When I was growing up as a kid, I mostly watched WWF. However, there was always wrestling on another channel and we watched that some, too. Even though I had dreamed of being a wrestler for New York, I of course would have also jumped at the offer from Georgia, if there was one. Wrestling was wrestling and that was my dream.

Just as I was getting into the wrestling business, one of my possible options for employment was going out – *going of business, that is.*

I think there were a lot of factors that brought about this change in the formula.

History shows that Ted Turner always liked wrestling. It was a cheap form of entertainment which he kept in his programming for decades. All you had to do was point a camera or two at a ring, send some bodies out there, and you had a show. It was easy to produce.

Turner went into business with Vince McMahon because he loved wrestling. This was obviously way before WCW even was a thing. Back in the day, WWF programming was featured on Turner's network, and the partnership was healthy. However, that didn't last. What happened was, McMahon got offered some money for programming from a competitor's network and jumped at the chance. He rocked the Turner boat by putting a show on at the same time as the other one he had playing over on Turner's channel.

Turner took McMahon's move as an insult. He did not want WWF to be broadcasted on any other networks as that watered down ratings. He was under the impression that McMahon would work with him exclusively.

Subsequently, Turner dropped McMahon's brand altogether and brought in the National Wrestling Alliance (NWA). NWA had a built-in wrestling audience that enjoyed traditional in-ring action and less of the cartoony stuff that McMahon was engaging in. The NWA had years and years of history behind it and was a clear competitor to its counterpart in New York. Turner's strategy then was a very "turnabout is fair play" type move.

"Let the pissing wars begin."

CHAPTER 4 – TNA Wrestling in 2002

Turner continued to air NWA wrestling on his channel for some time until, one day, McMahon cut out the middle man. Because Turner refused to give McMahon a spot on his channel, Vince went to the NWA and made them an offer they couldn't refuse. He bought their syndicated timeslot right out from under Turner's nose.

When Turner turned on his TV that first week that McMahon took over NWA programming, he wasn't alone. Along with countless others on that one particular Saturday morning, he was surprised to see that McMahon on his screen explaining the upcoming changes. Unbeknownst to Turner, a change had been made on a third-party level.

This event went on to be called "Black Saturday" and it ignited the feud between McMahon and Turner.

Vinny Mac was delivering what Tycoon Ted perceived to be junk. Gone was the NWA in-ring format, and in its place was something more like an infomercial. The new footage was mostly clips and hype stuff from WWF programming elsewhere that ultimately was acting as a big commercial for their first ever PPV, *WrestleMania*.

Once the WWF accomplished the national exposure they wanted, they bailed. Turner felt used and was pissed.

As you probably know, the WWF created a network of national syndication and took over the whole game. They grew and grew and started killing off all of the territories one by one. There was practically no competition, but Turner was still angry and wanted revenge.

In 1988, Turner bought McMahon's biggest competition, Jim Crockett Promotions, just to get his goat. He created WCW. The company remained private for eight years and was mostly a money pit. However, in 1996 when WCW became public, things began to hit. Turner started using McMahon's tactics against him. He began paying big bucks from to take WWF's talent away from them, the same as they had done – cherry-picking the best from every territory.

Eventually, WCW stole Hulk Hogan from WWF and made a major impact with mainstream fans.

Money was spent and WCW finally found success, finally beating the WWE in the ratings. Not too long after that, the nWo faction debuted. Ted Turner's company offered some very lucrative contracts that wrestlers loved (which I would have loved myself!) They say Eric Bischoff was allowed to write blank checks to get the talent he wanted, like he had permission to virtually write whatever number he needed to exact talent away from Vince McMahon. This set McMahon back big time.

The Monday Night Wars started. WCW won for 80 plus weeks.

However, Vince didn't just sit back and take it. WWE reinvented itself. They targeted a more grownup audience to bring in more ratings. After some time, it worked. WWE's then head writer, Vince Russo's writing brought in "The Attitude Era," targeting an older crowd, and it worked. Add Steve Austin and The Rock to the mix and the WWE was back on top. What happened then was WCW programming took a hit, and WWE was in a position to pull back the best talent to New York.

Eventually, America Online (AOL) and Time Warner came into the picture. They merged and took over Turner's networks and this was the straw that broke the wrestling camel's back. Their CEO, a guy named Jamie Kellner, wanted nothing to do with wrestling on their channels. This that ultimately ended WCW and ended WWE's competition.

WCW suddenly closed its doors. People tried to figure out who was to blame. Fans accused the use of too much shoot stuff in promos. Others said David Arquette winning the WCW title was bullshit. People also hated the "finger poke of doom" which was a lame title change amongst friends in a match between Hulk Hogan and Kevin Nash. Russo made the jump to WCW in its final years, and many claimed that his writing having no filter deserved all the fault. But in the end, most now agree that it was all the shirts and ties in a conference room somewhere that killed the promotion.

Whoever was at fault, it ultimately didn't matter. Come 2001, WCW was put up for sale and WWE was right there to buy them.

With the purchase of WCW, all was made clear. McMahon had no more competition and could do whatever he wanted again. The only question that remained was: "Who would step up and be the next WCW?"

EARLY TNA – A NEW WWE ALTERNATIVE

When WCW was gone, something in wrestling was missing for sure. WWE had won, but that didn't mean they would just absorb all of the wrestling fans out there. Wrestling promotions were like different flavors of ice cream, and the WWE ice cream bar just left a bad taste in the mouth of many.

A number of different promotions wanted to replace WCW's spot in the hearts of many. Many wanted to become the alternative to WWE, but nobody really had a chance. Wrestling promoters for promotions like Ring of Honor (ROH) talked a big game, but nobody could really compete with the WWE. WWE was already a machine. Nobody had the money, or the platform, or even the television deal needed to even come close. If you tried to single out any of them, each would be like pitting Walmart vs. a mom-and-pop shop.

The only way something could come close to becoming an alternative was to actually be a true alternative. They couldn't beat WWE at their own game; they had to be different.

One day by chance, Bob Ryder, Jeff Jarrett and Jerry Jarrett got together and did what rednecks do best. They went on a fishing trip. They got to drinking and figured that they were basically a couple of good ole boys that the professional wrestling business had left behind.

Like many other promoters, they had some big ideas, but the difference here was they knew those big ideas were dreams, not goals. They knew this from experience. All three of them had worked for the big two promotions: WWE and WCW. Life after WCW felt like a forced retirement for Ryder. The Jarretts, as many of you know, were the driving force for countless years of Memphis wrestling. They knew that there wasn't a whole lot one could do to offer the fans an alternative without the kind of money needed to really get a new product out there.

During the Monday Night Wars, Ryder co-hosted *WCW Live* with Jeremy Borash. He was also pretty close friends with Bischoff, so he had some good experience with things behind the scenes.

While they were fishing, Ryder said he didn't think it was the right time to pitch to a TV network because WCW just went out of business.

"They (networks) might not look at wrestling as the right business right now to gain commercial sponsors for TV," he said. "But maybe we don't need them."

"What are you thinking then?" Jeff Jarrett asked.

"Maybe we could run some shows, tape them, and just have all of it go straight to pay-per-view?"

That was genius. The Jarretts loved the idea, and they all decided to do just that.

Soon after that, they put the wheels into motion. Russo joined Jeff and Jerry Jarrett's upcoming promotion as a creative writer and would assist in the writing and production of the shows. Russo came up with the name "Total Nonstop Action," as being a clever play on "T&A," because he of course was a perverted son-of-a-gun that knew sex sells. They agreed that if they were going to be an alternative to WWE, and that if they were airing exclusively to PPV, they might as well do stuff the WWE could never do – because they could. They were hoping that fans, in turn, would view the new promotion as a more adult product than WWE was, or ever could be.

Next, they contacted NWA for street credibility with the fans. They paid in to operate under the historic wrestling banner. They got the licensing to run with NWA title defenses with a straight-to-pay-per-view platform promotion under the name *NWA: TNA*.

TNA's PPV series was banking on a regular weekly event to air every Wednesday night as the company's main source of revenue. This differed from the monthly format that most wrestling promotions fell into for their events. It wasn't a show on cable. If you wanted to see it, you had to pay. They knew that this could make the shows feel special to fans, but they also knew that the shows needed to be cheap so that fans would continue to tune in regularly.

To keep things affordable, TNA set up a deal with the Tennessee State Fairground Sports Arena in Nashville, Tennessee to be the venue to save money. They nicknamed their new home "TNA Asylum."

CHAPTER 4 – TNA Wrestling in 2002

The Jarretts got everything together and were finally ready to debut its first show.

The first show hit in the summer of 2002. That night, a dark warmup match went on to get the crowd fired up. A 450-pound wrestler named Cheex hit the ropes and one of the ropes hit the floor.

You see, Cheex's rather rotund ass was so large that he broke the freaking ring.

"Did you see that?" Vince Russo asked Jeff Jarrett who was staring at a monitor backstage and couldn't believe his eyes. "Bro, that fat fucker broke that shit and messed everything up!"

"Now what are we going to do?" a producer asked.

"Holy shit," Jeff Jarrett said when he heard the news. "We are going on live in like what, 10 minutes? How long will it take to fix?"

The ring crew sped out to the scene of the accident. The ring posts were pointing inwards. The rope had snapped. The turnbuckles were broken. The support pulley under the ring was off, as well.

After taking inventory, they returned back to the awaiting TNA officials by the curtain.

"What's it look like, bro?" Russo asked one of the boys shaking his head.

"It's pretty bad," the ring guy said. "Probably at least a half an hour, maybe an hour if we don't have all the parts."

That answer stunk up the place in an instant. Everyone shit their pants, long and hard.

Backstage, the producers ran all over the place spewing verbal diarrhea. They quickly put together some non-wrestling segments to stall for time and hoped for the best.

"3-2-1, and we are live," said a producer.

First, they sent Don West out there with Russo's writing partner Ed Ferrara. They hammed it up and worked the crowd as the ring crew went to work behind them off camera.

"Are you ready for some TNA?" Ferrara asked the crowd. "I know I am, and I don't just mean Total Nonstop Action."

Nice improv, right?

As part of the sex appeal that TNA promised to deliver, there were cage dancers brought in to spice up the entrance way. They were like the WCW Nitro Girls only their dancing was more stripper-ish. So the director put the camera on them and gave them a little more time that planned.

Then, Mike Tenay came out and cut a promo. Then, they sent it over to Borash. Then, rather than show a bunch of guys there in attendance for a group shot – they each got their own introduction to draw it out. Borash went into a "Hall of Fame" like lineup that was scheduled for later on, where he called out Harley Race, Dory Funk, Jr., Jackie Fargo, Bob Armstrong, Corsica Joe, NWA President Bill Behrens, and Ricky Steamboat to celebrate. This was actually a great move. The fans had no idea that there was an issue with the ring.

While the ring guys were figuring out how to fix a bent loop on the ring post, Jeff Jarrett jumped into the improve mix and came out to shit on all of the NWA guys …then Ken Shamrock… then Scott Hall. Then, a midget wrestler backstage.

The idea of all the frontloading of talent, again, was not ideal but it worked. It made a hot opening for the pay-per-view and it also gave the ring crew some more time, however the clock was ticking, and they were short on hands.

Fortunately for TNA, two 6'5" monsters came to the ring, each with massive hands.

"We can help."

Ron and Don Harris, aka The Harris Brothers, went out to ringside and literally muscled everything back together to save the day. Who needs a wrench? Those two big crowbars squeezed and pulled the ring back into working condition with their bare hands.

Way to start the promotion off with a bang!

As far as the girls were concerned, a Lingerie Battle Royal also went down, but wasn't shown that night. Yes, they taped it during that first *NWA: TNA* weekly PPV on June 19, 2002, but it wouldn't air until their second PPV the next week.

The Lingerie Battle Royal was as bad as it sounds; it was very jiggly. Some would argue that it was kind of a sleazy way to crown the first ever "Miss TNA." Taylor Vaughn won and defended the title against Francine, who soon afterward abandoned her pursuit of the title and engaged in a brief feud with Jasmin St. Claire.

St. Claire, as some of you strokers may know, is a legitimate porn star. In her industry of trade, she held a different kind of title: banging the most men ever in a 300-man gang bang. That victory, however, has a little asterisk next to it in the records books. It seems that the shady skin-flick promoter was not unlike that of shady wrestling promoters and may have pulled a big work on everyone. It seems that he bumped up the actual number of comers to the "record-breaking gang bang event taping" to get more attention to his video. Only a handful of the bangers were tested and met all the criteria. By the time cameras were ready to run, they came up short, so some of the guys had to come up again for sloppy seconds, thirsty thirds, and filthy fourths to get to that magical 300 number.

St. Claire herself said it was all a work, and she would later refer to this endeavor as "among the biggest cons ever pulled off in the porn business." I guess by the magic of television, there were only thirty guys there (not 300) and they were strategically placed and shot by different camera angles to make it look like far more. In the end, only ten of them got to actually make contact with her.

Nice, right?

For about six months or so, NWA: TNA ran the Wednesday night PPV show like clockwork and didn't fudge the numbers. Borrowing a page from WCW's use of the luchadores, TNA built up a decent following using smaller faster stars like Jerry Lynn, Low Ki, and AJ Styles to stand out from the "land of the giants" over in the WWE Universe. They created the X-Division for some action-packed matches, and things started to take off for them.

Anderson and I watched the first show. No, we weren't backstage, however. We were on our couch back in Minnesota. We had heard the hype and purchased the $10 PPV show to see where the business was going.

"The production is really good," Ken noticed.

"Yeah, it is."

We watched and had no idea that the ring was fucked up. The cameras stayed tight on the promos until the ring was ready to go, and then they put on a pretty decent show, I must say.

Right from the start, Anderson, Daivari, and I knew that this new formula could be what it was going to take to replace the missing WCW in the eyes of the fans and we wanted in. Wrestling was still big and there were loyal WCW fans out there without a home and who didn't want to watch WWE. We wanted to get booked on the show so those fans could see us.

We tried everything, but we couldn't get booked at the very start. They were focusing on bigger name talent to bring eyes to the product, and that was understandable, but we didn't give up. Banking on the exposure that a weekly PPV show could bring us, we decided that it would be worth the road trips to Nashville to try to be a part of this new idea, even if we were turned away some at first. We went a few times, and of course, we had our gear conveniently in the trunk just in case there was an opening. (This is old school folks, but it works!)

We made a few disappointing trips hearing "we have nothing for you," but we knew that this was going to be the most probable outcome anyhow. The good thing was, our faces were getting known. We were showing we wanted it.

Come October 2002, Panda Energy International came along. To get to the next level, TNA needed money. The right offer was made and Panda purchased a controlling interest (72%) of TNA.

In one of their first moves, they paid for a television spot. A new show called *TNA: Xplosion* launched on November 27, 2002. This was TNA's first regular cable show. It was a bit of a magazine show at first. It put over the PPVs and also featured some exclusive matches and interviews taped at the TNA Asylum.

CRUSH

Come the end of 2002, we still didn't have an "in" with TNA. I kept my ears open and heard that an all woman's promotion was starting up. I did some networking and got on a show that was said to possibly become a series in 2003.

This is where I first met Traci Brooks.

Traci was like me, a big personality from a small town. She grew up on a pig and chicken farm up in Canada in St. Marys, Ontario. In 2000, she won the Toronto Sunshine Millennium Calendar contest which led to her being named Miss June 2000. That got her into promotional modeling working with Molson, Labatt and Budweiser beverages. You know I like my booze, which is probably another reason why we would eventually hit it off just fine.

In a Toronto newspaper interview before she even started wrestling, she said that one day she would be "the next WWF Superstar." That led her to being introduced to Ron Hutchison, a promoter with a wrestling school in Canada whose students included Edge, Christian, and Trish Stratus to mention a few.

After training and working some with Ron Hutchison, Traci then switched over to another trainer, Rob Fuego, at Squared Circle over in Toronto. There, Traci met up with Gail Kim and really hit it off. They did everything together. They became drive buddies. They were work wives.

Eventually, there were some tryouts going on in WWE up in Toronto. I don't remember if this was when Gail got the job or not, but I do know that Traci went and was there sitting, waiting for a show when Molly Holly walked in. Traci was set to work with her that night. They were just shooting the shit and Molly was talking about an independent show she did somewhere. She mentioned to Traci about working with this wonderful new talent called "ODB."

"What a weird name," Traci said.

Fast forward a few months, and Gail got picked up by WWE. Traci was all alone. That is when she set out to work for a new promotion called CRUSH.

I guess she had put her name out there to go work for this new promotion by some of the same people who used to run Gorgeous Ladies of Wrestling (GLOW). The new promotion was supposed to carry on the lineage of the old one, with a new name, catering to the next generation of women's wrestling fans.

Seeing how it was in Minneapolis, I wasn't far away from that one, either. The promoter was actually former GLOW host, Johnny Cafarella. Cafarella was gearing up to pitch his television series that was loosely based on the original concept for GLOW. He was all ready to have CRUSH start filming shows to be compiled into a pilot, I believe, for the tail end of 2002.

When we all showed up one day for casting, he took one look at me right away and nodded. I was big and jacked and looked like a wrestler.

"You are hired," he said without hesitation.

Soon after that, a live audience was booked and I was ready to debut.

Not liking the name ODB, they decided to repackage me as Mekka the Warrior, which was badass mythical *Xena*-like character ready to kick some ass.

Backstage at the first show, we all did the walk around handshake. We wondered if the promotion would take off and if we would be working with each other a whole lot more. That was the first time I met Traci, and we hit it off right away.

"Hi, I'm Jess. But here they are calling me Mekka the Warrior."

Traci introduced herself, "Good to meet you, Mekka."

We hung out all day shooting promos and all kinds of footage and then eventually got ready for a match. It was then that I mentioned to Traci how the new gimmick was much different than my ODB character.

"Wait, you are ODB? One Dirty Bitch? The same dirty girl Molly Holly talked about?"

"Oh wow. Did she?" I asked. "Hopefully good things."

She laughed and that was that.

I made connections at CRUSH and some friends that would follow on with me throughout the rest of my entire career. There was a lot of unsigned female talent there including Melina, Jeanne Basone, and Cheerleader Melissa. I also hit it off with Christie Ricci who they were calling Glory there, but hands down, Traci was the real find.

Traci saw right away that I was a little different than the other girls. As you know, I didn't care about diva type stuff. Traci liked that I was real. She learned that I cared more about where the next drink to touch my lips was coming from, than what kind of lipstick I should wear. She loved that.

A guy named Steve Blance and The Flying Farley Brothers (brothers of the late comedian Chris Farley) were brought in as part of Cafarella's team. He started bringing in even more girls from all over the place to both film matches for the pilot episode, as well as shoot promos/vignettes for this upcoming "all-women's wrestling/sketch comedy television series." Traci and I were around for all of it.

Jimmy Hart was booked to do promotion for the company. As the new hype man for the show, Jimmy became the familiar face and mouthpiece for press interviews. He announced the series would debut on Comedy Central in the Fall 2003. Jimmy revealed that Tom Arnold was to also be involved with the series. However, just like I'd seen many times in the past, none of these big plans panned out.

Quite often in wrestling, you know, there is a buzz by some promoter suffering from delusions of grandeur. There is always the promise of a big overseas tour, or a television deal that sounds "too good to be true" and usually that is because it is. What happens is the promoter puts together a lethal mixture of hype, work, and ego together and drinks it down hard. Then, they believe their own bullshit. When this happens, their own believing makes it tough to see through the hoopla and pipe dreams, and wrestlers who want to believe the vision believe it, too.

In the case of CRUSH, the new revolutionary promotion that was going to change the face of women's wrestling didn't. The pilot was never sold to any networks or distributors. It just died like a fish in a barrel, and unfortunately went nowhere. (As a side note, however, down the road in 2008, Cafarella and Hart tried again. This time they partnered up with a guy named Jonathan Vargas who had just won a Powerball jackpot of $35.3 million the same year. With more money to dump into it, they repurposed some of the CRUSH characters for a new series they called *Wrestlicious*. It lasted one season on DISH Network.)

But just like that, our dreams of working for CRUSH, an updated version of GLOW in 2002, were crushed.

One thing I did get out of that gig, however, was Traci. She would soon play an even bigger part in my career.

TNA FIRST SHOT

Eventually, after some persistence, we finally got booked by the carload (Anderson, Daivari, and me) by TNA.

On February 26th, 2003, we were all debuting for their weekly Wednesday PPV, #33 to be exact.

In front of 1,500 plus fans live and on PPV, I was set to take on a wrestler named, Trinity.

Now, Trinity had been booked by TNA to do some intergender matches with Kid Kash. It was similar to what Daivari and I had done a lot of on the independents, and even more like what Andy Kaufman did in the 1980s with women for cheap heat. Trinity came to the business from the movie world where she did a lot of stunts for actresses.

Trinity was cool. When she mentioned TNA's plan for her and Kash backstage, I shared with her some ideas of what Daivari and I did to make our matches a success. Now, a lot of the girls were catty and didn't look out for each other. There was always someone jealous for your spot, and perhaps even more so with the women because there were less spots to have. But I wasn't like that. My philosophy was if you could help someone out, that is what you should do. It was like karma; if you do good things for others, good things would come back to you.

She was all ears. She was grateful and said she would use some of my ideas for sure.

Trinity did just that and later thanked me for some of the tips I gave her that night. It was super rewarding to hear.

"She always wanted to take everything at full force and was very willing to do the angle," Kash says about his spots with Trinity, today. "Her toughness and stuntwoman background was incredible. She would have me hit her with chops as hard as I ever hit any man. It was ridiculous." He says that other than Jazz, Trinity is the toughest woman wrestler in the business. That is because, he of course, never worked with me, haha!

Anyhow, for my first TNA PPV, I was booked to put over Trinity, and that I did. After that, Mike Sanders and "Disco Inferno" Glenn Gilbertti beat Anderson and Daivari in the second match of the evening. Mission accomplished!

We got seen. That is all we wanted.

After that, we weren't called right back. Dixie Carter was appointed President of TNA Entertainment the spring of 2003. I don't think she liked my look. My plan then became to work harder on the road until they had to notice me.

OUT ON MY OWN

Our gut feeling had paid off. A few months after the TNA PPV, and we were living off of the fat of the land. That little blip got out there and promoters were booking us more than ever before. The exposure was like a commercial for us!

Come the summer of 2003, we came across a weekend where we didn't have a booking which was becoming few and far between. To take a little break from it all, I decided to take Anderson out for some much-needed alone time. Between his personal training and wrestling, we had a lot less time to unwind – just the two of us.

We booked a little cruise. A few minutes before our three-hour-tour, my "spidey sense" started to go off, as well as my phone. I looked down, and I didn't like what I saw.

We boarded. We were hanging out on a boat in Minnesota, when that gut feeling really hit me. For all the girls out there reading this, I'm sure some of you know this gut feeling. We have all been there before, and it sucks.

I was experiencing that "oh shit" moment, when the stars and the planets no longer felt like they were aligned.

Yes, it felt like my man was cheating on me.

Now, it was not the ODB way to beat around the bush. I didn't do that with much of anything I did in life. So, once I had him all alone, I was going to confront him.

There was something I didn't like on the cellphone.

I think it is worth noting that technology wasn't like it is today back then in 2003. Not everybody and their grandmother had an iPhone back then. In those days, relationships were not being made and destroyed by companies like Apple and Facebook. It was still kind of new.

The reason we bought a cellphone in the first place was for road trips and bookings. One day, Ken and I were walking through the mall and saw this thing in the window.

"Let's do it," he said. So, we splurged on the new cutting-edge technology of the time and got an illustrious flip phone. This was way back when. I don't even think that motherfucker was a BlackBerry. It was a Nokia or something, but it was badass and it could even take pictures.

Well, we got that phone to help communicate for bookings while we were on the road. It also would come in handy in a time when there wasn't GPS systems in most cars.

We saw no mistakes in buying a cellphone then. The only mistake would be from Ken's perspective later on, in that we bought one phone together to share – not two.

This is way before cheaters figured out that their cellphones could easily get them into trouble.

When we were finally alone, I reached into my bag and clicked the word balloon message icon.

"Hey, Ken." I asked. "Who is Leiah?"

"A client," he said taking a nervous sip of his beverage.

At that, there was turtlehead action, I could just tell it. He looked away, he swallowed, and then an inch of a turd log made its way out of this asshole's asshole before he quickly sucked it back into place.

"Really?" I asked.

"Really," he said, squirming in his now soiled pants. "She is. Legit."

"Okay, really," I said. "But is that all that she is?"

Now, this was all going down at a time when Ken was working at the gym, and I was still working at the Crab Shack. My thoughts back then were exactly what you are probably thinking they were. When I was out selling crabs, Ken was out there almost catching them.

"Funny, Ken. The screen reads 'When are you alone?' Do you always train chicks better when nobody else is around at the gym?"

Ken shrugged.

"I mean, you really should answer that. You are pretty close to being alone right now," I said.

"She likes quick access to the machines maybe? I don't know."

"Quick access, right?"

"I don't know what the hell you are talking about," he said, as his asshole puckered up. He went to reach for our phone, but I quickly pulled it out of his reach.

"Neither do I," I said, putting the gnarly Nokia back into my bag.

I waited for a response.

Ken said nothing.

"Neither do I," I continued. "Because that is not all the message said."

He reached for the phone again to see the next text, but I pulled it further away.

"Well then, what else does it say?"

"After that, it says something about going out for drinks."

"It's just a client," he responded. "We went to a bar after the gym with some of the other members. Maybe it's that, again, what she means."

"But I thought she wanted to train alone."

"Goddamn it, if you don't trust me, I might as well cheat."

And that was that.

The conversation was done.

...*We were done.*

The whole thing sucked. He was my first real long-term boyfriend so I hated to see it end. I hated to see him go. He was a great friend to me. We had so much in common. He had helped me with wrestling. He had helped me get into the best shape of my life. He was a great partner. He was funny. He was fun to be with. He had helped me move forward in my career. But, after all that, I had to help him move forward out the door.

It sucked.

Don't you worry about Ken Anderson though. When he moved out of our apartment that next day, he wasn't "alone" for long.

I figured it would be weird for a very social guy like Anderson to have to go back to living alone. It's weird that he moved right in with this Leiah girl. Isn't it?

It made sense then though. Then, they could be alone together for whatever workouts they wanted.

I probably could have fought for him, but that was not what I was going to do. I would be lying if I said I wasn't upset. I would be lying if I said it didn't bother me and I didn't lose sleep over losing him. I did. I mourned our relationship the same as anyone would.

But I didn't let it break me.

I didn't quit wrestling.

When I would go out to do a show after that, I knew I would miss him sitting in the seat next to me. I knew I would miss our rituals on the road. Even if he took his love away, I wasn't going to let him take my love of wrestling away from me.

I didn't quit wrestling.

Anyhow, I knew Anderson was going to still be around after that. I knew we rode in the same circles. I knew I couldn't avoid him. I was going to have to see him if I was going to keep taking bookings. I soon decided, "Fuck that talk." I was going to have to see him?

NO. HE WAS GOING TO HAVE TO SEE ME!

I read books on breakups. I learned what I had to do to mentally and physically get over a breakup. I did what they said and it worked. I got over him, and I was stronger for it.

I continued to work the independents, sharing custody of Daivari like he was a family dog from a broken home.

Daivari was both of our friends, so he stayed out of our shit while stuff was still touchy. Sure, I milked him for some info during our road trips on what Anderson was up to, and I'm sure Anderson did the same to him during our "I'm not totally over you" phase.

"So, how are things going with Ken?" I'd ask Daivari on the way to yet another show.

"He was booked on this show, too," he confided then laughed. "But I don't think from the sounds of things that we will see him there."

"Why is that?"

"He knew you were going and decided to sit this one out."

"Good," I said. "The fucker."

Daivari would laugh. He liked both of us. What else could he do?

Soon after that, Daivari and I were back in the car again. It probably hadn't been even a full month since the breakup.

"So, have you heard from Ken?" I'd ask Daivari, blunt as a mofo.

"Yup," he said.

"Well?" I said. "How is he doing?"

"Not so good," he replied.

"Dirt," I demanded. "Now."

He laughed.

"Okay, okay," I said. "Dirt now... please."

"Well, they had it out over something with money," Daivari said. "I'm not sure what it was, but he's been sleeping on my couch the last couple nights."

"And you didn't tell me?"

"I'm telling you now, aren't I?"

Daivari was like a cross between a family dog and the sister I never had. Also like a dog, he could really just be a bitch.

"I don't know," I said. "I don't think you would have told me if I didn't ask."

He laughed again.

"Well, good," I said. "Your cheap ass couch is as uncomfortable as hell. Serves him right. I hope those springs poke up his ass and fuck up his back."

"Be nice."

When it comes down to it, I really didn't wish Anderson ill will at that point. It sucked that we were no longer together. He was after all my first love and it hurt my heart when he left, but he didn't break it.

It was kind of tough on my family. My family would call and also ask to see what was going on with Anderson. They sympathized with me, but I somehow wondered if they were hoping for a reconcile.

Anderson had become pretty close with my family members. That is always tough because when you go through a breakup in a situation where your ex had become good friends with your parents and siblings, things always get strange. You have to almost ask your family not to be friends with someone you wanted them to be friends with in the first place.

Weeks passed. Daivari and I were off to another *First Avenue* show for Ed Sharkey. I put in a good word for Traci and she got booked. I figured that if I got to work with her, it could be a pretty good match. Much to my surprise, this is not what happened. Apparently, nobody had told Sharkey that Anderson and I were no longer together. When I got there, I looked up to see the poster announce: "Traci Brooks & Ken Anderson versus ODB & Shawn Daivari."

Oh boy. This is going to be great.

I was getting ready to leave the area so my family all came out one more time to see me live at a local venue.

Being recently single, I decided to go ahead and move down toward Nashville to look for more spots with TNA. I had talked some to Traci about it, and she thought it was a good idea. So, without anything holding me down, I said that I "was in" for just about whatever.

Backstage at that last show, it was actually quite easy to stay away from Anderson until I absolutely had to. He knew not to come looking for me right away, but he knew he was going to have to, as I was not going to bother if he didn't. We were working together, after all, and he knew how stubborn I could be.

Eventually, he grabbed Traci and slowly headed toward me.

When we finally got together to talk about what we were going to do, I saw Daivari sneaking a peek at us from around a corner and prolonging it. Anderson had his back to Daivari, and Daivari knew it was all awkward, and he loved it.

"Hey Shawn" I said, calling for him. He put his hand up to his mouth and made the giggle face, but didn't come right over. I made eye contact with him from across the room, then scratched my forehead with my middle finger before he finally came over. "Thanks for joining us, Shawn."

All the while, Anderson was talking to Traci but hadn't said anything to me yet. Then, that moment came.

"Hello, Jess," he finally said cordially with his tail between his legs.

"Hello, Ken," I said, in a very Jerry/Newman from *Seinfeld* moment.

And that was about it. We got over the hump. I was over him, and he knew it. He was now in the coworker zone, and everything else was just that.

When I walked away, Traci ran over to me.

"You okay?" she asked.

"Yeah, of course I am," I said. "Maybe you should ask him though, he's probably off crying in a corner somewhere now."

"He actually might be," she said.

I laughed.

"Listen, you are doing the right thing, girl. Fuck him," she said. "Soon we will be in TNA."

"That's right," I said.

When our match finally came, to my surprise, Traci wasn't the only one showing me support. My whole family was sitting in the audience. Represent. They were all there in full effect making noise, and everyone knew it.

There were a number of regulars in the audience. They knew Anderson and I had been a couple for some time, and before the end of the night, they were going to learn that we no longer were. They were going to learn this whether I had a say in the matter or not.

"Cheater!" my brother yelled.

Now mind you, this accusation of "cheater" was probably not the first time something like that was yelled out at a wrestling show. So, the first time it was shouted, nobody batted an eye.

"You suck! I hope you die!" my dad yelled.

That too was a regular outburst from a fan to a heel, so again, nothing seemed weird.

However, then my family started to lay in on Anderson. REAL HARD.

"Is that the girl you cheated on her with?" my brother yelled, knowing damn well that wasn't the case, but he was just trying to get Anderson's goat.

After that, my family put so much "cheater" heat on Anderson that there soon would be no question that they weren't implying that he was a rule breaker in the ring. My family meant exactly what they were saying, literally.

The fans looked at Anderson, then looked at me. A lightbulb went off. Even though some wrestling fans weren't the brightest people in the world, they immediately understood the shade my family was throwing.

I looked at Anderson and laughed. He was turning red, not from anger, but rather embarrassment.

Daivari, the smart ass that he was, threw gas on the fire when he deliberately threw Anderson over to our corner.

"Uggg," Anderson said to me as he hit the ring pad. Daivari grabbed his head. Under his breath in a headlock, Anderson looked up at me and said, "Come on, Jess."

"It's not me," I laughed.

"Can you ask them to lighten up?"

"They are doing that shit on their own."

Daivari tagged me in, then I laughed even harder.

The spot was not planned, but the fans along with my family figured out what was about to happen.

Daivari hopped over the ropes, hooked the arms, and held Anderson in place.

"You son of a bitch," Anderson said, laughing under his breath, knowing damn well he was off to Chop-Fest.
I stepped into the ring and spit on both of my hands. Then, as he predicted, I chopped the living shit out of him.
SLAP! SLAP! SLAP!
Man-boob hamburger meat.
The crowd went crazy.
That was some sweet closure. I have to say, if you can ever get some knife-edge chops in on your ex before you move away, it really is a great way to get over him and get over in a match at the same time!
My family popped like I was the second coming of Christ, and so did the rest of the audience.
Anderson was a great sport about the whole thing and took his punishment like a man.
When we got back to the locker room, even his tits were crying.
We all laughed at Anderson's expense and congratulated each other for a good match.
"Okay," Anderson admitted. "I had that coming."
We hugged it out in the back anyhow, and to his credit, he laughed at the whole situation.
We were done, but what a way to finish.

MOVING ON

I moved on, and Anderson moved out – out of the state actually.
There was lots of good news. Daivari was off to WWE. They had a manager role that he fit the bill perfectly for so they were ready to hot-shot him in as an Iraqi supporter with Muhammad Hassan. This was huge, and I was so happy for him! Finally, his hard work was going to pay off.
Anderson found a connection at Ohio Valley Wrestling (OVW), the new WWE training farm league. He too was off to Kentucky to polish up for a possible WWE TV run. This too was really a big deal.
A little before this, we had both worked some with Tommy Dreamer. He had been hired by WWE and was also working for them as a talent agent. Every few months or so, I would call him up (as did many other unsigned talent) every so often looking for work.

"Hi, Tommy, it's ODB," I'd say.

"Hey, ODB! I have nothing for you, yet," he'd say. "But let me say, you are looking pretty jacked these days!"

On a similar call after the break up, Anderson got a different reply. His hard work was finally paying off, as well.

I legitimately felt happy for Anderson.

No WWE calls for me, however. I didn't fit their mold.

I had had a taste of TNA, so that became my goal.

TNA was a realistic hope of bigger things to come for me at this point in my career. I had found a few spots there with Anderson. My new friend Traci also worked some manager spots, but neither of us were seriously being looked at. However, TNA was running regularly, knew who we were, and had more money behind them than anyone else I had been working for. This was good, so around this time, we started to pack. Traci and I figured that migrating in that direction toward the work was the way to go.

TNA kept gaining steam. They were getting a buzz and getting their product out there with regular weekly PPVs to hardcore wrestling fans who were willing to pay money for it. Predating what would become the Knockouts division, we were told that they were looking to expand their Miss TNA division and that they would book us for sure if we could commit to being available more often.

So, on a wing and a prayer, I decided to leave everything behind in Minnesota. I set my mind on finding somewhere to live near the TNA fairgrounds.

ROAD TRIPS WITH TRACI

Now, a lot of people know that Traci is now married to the love of her life, Frankie Kazarian. However, what people don't know is that Traci Brooks was "married" twice before that. Her first marriage was with her work wife, Gail Kim, in a Canadian affair, and her second one was about to begin with me.

We both decided it was time to relocate to the music capital of the world – Nashville.

When I got down to Nashville, Traci and I teamed up again to save money. We started by renting a room from a wrestler named Christie Ricci, who was already getting some work in TNA. She lived right near the Fairgrounds where TNA was running regularly, so it was perfect.

A TNA contract was the goal for both Traci and me, but we were realistic. We knew it could take some time so knew we should look for other work in the meantime.

Once I got settled in Nashville, Traci and I hit the road. We started to make our way around the indy scene in West Virginia, Arkansas and Memphis. We got a good little match put together, and convinced promoters to book us by the carload. Between gigs, we would show back up to our temporary home base with Ricci, and recharge. During the week, I also took some random bartending gigs, and Traci waited tables. We continued to look for gigs and would be off again on the weekends.

Over in Memphis, Jerry Lawler loved us. The United States Wrestling Association (USWA), for a time, was all about us. We were always used for his obligatory girl's match. After working there, we would sometimes circle around and head back north.

We also worked some back then for Harley Race. Harley ran a promotion called World League Wrestling (WLW). His independent promotion ran shows near the former NWA champion's hometown of Eldon, Missouri, as well as other surrounding cities including Kansas City.

Just like Lawler, Harley liked us, too, but Harley didn't like my ODB ring name. He preferred to call me Jessica Dalton, which was also a character's name from the movie, *Road House*.

With Gail Kim off doing her thing, I became Traci's new road buddy. We became the perfect new team. Traci was the yin to my yang. We went together like peas and carrots, and shit. In our case, Traci was like The Fabulous Moolah, and I was like Mae Young. I was all about the wrestling and performing side of things, and Traci was all about the business.

"Did you go over the contract yet?" she would ask me.

"Okay, mom," I would say.

"What? You have to make sure that stuff is right."

"You are probably right," I would say. "But such a Debbie Downer."

Traci was good though. She handled the money. She always dealt with the promoters and worked hard getting both of us gigs. In return, I provided a car, and handled the driving and all the road stuff.

Now, I will make a confession here. I got so comfortable with Traci that she got to see the real me. And guess what? She loved it. (What's not to love?)

The real me loved 98 Degrees and other boy band shit like that, so that is what I always played on the radio. I have fond memories of us singing to stay awake to the lamest pop songs you can think of with her on the way to USWA shows, and any other small promotion that would have us back in those days.

For the first few weeks on the road together, we were living on friends' couches and sleeping in truck stops. Life on the road was tough. I remember taking what some called "whore showers" back then. We would go to a single stall bathroom at a gas station and take turns washing our asses in their sinks. We would lather up our armpits and any other places that needed a cleaning, and call it a day before getting back on the road.

Yeah, the wrestling life was trashy, but we both loved it. We were like that TV show *2 Broke Girls*, legit. However, instead of trying to make a cupcake business, we were two cupcakes looking to make names for ourselves in the wrestling business.

I wouldn't have had it any other way. We were learning the ropes on the road, just how it should be.

While I think Traci might disagree, I personally think the current WWE Performance Center wouldn't have been for us, because back then there was more element of improv in pro wrestling. That, to me, made matches feel more real. You have probably heard about this concept before. We referred to that spontaneity as "calling it in the ring." Everything is so scripted now and written out to the even smallest of details for newer wrestlers today. It would have been tough to get a well-rounded education for every little thing that could go wrong if everything was all handed to us back then on paper.

Traci told me a story once that also showed she had the same mentality as me when it came to matches. One time early on when she was still married to Gail Kim on the road, she was on a show with Beth Phoenix (aka The Glamazon) out in the boonies somewhere. She said they had all this vocal stuff worked out where they would be talking shit to tell a story before their match and during it, then realized none of it was going to work.

"When we got there, we found out that we were working at a deaf school!" she exclaimed.

I guess they started to freak out, but then found sage advice from the greatest Intercontinental champion of all time.

"No problem," said The Honky Tonk Man. "Just do pantomime." He showed Beth Phoenix and Traci his version of what they were already going to do, but only using body language.

"Wow, that's great," Traci said. "We can totally do just that! Thanks so much."

Honky nodded, then probably went back to a corner to be the grizzled ring vet that he was.

Sometimes we forget. These guys have so much to teach us. We just need to ask.

The same thing was going on when it was just me and Traci on the road, after I stole her from Kim. We realized the importance of specific little things like knowing your crowd, and learning all the essential lessons from the road. We realized the more ring time we had, the better off we were going to be. That time we had together on a show was far more valuable than any amount of money a promoter could pay us.

We were still in the learning phase and realized that what we were learning on the independents would pay off hopefully later on down the road. Therefore, we would go just about anywhere for almost nothing to get in a ring. I remember driving even as far as from Nashville to Philly to work for World X-treme Wrestling (WXW). That wild type of haul, for example, was worth it though because it allowed me to work for Afa of The Wild Samoans, whose input was just priceless.

Looking back now at how we lived, it seemed like it was us who were the WILD ones.

We each had no money and would work any old place to get our names out there. Our minimum was like $35 each and a hotel room, though admittedly there were decent promoters who would pay more. (They weren't all bad!) So, yeah, while we were learning the ropes and mastering our crafts, we had very limited money. Sure, we would be sleeping at rest stops in dangerous areas, or beat up "no tell motels" that I probably would never consider stepping foot into today, but we considered the biggest part of our pay was *the experience itself.* We knew more would come later if we did it right.

    We had this pre-show ritual. When we got to town, we would always first go seek out the hotel room. If we were early, we didn't shop. We didn't go see a movie to kill time. The moment we would show up to the show, we would immediately get to our room and open up shop. Set it and forget it. We would lay out our gear and makeup for quick accessibility later, and be ready to go on a dime. Then, we would just go relax in our luxurious hotel taking advantage of whatever amenities they had.

    We were cheap dates. It was the simple life we loved.

    The room accommodation paid for by the promoter was usually part of our deal that Traci always fought for. We never paid for a room; we lived for the room the promoter provided. When we were on the road, we were basically homeless. That hotel room was our "home away from no home."

    No matter what room was given to us by a promoter, when we got our keys, we rolled up happy into that joint, no matter how crappy it was. Because we slept in the car most of the time and washed our asses in gas station sinks, so staying at even the cheesiest of motels was like sleeping at the Ritz Carlton to us. It didn't matter if the room had matted shag rugs, broken creaky beds and mirrors on the ceiling, the day of a show and that night, we would chill there like queens. That part of the trip, compared to sleeping in the car, was finally living the easy life.

    After the show, we would collect our $35 and I would get us some Pabst Blue Ribbon. That, of course, was the drink of choice because it was the cheapest beer. After making our necessary purchase for survival, we would go to our hotel room, strip off all our clothes, and squat. Now, if we couldn't find anything on the shitty TV that we wanted to watch, that was okay. I was prepared to offer high-quality entertainment at low-budget pricing.

I had me a beat up little generic portable DVD player. I think the brand name was Dynexx, probably because it was so cheap they figured after you bought it – it would "die next week." Anyhow, I would take that little gadget and fiddle around behind any TV for a few minutes and I could figure out a way to make it work. After twisting some wires together and shit, and we would soon be watching a luxurious disc of *Beverly Hills 90210*, complete with Tori Spelling and everything.

When that TV was on, that was it! Nothing else in the world mattered. We would totally immerse ourselves in the lives of Brandon, Brenda, Kelly, and Dylan. It was messed up, but hilarious. I will admit, I was a total mark for Luke Perry. I even had an old *90210* blanket that Traci got me as a rib that I cuddled up in to watch the show. I guess for a time I was like fucking Linus Van Pelt from *Peanuts* and Snoopy with that thing. I brought it with me everywhere.

The next day, we would be either off to the next show, or driving back to Nashville. I don't ever remember shopping for clothes with Traci, ever. We only really needed food, so we would eat and then maybe do some gym stuff. We did have gym memberships, but aside from that treat, we were like the Netflix *GLOW*'s Welfare Queens by every definition of the word. We spent NOTHING!

When it was a choice between beer or gas, beer always won. We were so cheap, we pretty much drifted to places on fumes. I was always running out of gas. Why would we invest in a full tank? That was wasted money when an extra gallon was just sitting unused in the car. One time, I remember we ran out of gas near a Hooters in Nashville. We had absolutely no fuel at all, but had to get to the gas station. I remember Traci recruiting a couple of guys away from the cute waitresses using a little charm and having them push us a block or so to the crest of the hill, then let go. We coasted our way downhill saying a prayer to get to that gas station in neutral. We rolled into the place so slow, I didn't think we were going to make it, but we did.

Eventually, however, we agreed that sleeping in the car sucked. We agreed that living on people's couches and depending on a promoter's shoestring-budget hospitality was the shits. So, at some point, we decided to shell out a little of our earnings to finally pay for a bigger place.

LOLLIPOP'S ROOM

Lollipop was a TNA cage dancer, which sort of was like WCW's Nitro Girls. She was also just starting to valet a little from time to time, and needed a place to stay.

She set things up smart, sharing a big apartment with Cheerleader Valentina, a wrestler based out of California, who was already there getting steady working with TNA. She was also dating some guy named Ryan who incidentally would years later go on to do some producing for NXT. He had the ear of some of the bookers. This was all good for us.

Cheerleader Valentina had one of the nicest rooms in the apartment claimed already. After all, it was her place and we were all technically just squatters. However, the bedroom that Lollipop was camping out in was just enormous. There was plenty of room, so Lollipop was happy to split the bills with us in the mix and give up an unused corner.

Valentina didn't have extra furniture for us when we first came in on the scene. She had a big apartment and a lot of space, but that was about it. We were kind of leeching on her single girl accommodations. So we did some digging and dragged in a secondhand futon and an air mattress. Then, we were good for the time being.

One day in Nashville, I was getting ready to go work at a bar somewhere. We were driving together going somewhere, and we looked off to the side of the road at a sign. It read "FREE." That was the magic word.

We were driving through an area of extremes. We were in an area that could have been very rich, and then right down the block, it could have been very poor. So, we pulled off to see what exactly was going on with the freeness. There was a cardboard box with the typical yard sale reject shit in it. You know, it was filled with old glasses and plastic drinking cups and shit nobody wanted. However, just to the left of that was the Mecca, the holy grail, the Shangri-La of furnishings, just the accommodation that we needed.

"Bunk beds!" we yelled together in ecstasy.

Yes, we found bunk beds on the side of the street. After living out of a car for so long, to us this looked awesome, but to everyone else it was plain gross. Not only did we take the beat up, half-assembled frame and throw it in her car, but we took the mattresses too.

Telling this story is somewhat embarrassing, awesome, and disgusting all at the same time. Those mattresses looked like something evil was conceived on them, something sinister. They had various stains on them that could have been blood, sweat, tears, and/or even feces.

"What is this stain right here?" I pointed at some discoloration on the fabric.

One of those spots looked very suspicious.

To our defense, however, one of the yellowing mattresses looked like it had some strawberry milkshake looking spillage on it so we focused on that to make everything feel more innocent and safe.

"Probably just a couple of kids had these before," Traci speculated, repulsed even more at what we were doing than I was.

"Yeah?" I asked. "Good kids?"

"Nice kids," she repeated.

"Okay, it is settled then," I said. "We have furniture!"

"Yay?" Traci said, wrinkling her nose up a little.

Those things were brutal. In hindsight, as kids ourselves, we were overly positive in the way that we perceived the world. We were bright-eyed and bushy-tailed, to say the least. In hindsight, looking back now as an adult at why we would ever have considered something like this is beyond me. It was a used mattress for Christ's sake. They had been sitting outside in the elements for God knows how long. Bed bugs would have been the least of our worries. There could have been spiders. There could have been mice. There could have been rodents inside the padding. Hell, there could have been mating raccoons inside, but we didn't care. We dragged those shitty mattresses to Lollipop's place, hosed them off, and polished that turd the best we could with a ShamWow.

You know, come to think of it, I don't even remember buying sheets. Maybe we didn't even have them at all and slept right on top of the mattresses. I had my trusty *90210* blanket to protect me, so who knows?

I did know this however, Traci was my bunkmate and I couldn't have asked for a better one. We made a bunkmate contract, not unlike Sheldon's roommate agreement from *The Big Bang Theory*. We decided that Traci was going to always take the top bunk, and I was going to always take the bottom.

"What happens if a boy comes over?" I joked.

"With me?" Traci asked. "Might want to pull that blanket over your head."

The very first night we slept in that repurposed bunk bed, all she wanted to do was make jokes.

"Hey Jess?" Traci asked, waiting until I was almost totally asleep.

"Yeah."

"Do you think maybe a bum peed on your mattress? It smells kind of funky."

"Oh boy," I would say. "Go to sleep."

Traci would get quiet. Then she would wait until I was almost asleep again, then continue, "Hey, Jess?"

"Whaaat?"

"I feel like something is moving inside the mattress!"

"Huh, wait, what?" I asked waking up concerned.

"Ugh!" her voice yelled from above where I couldn't see. "There is something nested in it!"

I jumped out of bed all itchy and looked up at her. Then, I felt something hit my head.

Traci was throwing stuffed animals at me.

"What in the heck?" I said looking at the toy. "Yeah I'm sure there is an octopus and an elephant in your mattress you bitch! Now go to sleep!"

BEFORE THE CONTRACT

Before I was officially getting booked by TNA, I was mostly just going down to the shows and making my face known. They were cool and let me hang. From time to time, I got a spot here and there as an extra on one of their Wednesday PPVs, but nothing more than one-offs.

Eventually, they offered me a spot as one of the cage dancers, one night. They figured I could dance with our new roomie Lollipop, but I politely declined. I mean, it was work and Lollipop had been doing it since August of 2002, but it was not the kind of work I wanted to do. I didn't want to just be the literal T&A part of the show.

Lollipop herself got "the bug" to be more that eye candy and wanted to become a wrestler. She decided she wanted to be at least knowledgeable enough that if they wanted her to step outside of the cage for an angle, she could. Therefore, she took a few months off to train as a wrestler, taking lessons from Leilani Kai.

Soon after Traci and I moved in with her, Lollipop (whose real name was Jaime Lynne in case you were wondering) asked us for some advice one night over some takeout pizza.

"Listen, guys," she said. "Vince Russo made me an offer."

"The boobs bonus?"

"How did you know?"

Traci pointed at her chest, "I got 'em too, you know."

We all laughed.

Apparently, Russo had officially gotten the green light to show the "T" part of TNA on PPV.

"If any of the girls are willing to show the girls, I'm just saying," he said in that ridiculous Brooklyn accent of his. "If you are interested, they are willing to pay a pretty penny."

"Well?" Lynne asked.

"Not interested?" Traci said.

"No, I mean, do you think I should do it?" Lynne said. "As Lollipop."

"If you want to be remembered for that," I said. "Go ahead. But that is what you will be remembered for. You will forever be the chick that got her tits out."

We laughed again.

We shut the lights off, but Lollipop didn't shut the lights off on that idea. In my mind, she sat there probably for hours scratching her chin, and maybe squeezing her boobs thinking about that bonus.

It wasn't long after that that Lynne obviously didn't give a shit about being remembered for her assets, or in this case, chest-etts? Coming from a dancer background, she figured people had seen them before, so what was the difference?

When she accepted the "boob bonus," she was immediately written into a spot and thrusted into the spotlight. They pulled her out of the cage, and put her into the ring.

She got a match with another buxom blonde vixen named Holly Wood of Sports Entertainment Xtreme (S.E.X.) Then on a TNA PPV, Wood ripped her shirt open and exposed Lollipop's sweet suckers to the world.

Brooks and I watched from a monitor in the back.

When her boobs came out, our jaws hit the floor.

"Holy sweet mother of Jesus," K-Kwik (the future R-Truth of WWE) said.

"Wow is right!" Hacksaw Jim Duggan said from somewhere behind us. (He probably should have said, "Hooooo!")

"Oh boy," I said to Traci who was laughing her ass off.
There you have it, boobs.

The fans popped hard, and so did their boners.

Lollipop was the one to finally take one for the team. She (and her boobies) were to be rewarded.

After that, Lynne was written into more spots. They gave Lollipop more TV time. They gave her a feud with a new all-female stable known as Bitchslap, which consisted of Nurse Veronica and Traci! The creation of that team was the beginning of more women being used as they had promised.

More importantly for us, yes, my girl Traci started getting more regular work with TNA.

ODB IN MMA

Before 2004 rolled around, there was also a $500 offer on the table. It was a paying gig, but for a Mixed Martial Arts promotion in Wisconsin. They had been sending some messages out to the professional wrestling world to spice things up a little and make one of their regular girls look good, so I said "fuck it" and took the gig.

There, I was set to do a worked-shoot, meaning a real fight that was actually fake. This was right up my alley. I was set to take on a girl named Kelly Kobold. The problem was, I don't know how much of the worked-shoot message was relayed to my opponent who was not from my world.

When I got to Ring of Fire (ROF) Championship Fighting, I realized it was a huge deal. This event was much bigger than many indy promotions I had worked for in the past, as far as what it was drawing fanwise. There were tons of bloodthirsty asses in those seats just waiting to see a chick get punched in the face for real.

For this particular MMA event, there wasn't an octagon, however. It was just a traditional boxing ring. When I got into that ring, I felt the urge to run the ropes, but resisted. We started the match.

We went to tie up, kind of, and then it quickly turned into slugging. There was a little chain-wrestling action after that and then we broke it up and stepped back. Then, all of the sudden…

WHAP! WHAP!

Even though it was supposed to be a work, this bitch kept kicking me.

WHAP!!!

"Hey girl, lighten up," I said, but to no avail.

WHAPPP!!!

I got hot.

Like a bull seeing red, I had had enough. So, what did I do?

I kicked the living shit out of her.

Once I had my fill, I let her put an armbar on me. At this point, I was going to make the match run longer than they had requested, because that was what the promoter truly wanted, but I started selling her move like a wrestler.

The ref thought I was tapping out, and called the match.

Oh well. It was worth it for $500.

PREPARING FOR TNA

TNA was using me sparingly for little side spots, but I still was only being treated as an afterthought.

I started to get nervous. I saw that Traci was getting booked, and she was more of a manager. Not to slam her at all, but I definitely was a better in-ring wrestler than her, but yet I still wasn't getting used.

What does Traci have that I don't have?

I put on my thinking cap. Now, I am not a mathematician, and I am not a biologist. But when I plugged in all the numbers and variables into the scientific equation before me, two things hit me right in the face.

Oh shit. The answer is obvious!

Boobs.

My muscles and fitness training set me apart from the girls, but maybe not in a good way. I didn't look like the girls, and the name of the promotion was TNA.

Duh.

After I dated Anderson, I had insecurities. As any young impressionable girl would do, I started to question why he would have strayed in the first place.

Was it something I did wrong?

I wondered what I could have done differently to keep his attention. I wondered what I could have done to keep him from wanting to cheat. I wondered what I did wrong.

I am here to say now to any young girl that finds herself in the same position: push these stupid thoughts out of your head. This is social programming. It's a man's world and that is why you are thinking like a man. You wonder what you did wrong, BUT YOU DID NOTHING WRONG. It was his fault he left, because he was a fucking pig.

Anyhow, I didn't have this wisdom as a kid. I had insecurities. And after the breakup with Anderson, I wanted answers to these questions. I wanted a preemptive means to get ahead of this problem if I were destined to experience it in the future, so I would never have to deal with it again. I just didn't realize that, as a woman, there is no way to control this. Some dudes just really suck.

Anyhow, after seeing the success Lollipop had with showing off her suckers, I started thinking about what having some bigger titties would do for me.

More and more, I decided that it was possible big breasts would make me feel more womanly. They might have helped me in my relationship with Anderson, and they could possibly lead me further in my career in wrestling which truly was a cosmetic sport.

At the same time, I heard that another girl was contemplating the same thing.

Angelina Love and I talked about our insecurities one night. I found out that I wasn't the only one that felt the way I did. While we were talking, one of the cage dancers interrupted us with her words of wit.

"I don't want to be nosy," she said, "but if you want to get fake boobs, you should go to this place I went to in Alabama."

We laughed, but she did have a nice rack.

"Can you show us the work?" Angelina asked as a joke.

The cage dancer didn't skip a beat. She pulled up her shirt, and there they were.

They looked beautiful.

I was shocked. She looked just like a pinup girl or a *Playboy* model you would see in the magazine.

I want that.

"Those are nice girl," Angelina said.

"You wanna get on TNA? Then you have to have some TNA," she said.

"She's got a point," Angelina said.

"Actually, two of them," I said.

She flashed us again. Now, I'm not gay, but those were hot, I had to admit.

"Bitch where did you get yours?" I said to the busty cage girl.

She told us. We immediately took notes.

The very next morning, Angelina put in her order at Boobs 'R Us. I let her be the guinea pig, but the moment she was back I was ready to check her out the same way we did for cage girl.

Angelina showed up at my door. The rest of the girls were out, which made for a perfect opportunity to get her girls out.

"Okay," I said. "Whip those suckers out."

Angelina was a doll and did just that. If you could have added a sound effect to add to the moment, it probably would have been a cartoony "Boinggg!" She was so generous. She even offered to let me get to second base, which I did for scientific purposes, solely. (You fucking pervs!)

They of course were beautiful, and felt like the real thing.

"Are you happy with them?"

"Totally," she replied. "And I totally recommend it."

Angelina Love was already as beautiful as a doll, but with her two new companions, she was the total package. Her decision certainly allowed her to enter the beautiful people club.

The very next week, I woke up. I sat up on the table, and I couldn't see my feet.

I walked over groggy to the big full-length mirror in the plastic surgeon's office.

WTF!

I was still jacked, but now I HAD pecks. When I looked down, there they were – my two new best friends.

THE DOUBLE D's.

A week later we were back to wrestling in the ring! Angelina and I were both fresh with our new fake boobs, and taking bookings. It wasn't hard to do. We just worked around the boobs. No splashes. No chops.

We were good to go.

The advice was good. Soon after the operation, my phone started ringing off the hook.

MY FIRST SHOTS AT TNA

My investments worked.

Now as I've said before, I don't think I was Dixie Carter's ideal image of wrestler, but others professed value in me. Jerry Jarrett, for one, liked my look. He said that I looked like a better looking "mini Chyna," so they decided to give me a spot like that. Vince Russo also said that it would be good TV to have a jacked wrestler around to "beat on the little hotties." It would give the fans all the reason more to like the more girly wrestlers of TNA.

However, despite the fact that they were going to use me, it was clear that someone else didn't like my name. Even though TNA was catering to an older, more adult crowd, someone higher up didn't like the idea of me being called "One Dirty Bitch" on TV. It was the same thing that old school wrestlers/promoters like Jerry Lawler and Harley Race were saying; the name was just too filthy.

THAT GIRL IS POISON

It was Abyss who noticed all of the band shirts I liked to wear. I also wore a bandana and he thought I looked like a female Bret Michaels when I did so he suggested the name *Poison*. Manager/promoter Bert Prentice was amused at the idea, so that was the new name they christened me with.

Traci had already been doing the legwork for us. She had been working for TNA on and off and was getting paid as a manager before the expansion of the new Knockout division was even a thought. She was friends with Angel Williams, who gave us a verbal promise that we would appear on most every Wednesday PPV. Verbal promise was the key words there. We had nothing in writing, so while the spots were set, the money still was not.

As Poison, I did a lot of spots with Trinity and a lot of mixed tags. I started getting TV time and that was all I was concerned with. I figured you have to start somewhere and it was better than showing my boobs. I was getting a little bit of pay and figured the rest would come eventually, after I caught on with my new character.

In the meantime, I started bouncing at a bar in Nashville during the week, sometimes until 4 a.m., to pay the bills. You heard me right, bouncing, not bartending, and not bouncing my boobs like some of the other TNA girls were doing.

As a female bouncer just as a male would do, I would stand at the door of the bar and I would stop fights when people got out of hand. Most of the time, I was the one throwing the shitfaced whores out of the bar. Nine times out of ten, it was the girls who would be the ones actually starting the fights, so the bar realized that they liked having a female bouncer who could kick a girl's ass when she got out of line. Guys, after all, couldn't touch them.

It was funny though, some nights as a female bouncer, I would be tasked with having to deal with a dude. A lot of times, the dude was smaller than me, so I didn't care. There were plenty of times I would just pick junior up by the seat of his pants, give him a wonder wedgie, and throw him out on his face. That was definitely one perk of the job.

Other times, drunk guys would carry on and start trouble. I would come up to them from behind and tap them on the shoulder to help see them out. They would act all "Billy Badass" like they were going to hit me, until they would see that I was a girl and stop. From my training on the job, I learned that the moment they realized I was a girl – that was the best time to catch them even more off guard and strike.

For instance, one time some dude went to hit me with beer bottle. He saw that his target wasn't a guy. He was, instead, a man standing up against a jacked-up girl.

"Thou shall not hit a girl." Everything he learned from Sunday School apparently flooded his already inebriated brain, and he stopped for a second. That one moment was all I needed. I, on the other hand, didn't hesitate. As his catholic guilt kicked in, I kicked him in the rosaries.

"Oh God!" he cried, praying for the pain to stop. Then he, like many others before him, dropped to his knees. As he was trying to unscrunch his sacred sack from his penance-paying pelvis, I rolled him and his battered balls right out the door.

Anyhow as you could guess, between my bouncing and my wrestling, my Wednesday nights back then were long.

First, I would go to work for TNA at the Fairgrounds. I would beat up bitches and get beat up. Then I would head over to my other job, where sometimes another fight would break out. That double shift toughened me up fast.

The good thing is, eventually word got out in the locker room about my moonlighting, and I got even more street credit with the boys for my endeavors. Sometimes after the show, some of my coworkers would head over to the bar right along with me. It is quite possible that a few members of the TNA X-division helped the new girl escort a drunk or two out of that establishment back in the day with style.

MAKING AN IMPACT

In May of 2004, TNA introduced its second weekly television program, *Impact!* This show was set to be filmed at Soundstage 21, at Universal Studios in Florida for broadcast on Fox Sports Net. I was more than ready to enter the "Impact Zone."

With the show's premiere, they wanted to look different from the product on the other channel. They wanted no confusion about it, TNA was not WWE.

The first step to make this happen was that TNA would introduce a six-sided wrestling ring; an idea stolen from the Lucha world.

I remember when I first saw that thing, it blew my freakin' mind.

"How the hell do you hit the ropes?" I asked AJ Styles.

"I don't know," he laughed. "I was just going to ask you the same thing."

I watched his gears move a little as he bounced his head and made some calculations. He showed me what he was thinking and I guess it made sense – the best sense one could make out of something as fucked up looking as that.

On top of the new weird ring, they brought in something they called "The Fox Box." This is where they could shoot and display competitors. And in a more sports-like style than the WWE, they displayed a ticking clock to show the timekeeping for matches.

In Orlando, I got to work with Traci Brooks. I think I really impressed them because after that, they started to fly me in! I was flying high on cloud 9. Never once had a promotion thought so highly of me that they were willing to splurge on a plane ticket. That was a great sign. More TV was good, but when you were also getting flown, that meant that you had some kind of value to a promoter. It really meant something when you were worth a plane ticket to the office.

Traci and I were growing up in the business together. So, when we both started getting work in TNA, we felt accomplished. We appreciated each other and loved each other, and protected each other.

The boys there at TNA appreciated us. Most of the guys knew we were paying our dues and they respected us more than the other girls because of that. They protected us like we were one of the boys too. We were living the same lives they were and they recognized that. We weren't like the divas that only wanted to wear fancy clothing and be on TV. We wanted a life in wrestling and did what we had to in order to work.

As far as getting paid by TNA went, unlike some previous indy promoters we'd encountered, there was never an issue. They were totally professional and we never had to worry about a hotdog and a handshake as our payoff there.

In fact, I guess there was even the idea amongst the women wrestlers that the TNA promoters could actually be paying the girls even more than the guys for the same amount of work. In a world where women traditionally saw less money than their male counterparts, why would this be, one might ask? Maybe because the people paying us were men, haha! Just sayin'.

You know why a waitress takes off her wedding ring before starting her shift at a restaurant? Someone figured out that men like a single waitress and will tip better, in turn. Now, I don't think in every case that the customer really wants to hook up with their server and thinks they have an actual chance with their waitress, but maybe they just like the idea that they COULD have a chance with them. I don't know. Guys are weird. There really is some truth to the fact that waitresses do get more tips when they are perceived to be gettable, so maybe that's why our envelopes were slightly bigger. *Impress the girls.* Who knows? There was never any foul play so I wasn't complaining.

I should mention that a lot of times the locker rooms didn't have much privacy, but the guys still respected us. The guys didn't just do their thing ala boy's locker room style. They changed under towels in the darkness of a corner when we were around, or often even left the room out of respect. They were all pretty considerate.

I remember, one time, we were booked at a show in a minor league hockey arena. It was just one big locker room, so we excused ourselves to go and get changed for our match. The doors were already open, and we didn't want to break kayfabe and go change in the ladies room together with the fans. We looked around, and Traci found a concession booth.

"How about in there?" she asked.

"Looks as good a place as any," I confided.

We went over to this big wooden box on cinderblocks and asked the boys running the place if they could take off for a few minutes so we could change. They agreed.

The plan was to have one of us stand in front of the box's serving window to block the view of the other one changing.

It went pretty well until a customer came up to the window. I was sick of blocking and waiting for my turn in the back, so I just started changing right there. When I saw the hungry fan come up to me, I decided to play cashier. I just held my clothing against my chest, and stuck my head out the window at the person looking for food.

"What can I getcha, babe?"

"Um, oh I am sorry," the fan said blushing.

"No, no," I said, pulling on a top and ducking down just a little bit as to not give him a whole peep show. "What can I get you? Really."

"Um, are you sure?"

"Yeah, yeah. Whatever you need. You want nachos, a hot dog?" I said, pulling up my tights over my butt under the counter. "Whatever you want."

"A hamburger?" In my first food truck-like experience, I made that guy a bomb-ass triple cheeseburger with all the best trimmings, all while still lacing up my boots.

Now that is both class and multitasking at its best.

We were great together. When the Knockouts push became a thing at TNA, Traci looked down at my shitty worn out boots and saw that I had beat the crap out of them. They were so bad that they were duct taped together. Now, she didn't want to have her girl showing up for the new *Impact!* booking looking like a hobo from the knees down, so she gave me a pair of her boots!

Hand-me-down boots? I had no problem with that.

We were becoming famous with the boys for being cheap, but they loved it. One day, for example, I remember AJ Styles busting our chops for washing our clothes in a locker room utility sink with no soap, just water.

"Water is free though," we said. "If there is no soap, you just scrub a little harder is all."

In the end, however, being cheap paid off and this is something all wrestlers needed to do. We learned on the road that by getting as much experience as possible and not worrying about the pay days was everything. Pay would come later. Being economical surviving on the proverbial tuna out of the can was all part of coming up.

I will say it again, in these early days of my career, Traci was just what I needed. Traci was Moolah, the money bitch. And I was Mae, the drunk chick in the boots. She was and always will be my plus one to any party.

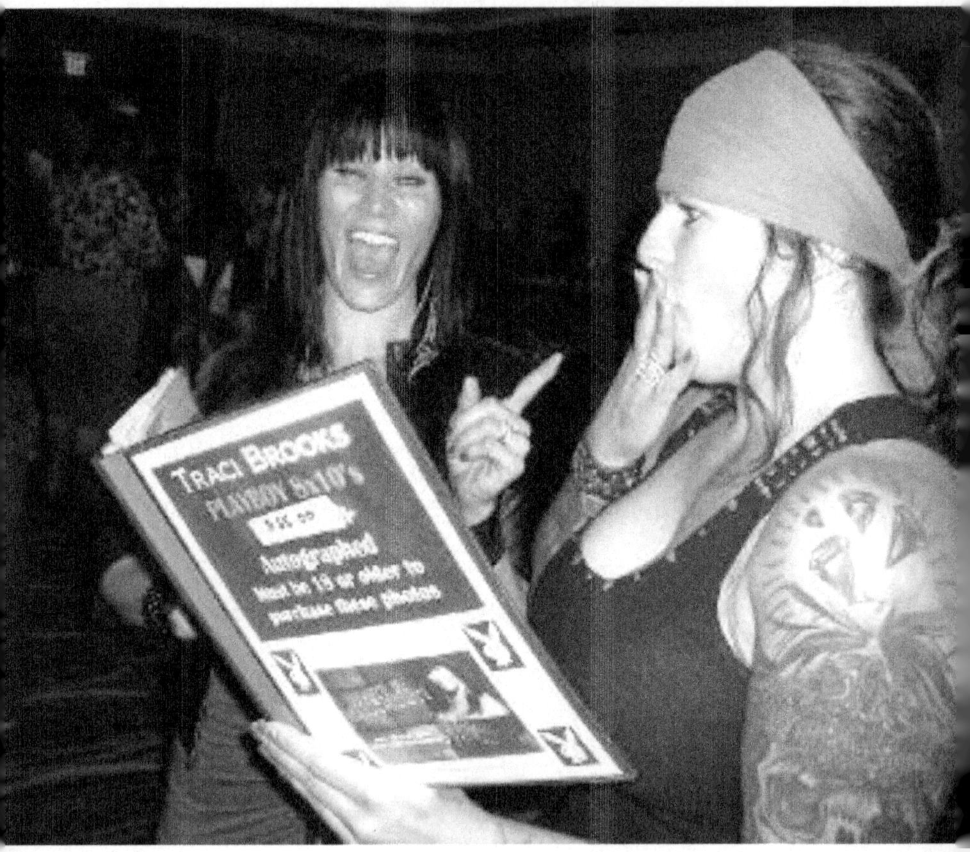
TRACI BROOKS
Autographed

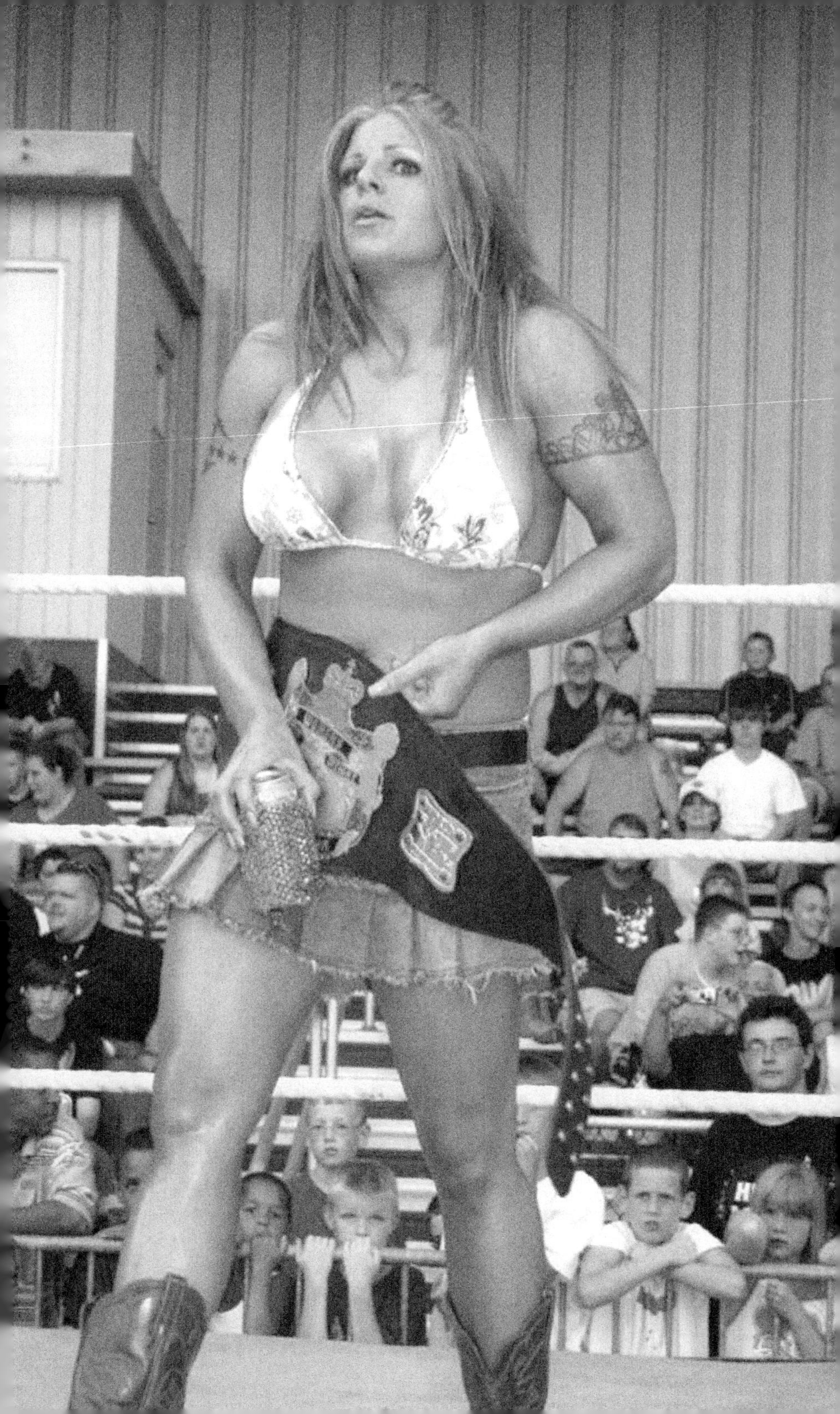

CHAPTER 5 - OHIO VALLEY

Back while I was trying to get an actual long-term money deal in TNA and begging to climb up the ladder in their women's division, I was still working elsewhere. The exposure I had as TNA's Poison on national television increased my bookings, and each week they had used me became like a new commercial on why a promotion elsewhere should book the ODB.

I was still at every single TNA taping, like clockwork, looking for work. If you didn't see me on TV in a match, or a pull-apart breaking up a fight, I was probably backstage hoping to get used.

I continued to work as much TNA as I could, but eventually, TV stuff dried up. I am not sure why, but I think in hindsight that Dixie wasn't a big fan of mine. While stuff may have been running idle in Nashville, I was still getting booked all over the country off of the few bones they threw me.

It was nice getting paid to sit backstage at TNA, but it did me no good. Wrestling fans had a short attention span and an even shorter memory. I knew if I wanted to keep the ball rolling, I needed to be seen.

After *Tough Enough*, I had stayed in contact some with Al Snow who seemed to be supportive and a champion for my cause. On more than one occasion, he suggested that I should come check out OVW, but I still had family in Minnesota and my new posse in Nashville. I wasn't sold on moving yet again.

"You really need to get seen though," he told me at an indy show. "Take whatever you can. Even be an extra. But sitting backstage isn't going to help your cause. You need to get out there."

Many people were concerned about being typecasted. There are a number of guys that did such a good job putting someone else over that the major promotions only wanted to use them as enhancement talent, thereafter. However, Al thought I should give it my all, so that is what I intended to do.

When I heard that WWE *SmackDown* was coming to Minnesota in 2005, I was willing to do whatever I could to get seen. It would be nice to go see my family and get a gig at the same time.

CHAPTER 5 – Ohio Valley

I called Tom Prichard and he said he "really didn't have anything for me." He was nice, but he had heard the show was "booked pretty solid," but he told me to try back again soon. At this time, the roster was massive and guys on the payroll wanted to work and weren't all being given any time. I believed him.

After that, I called Tommy Dreamer for the 700th time. He was in the WWE office still, and he knew I was getting the runaround at TNA. With some more experience under my belt, I think he felt he could do something for me. He made a few calls and got me an "in."

I was officially booked as an extra for the WWE.

Now, I know this isn't a big big deal. It was just a one-shot deal. For some people, they think being an extra for the WWE means they made it. This mentality is the furthest thing from the truth. WWE is willing to book anyone and their mother as an extra if it makes sense at the time, so it isn't a real accomplishment. But it could, I guess, be a help if you use the time well and network.

God, I hope I don't become the new female version of Iron Mike Sharpe.

A lot of times when you were booked as an extra, you would get there and sit backstage, much like I was already doing at TNA. Sometimes you got a match. Most of the time you didn't. Quite often, the show was being written while it was happening on the fly. As an extra, you had to realize that at any time you could lose your spot to someone else with a contract that wasn't being used anywhere at the last second.

Getting that extra spot was bittersweet. You would get excited for it, and if you did get a match, you knew it made you look like shit. Your assignment overall if you did make it to the ring was to make contract talent look good, and pretty much just be a crash test dummy. You didn't want to take too many bookings like that, or else the exposure that it would garner would work in reverse.

I was hungry. I was ready to take the risk. I was ready to change things up and take whatever I could get.

In this case, however, false expectations were not even the case. Yes, I had pulled some strings and got that extra spot on *SmackDown*, but I knew that when I got there, they weren't going to have anything for me. Dreamer warned me that my spot was in fact a "just in case" spot.

Sometimes these extra bodies would make it on television, but fans wouldn't even know who they were looking at. As an extra, you might be asked to wear a police outfit with a SWAT team helmet, or maybe some kind of medic outfit. A number of guys got their starts with the company doing stuff like this. Montel Vontavious Porter (MVP), Wade Barrett, and Sheamus all had on TV appearances as security guards before officially getting on the WWE roster. Braun Strowman was one of Adam Rose's "Rosebud" dancers, not unlike the Godfather's "Ho Train" which started out both Lita and Victoria's careers. CM Punk was an extra dressed like John Cena (of all people) for a big elaborate intro with tons of other Cena clones.

When I got there, there were clearly some others in my boat, that is, people booked with no real assignments at hand. Before the show, we went down to the ring. A few of the guys on the card were practicing. They knew some of the indy talent who were being booked as extras as well, and they were running some spots together in the ring and catching up.

That is when I saw Chavo Guerrero, Jr.

The extras were standing around the ring looking stupid like usual as per tradition. They would get directed to the ring and eventually the office would send someone out for a little inspirational speech. In this case, we were being treated to "Latino Heat" Eddie Guerrero's nephew.

Now, I knew Chavo, and surprisingly he also seemed to know me even though we had never met before. I approached him and decided that if I was going to get anything out of this booking, networking was my only hope.

"Hoping maybe you can give me some advice?" I asked.

He nodded and agreed to help. "Al told me to come find you, anyhow. Give me ten minutes here."

After Chavo was finished greeting the extras on the show, he gave a little motivational speech. He played a good statesman for the company, then wished everyone luck.

I thought my shot to pick his brain was gone as he turned to walk away, but then he turned and motioned me to follow him.

Now is my chance. Don't fuck this up.

"So, I guess my question for you would be to throw it right back at you first," he said as we made our way to some empty seating in the arena to talk. "Why do you think maybe you are not being seen?"

Well, you got me there.

I didn't know how to answer that. I mean I was out on the road. I was working wherever and whenever I could. I was making an attempt to do the bigger shows for exposure. But still, I did not know how to answer his question. I decided that honesty was likely the best policy, and I was going to just tell him the truth.

"Honestly, I don't know how to answer that," I said. "I know Tommy and some of the other guys here, but I'm not sure how to get someone to want to look at me more."

"If I had to answer that, I would say, be around more."

"More?"

"More," he said. "Like, more. I'm sure you have heard of being in the right place at the right time. My guess is your odds for that happening go up drastically if you are around more and there when the moment comes when there is more of a need for you. Then, your opportunity to shine happens."

Well, that made sense. It was what I did with TNA.

"So how can I be there or here more?"

"You said you are from Minnesota, right?"

"That's right."

"Is there anything tying you down to Minnesota?"

"No," I said. "Not at all. Just family maybe?"

"Could wrestling be your family?"

I knew exactly where he was going, so it was no surprise when he suggested I contact Al Snow, and finally move my ass to OVW. I bet Al even put him up to it.

After that, it wasn't difficult at all. Getting into OVW only took one phone call. The harder part for me, a creature of habit, was packing up to move out of my familiar happy place I knew in Minnesota and moving to the unknown.

The deepest darkest depths of Kentucky.

OHIO VALLEY WRESTLING

OVW was a NWA affiliated promotion that started back in 1993 by Danny Davis. Now for those of you keeping track, I mean "Nightmare" Danny Davis, not "Dangerous" Danny Davis the famous WWE heel referee (whose book is also available by Kenny, the same guy helping me with this book. ...Talk about a Mick Foley-style cheap plug!)

The company ran shows out of both Kentucky and Indiana territories back then. In 1997, NWA: Ohio Valley ended its relationship with the NWA and subsequently rebranded itself as just Ohio Valley Wrestling.

Come the beginning of 1998, OVW started its own television show and more eyes came along with that. A year later, Jim Cornette became a partial owner of OVW. It made sense. Cornette was a native of Louisville and liked the idea of moving closer to his home. He hated living in Connecticut, where the WWE was based, and wasn't getting along all that well with coworkers Kevin Dunn and Vince Russo at that time.

Now, this history is important because even though Cornette was gone before I got to OVW, his presence there gave the promotion the street cred that it needed. When Cornette took on the role of booker while still having contacts in New York, the doors opened and the relationship began between both companies.

With Cornette at the helm, the WWE started sending some of their hot talent to work at the promotion. This in turn filled the OVW audience. After that, WWE sent new greener talent there to get experience working in front of a large crowd that they helped to create. In return, they got a great testing/training ground for new wrestlers.

OVW became the official farm ground for WWE and everything was great. With all the new talent, OVW's ticket sales grew and they even had to move to a bigger venue to accommodate all the new fans. It grew and grew. You would think that Cornette would have been rewarded for this, but at the same time that business picked up – bad stuff went down. So instead, come July of 2005, Corny was actually parting ways with WWE, which included being relieved of his duties overseeing OVW.

What happened was, there was an incident with Santino Marella where he was supposed to put over The

Boogeyman gimmick when they were both down in OVW. At the time, Marella was still green to the business. From what I understand about this story, he didn't know how he was supposed to play to Boogeyman's character, so he laughed at the odd character that he was portraying in the ring – he didn't take it seriously or play it like he was scared.

After this, Cornette was furious. When Marella came back to the locker room, he was pissed and the two of them had an incident backstage which led to Cornette being banned from OVW. Apparently, words were exchanged and Cornette slapped Marella. (The two have not been on positive terms since, even having a confrontation that went viral at an event both were on as recently as October 2017.)

Cornette was replaced by someone who liked my different look/approach since we first met at *Tough Enough*, WWE Trainer Al Snow.

Once I got Louisville, I had visions of moving into a very old school, Wonder Bread Kentucky Derby highbrow-like city. This image quickly faded when I found myself rooming with Shawn Spears in a two-bedroom apartment across from the tag team, The Highlanders. We were right down the street from OVW, but make no mistake about it, it was straight up ghetto.

Now, The Highlanders were super tight with their money, as was Spears. I can't fault them for this, because so was I. This is why we were all bunking up in the first place. All the contracted guys stayed in super nice places, but they were stupid. They were burning through money that they didn't have, I won't name any names, but okay: Dolph Ziggler, CM Punk, Ryback, and Cody Rhodes, just to name a few.

Cody was funny back then. He was the son, of course, of Dusty, who was a big booker for Vince back then. He knew he could do no wrong. He was super cool, but it would become tough to keep track of whoever he was dating, so most of us didn't even try. While he is a family man now, back then, he had a new "flavor of the week" practically every week – sometimes two.

The list continued. Other names kicking around in that class included Deuce 'n Domino, and The Major Boys Matt Cardona and Brian Myers.

We had chicks, too. Maryse, Kelly Kelly, and also Alicia Fox. It was funny to see the boys drooling all over the girls. Those blondes were the talk of the locker room for sure, if not the whole town any night that they went out. It would have been something to report here if one of the boys hooked up with one of those girls, but I don't think anything like that would happen until later on when The Miz ended up with Maryse, maybe? IDK. There were some crushes perhaps, but nothing would become of any of that.

Our new crew was pretty impressive, but before I start to talk about them, I guess I should talk about the alumni before us – the ones whose shoes we were about to step into. Do you who was in the OVW class right before me? The few years before us cranked out names that would become the face of the industry for years to come. These included Brock Lesnar, Shelton Benjamin, Batista, Randy Orton, and even John Cena. But even more importantly than all of those superstars, yes, there was someone else worth noting. You are right, a year before I got there, my ex, Ken Anderson, went through the ringer and was off to become Mr. Kennedy the illegitimate son of Vince McMahon himself, on *Monday Night RAW*. (INSERT KEN HAVING AN ILLEGITIMATE SON PUNCHLINE HERE.)

Thank God Anderson had already graduated from OVW, and he didn't stay back a year.

At OVW, I saw that Al Snow was incredibly smart from day one. The wrestlers that had amassed in Kentucky to be polished by the farm league were by no means newbies, and Snow knew it. The majority of us had been around, and we all knew the deal to some degree. WWE didn't book totally green wrestlers for OVW. A number of us, of course, had already been working in the independent scene quite a bit. Therefore, Al Snow knew he didn't need to go into a whole big diatribe about the business, and then hit us with drill after drill after drill.

Typically, the first day of wrestling school as well as a number of other seminars that I have seen around the world, were always the same. They get everyone together for a speech by the trainer on day one which involves an inspirational talk. This speech comes in various shapes and sizes depending on who is giving it, but for the most part it is always the same thing. It starts with some kind of story to build credibility, then it shows how brutal the business can be, then it finishes with all the words of encouragement in the world.

At OVW, however, Snow wasn't going to do that to us. When it came time to meet up with all of the new talent prospects, he only had one agenda.

"I don't really care what you do, but in the end, I want you to own this town."

That was it?

No, Snow also didn't want us to go out and be assholes, but he wanted us to look like legends. He wanted us to work on living life to its fullest and in turn become larger than life. It all made sense. If we acted like normal people, we would just be normal people. However, if we lived big – we would become big.

This is just what I am going to do.

This reminds me of a story Jimmy Hart likes to tell. When he spent his time in the music world with his band The Gentrys before his wrestling career, he talked to Dick Clark. Clark apparently gave him some great advice when he was brand new to the entertainment field. Clark said something to him to the effect that "you have to look like a star in the eyes of the people around you in order to become one." He told a young Mouth of the South, "You see you have to stand out. If you look like just any old person, you are just any old person. If you look like someone that just came up on the stage from the audience, you are going to end up back out in it."

After this, no matter how little money Jimmy had when he got into wrestling, he says he always tried to look different. He says today that if he only had one pair of shoes, he would spray paint them a different loud color every night he could so he was looking flashier than ever to anyone that would dare look at him.

Al Snow's idea of living large went right along with what Jimmy had once said.

After hearing Al Snow's words, we decided as a group that we all had to take what he said to the next level.

We trained hard during the week, and we worked hard on the OVW shows. However, no matter what day of the week it was, we would all go out and party harder than anyone. This became the OVW culture. This was the way.

Becoming larger-than-life and the life of the party was our collective motto.

There was a place called Four-Street Station which was in the heart of downtown. It had all the major watering holes lined up in tandem. I wasn't much of a clubber – but I liked the watering holes that were more like "hole in the wall" bars – the dirtier the better. That is where the good shit always went down.

Picture a pub crawl every night of the week. This was OVW. Now, don't get me wrong, we didn't just get shitfaced and stir up trouble. However, if there was trouble, we protected each other wherever we were.

As far as groups were concerned, Spears and The Highlanders went out with me a lot and not because we were neighbors. Our party preferences were just like our accommodations; we liked the cheap places and ended up seeking out all the dives that Louisville had to offer.

For one, we always liked to go to a place that was so basic, it was just called The Bar. There, you didn't have high end bougie peanut butter cup martinis with graham cracker rims and other various fruity chick drinks with umbrellas as their specials. At The Bar, you could get pitchers of beer for $5. That was our draw.

The crowd was a little rough, but that is what I liked about it. It had a regular roster of clowns, kind of like the list Billy Joel would spout off in his song "Piano Man."

Eventually after some persuading, we convinced Al Snow to let us have the official OVW Christmas party there. And no OVW party would have been complete without drunken karaoke.

Now, a lot of that night is just like the others, a big blur, but I do remember a little. Derek Graham-Couch aka Robbie McAllister from The Highlanders sang a bunch of metal songs, and Black Sabbath's "Crazy Train" was one of them. I remember that Al Snow sang The B-52's "Love Shack" with us, too. This says a lot about Snow. Agents don't do this today, but he was right there in the mix with us. Come the next year, he even used to throw his own shindigs for us and put together some of the best ever BBQs.

I remember one time, a bunch of us got together to go out and get a real flavor for the town. Louisville was ours for the taking, and Al Snow decided to help make that happen. He packed a bunch of us in a van and took us all out to the actual Kentucky Derby.

The Kentucky Derby is considered to be one of the most prestigious annual horse races in America. It initiates the first jewel of the Triple Crown of Thoroughbred Racing. Every year since 1875, the Kentucky Derby brings the world to Churchill Downs in Louisville for a week of excitement, suspense and spectacle. And on this particular year, with the OVW boys in attendance, you could add debauchery to the list.

The Derby is also known as being "The Most Exciting Two Minutes in Sports" and "The Fastest Two Minutes in Sports" because of its approximate duration. It is the first leg of the American Triple Crown, followed by the Preakness Stakes, and then the Belmont Stakes.

So OVW showed up to see "The Most Exciting & The Fastest Two Minutes in Sports." We were walking around and taking all the pre-game in. There was one particular wrestler who took even more in than probably he should have. This includes taking a girl into a shit house porta-potty where he would show her "The Most Exciting & The Fastest Two Minutes" of something else.

Yes, they did the deed in a porta-potty. And as we all know; that is one of the most intimate romantic places you could ever take a girl. Gross!

That being said, Kentucky Derby dignitaries probably wouldn't have liked to know what was going on behind a certain closed door. The good thing is, if two people were going into a porta-potty, things could have been explained away. The girl could have had to help with something behind closed doors, and so on and so forth. The idea that OVW wrestlers were having sex in a fly-infested shithouse would be a tough one to prove (unless they were very loud or if the proverbial van or in this case potty was rocking.) Therefore, we fortunately didn't get called out on this offense.

However, the smell of marijuana is pretty distinct, and because the potty tank wasn't filled with patchouli oil or any kind of air freshener, something happened that left us up shit creek without a paddle, quite literally.

In the end when the smoke settled, OVW got kicked out of the Kentucky Derby as a whole because one of us got caught smoking pot in an outhouse.

"Come on guys," Al Snow said, scolding us all as we were being showed off the grounds. "Did we really have to be the ones to put the POT into porta-potties?"

HOT WHEELS

Another interesting story that I would be remiss in not telling has to do with my ride. The ticket to my freedom while at OVW was an army green Ford Sport Explorer.

I am not sure if you remember him or not, but there was this one wrestler named Kasey James. James got his start training under a guy named Rockin' Randy in the North American Wrestling Federation (NAWF). After that, he traveled a little with CM Punk, Colt Cabana, and Adam Pearce. Before coming to OVW, he spent some time in Puerto Rico for the IWA, working with guys like Savio Vega.

After his time in OVW, he would show up in the WWE for what they call "a hot second." His debut was on *SmackDown* tagging with Aron Stevens (aka Damien Sandow) and being managed by Michelle McCool.

Anyhow, while in OVW, one night, James decided to throw a pretty good-sized party out of his apartment. Because he lived in a more well-off side of town, I grabbed The Highlanders and Shawn Spears and we headed over in my car. We had our pregame on to some degree back at our apartments first, and decided to show up fashionably late.

When we finally got there and cracked open the door, it was like we were opening the gates of party hell. I looked down and it looked like dry ice rolled out onto the floor and into the hallway like a haunted house. The reefer in the air was Snoop-Dogg thick. When we walked in, we saw that James had Jell-O shots, Fireball shots, and probably gun shots all going on simultaneously, that is if you could hear anything over the loud music.

"My kind of party," I said to the boys.

When we walked in, we soon learned that James also had a giant beer pong tournament going on. Most of the guys there were fully engaged, betting on the tourney, and the ones who weren't, were drinking from a big funnel in the corner. It was a mess.

The next three or four hours were kind of a big blur, but I think this party went down under the classification of "epic" as far as I can tell from what others have said about it.

Anyhow, eventually the night was finally over. When I say this, I mean, over for me. Once they broke out the midgets and the chocolate cigars, I decided to give my Irish goodbye and just take off.

When I went down to my car to make my getaway, however, something very odd occurred to me.

My car was not parked where I had left it.

I stopped. I looked around. I did a double and a triple take, and yet I still couldn't for the life of me figure out where my car was.

"Oh boy. Who the hell did this?" I laughed to myself. "And how the hell did they copy my keys? This must have taken some thought."

I immediately thought I was the victim of a rib – my first one in OVW.

Does this mean I'm in the gang now?

I ran back up to Kasey James' apartment. I looked around, waiting to see someone jump out from behind the couch and hold up an extra set of my car keys, or something.

No dice.

After a minute or so of waiting to be debriefed and nothing happening, I noticed that someone was conspicuous by their absence.

Dolph Ziggler was nowhere to be found.

I rushed back down the staircase, expecting to see Dolph out on the sidewalk with the grand reveal: my car parked and waiting. Still, nothing happened.

After some time had passed, I knew I had to start thinking the worst and I did.

Eventually, the cops came.

Nervous that I was going to get one of the boys into trouble, I was leery on filling out the police report.

What if it is one of the wrestlers, after all? If I fill this out, am I going to get them sent home? Am I going to get bad press for the company if the truth gets out and I wasted the police's time with some big practical joke?

As the boys departed the party, everyone seemed generally concerned seeing me filling out the paperwork. As much as I hated to think my car was stolen, at least the idea that I was perhaps stooging on some prankster was moving further and further from my mind.

Losing your car sucks.

Let me say that again, "LOSING YOUR CAR FUCKING SUCKS!"

After that party, any car that even remotely looked like mine was on my radar. No matter where I was, no matter who I was with, I became a total and complete bloodhound. Because I didn't have any clue what had become of my wheels, and because my freedom had been revoked leaving me to grovel for any kind of mercy ride I could find, I was constantly on the lookout hoping to stumble onto my car.

I remember right after it happened, me and The Highlander boys teamed up like Mystery Inc. from *Scooby-Doo* to look for clues. We went out on the town combing lots in their Mystery Machine. We drove everywhere, just hoping to find a trace of my beautiful lost ride. We explored every nook and cranny in Louisville to find my Explorer, but to no avail. (Jinkies!)

I even went so far as to put a picture of my car on a flyer, the same as you would a lost dog and put them up on some of the posts around my apartment. That avenue didn't work though, either. All I got was some weird calls in the middle of the night of some guy breathing and maybe beating his meat, as a result.

Note to self: next time, don't include a picture of yourself along with your missing car.

Then one day, it finally happened. About 20 something days or so later, I got a call from the police. It seemed they had found my car, or at least one that looked like mine. It was parked under a bridge, and they said that apparently a family was living in it.

When I got to the scene being dropped off by one of The Highlanders, I just expected that I would show up, put in the key and turn away. However, that wasn't the case at all.

When I opened the door, the first thing I saw was baby shoes. I pushed them out of the way and rolled in. I couldn't tell if I was getting into a car, or rolling into a dumpster. On the floor was a foot-high pile of garbage that included every fast food bag you could think of, broken bottles, and cigarette butts. That wasn't the only butt I was smelling, however.

On top of all that, my car now smelled like a lethal combination of blunts and baby diapers.

This pungent pot smell was stronger than any strand I had smelled in my life, and I had been on road trips with RVD, mind you. There was no getting that smell out either. After that, my car smelled like it had once been used as an undercover Uber ride, transporting only Snoop Dogg, Willie Nelson, and Seth Rogen on the daily.

It was cool to get my car back, but in hindsight, it also sucked. At the 30-day mark of your car being missing, you would be able to tap insurance for a full replacement. At 30 days, they would write the car off for a loss and cut you a check for the full value replacement. However, at 28 days, you would take the car back at pretty much whatever condition it was in. And in my case, the condition was GROSSSSSS.

We never found the people who had taken ownership of my car, despite their names being all over the prescription pill bottles on the floor.

We did, however, find some very interesting baby shit skid marks all over the upholstery. At least they matched the army green paint job.

OVW SHOWS

As for shows, come 2006, I was getting a ton of work from OVW, as well as other promotions. My ODB character was developing and things were looking up.

In OVW, after running a program with Daisy Mae, I wanted to shake things up. So, whenever I got on the microphone, I decided to "take the brass ring." That is right. I declared myself as the OVW Women's champion.

OVW did not recognize a women's champion at the time, so me and my next opponent, Serena Deeb, took it upon ourselves to make up a title, because we didn't see any signs of one coming about any time soon.

Now, "going into business for yourself" is usually frowned upon by most promoters. The idea that two women without contracts could come into a promotion and just create a championship for themselves to work an angle around should have been shit on in hindsight. However, to their credit, nobody said anything and they just rolled with it.

I repeatedly cut promos saying that I was the new women's champion, and OVW booker "Nightmare" Danny Davis finally laughed it off and conceded to my nonsense.

One day, Davis walked into the locker room. He had a shit-eating grin on his face and walked slowly up to me. In his arm, he was carrying a grocery bag.

When he was finally up to the bleacher where I was sitting, he handed me the package. I opening it up and pulled out a generic championship wrestling belt.

"What is this?" I asked looking down at the belt.

"You are looking at the new OVW Women's championship," he said. "What do you think?"

"Ha! Oh my God," I laughed. "This is great!"

"Congratulations."

Davis appreciated my spunk and decided to recognize me as the first ever OVW Women's champion.

I know it is all a work, but still, it was a super honor that a promoter would trust in me enough to do such a thing. It made sense. We had a number of girls around, so why not have a title? But letting me be the first champion was a very cool thing for me.

I held it for a bit and loved every minute of it. Then, come September 13, 2006, I dropped the title to Serena Deeb in a four-way, as not to be greedy.

I continued to work wherever I could into 2007. I took some decent paying gigs on the weekends when I could, and did OVW during the week. Doing OVW TV programming helped to polished up my promo skills for sure. It seemed I was practically doing wrestling stuff almost seven days a week.

Every other week, OVW would have a WWE office guy come down to check out our progress. Sometimes it was Dean Malenko. Other times it was Tony Garea. In theory, the WWE guys would watch our show and report back on what they liked, and what they thought could mean money.

I was waiting by the phone, but the call from the WWE never came. Then one day, there was a call from Terry Taylor. At this point in his career, Taylor had left the WWE and had more recently been working at TNA.

Taylor called me with a contract offer. It seemed the company was expanding their women's division once again and hoping to spend a lot more time on that type of programming. I didn't accept it on the spot, and I didn't decline it either. I said I needed to figure a few things out before I could answer, and that I would call him back in a few days if that was cool. He agreed.

I called Al Snow. "What do I do?" I told him I wanted to make myself available for WWE, but at the same time, I didn't want to turn something down if an offer wasn't going to be coming from them. He said he would try to help and find out.

The next week of WWE scouting came. Malenko wasn't there, and neither was Garea. This time it was Triple H. (I figured Al Snow probably asked him to come take a look at me, or at least talk to me about my situation.)

Triple H was easy to talk to. He was one of the boys, after all. Before I asked him what he thought about the offer, I made good and sure that I told him my intentions. I told him that I did not want to go back to TNA, because that was a step backwards for me. I told him that I wasn't discussing this with the WWE as a means of having a leverage stick, a bargaining tool, or any form of disrespect, and I believe that he totally understood where I was coming from.

Triple H was super cool, but admitted he just didn't think there was anything for me in WWE at that moment.

He more or less told me to take the offer and work hard, then to contact them again in a year or so.

I appreciated his honesty, and then Hunter bailed. Shawn Michaels stuck around for a bit, but he wasn't very friendly. I tried to talk to him, but he was unapproachable. I felt he was so dismissive of me that after our interaction I almost didn't want any part of New York.

The writing was on the wall. Even though I gained praise for my matches, WWE's head of talent relations, John Laurinaitis, ultimately thought that I just didn't fit in with the other WWE Divas. A small deal was better than no deal at all, right? After that, I was about ready to sign with TNA.

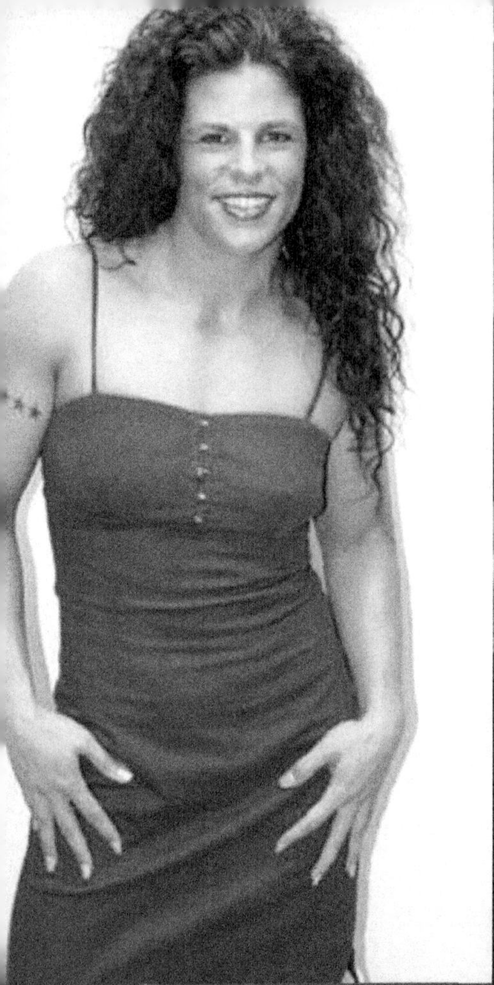

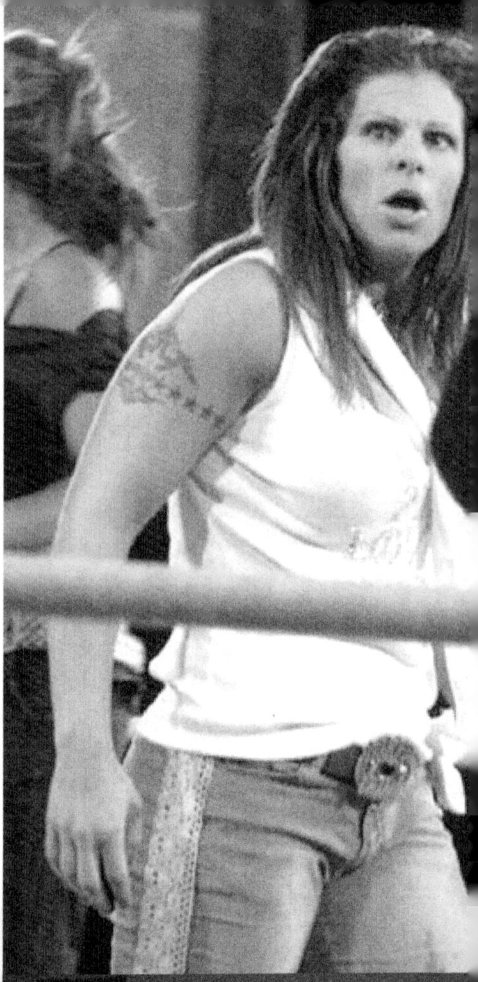

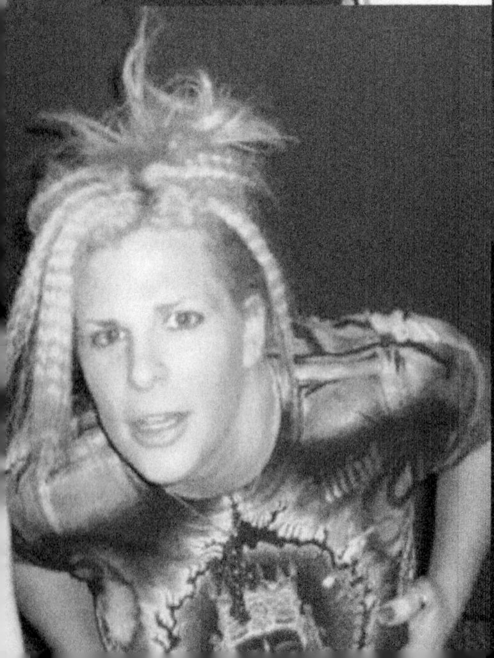

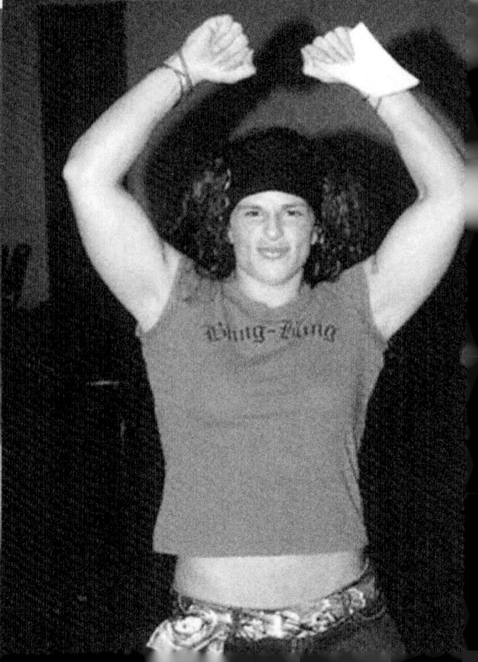

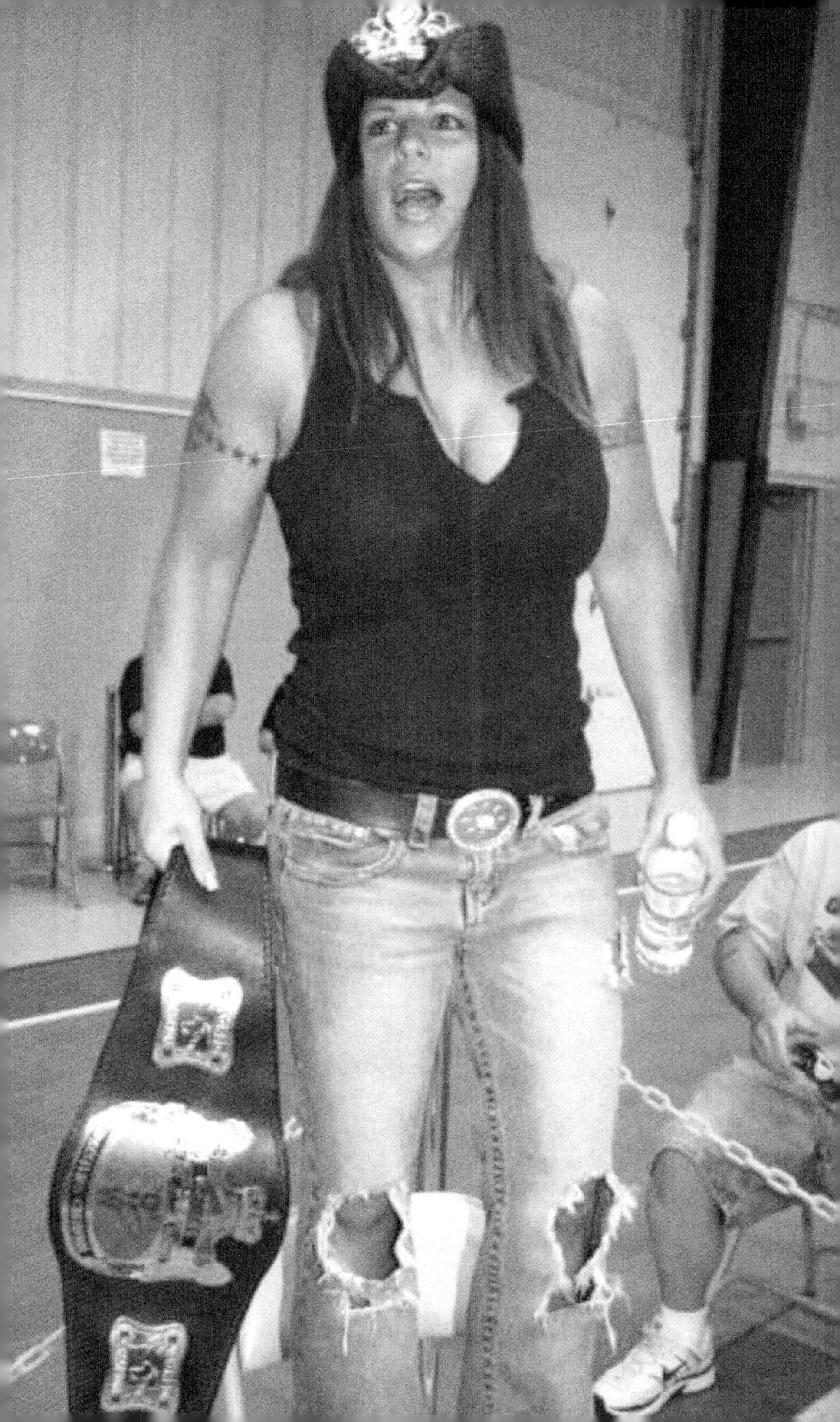

CHAPTER 6 - TNA CONTRACT

Before I accepted any deal from TNA, I got to check off one of the boxes on my bucket list. One box said "Japan," the other said "Mexico."

I was off to Monterrey City in Mexico. I got a call from Canadian wrestler, Taylor Wilde. Apparently, her and another girl from Canada, Sarah Stock, were off to take a booking in Mexico. They needed a third wheel, so I went along for the trip.

When we got there, there was a lot of training before the show. It was almost like they threw us into a class, or seminar to make sure that we would do a decent job in the Lucha world. Lucha is definitely a different style. I knew this, but I didn't know to what extent the differences were.

Lucha Libre dates back to the mid-1800's with the first fully-fledged promotion being established in 1933. The history of Lucha Libre is not only important to the cultural identity of Mexico, it's important to the evolution of professional wrestling worldwide.

I quickly learned it was fast-paced, super mega fast-paced to be precise. Fans in the states are used to a very deliberate pace to the matches they watch. We start off slow, pick up some speed, and build to an interesting finish.

In America, most matches evolve into brawls. It is what I knew. Everything in Mexico, however, was more of a high-flying, fast-paced style. I was told right away that rarely do Lucha matches turn into two people just "slugging it out."

"Well, you booked me to come from America," I said. "I am not Lucha."

I was bigger than most of the guys there so who was going to argue with me?

On the tour, it was set to be us three Americans (even though two of them were technically Canadian,) versus three Mexican chicks. We would work out a good match and do the same thing in a few different towns.

At the first show, we walked down the aisle and the fans loved us. They cheered. We were different and we got the response the promoters wanted even before we stepped in the ring.

Once we did, we looked over at our opponents who were standing on the other side of the ring waiting.

They were nasty-to-the-eye, I can't lie. They were rough. They were brute-looking. They looked like they could all use a siesta, and half of them maybe a shower.

However, it wasn't really the wrestlers in the ring that I was concerned with.

"Hey, Taylor," I said. "Look over there."

I wasn't really concerned with the wrestlers, but rather more where we were going to wrestle the wrestlers.

Ugh. The ring isn't clean.

In one of the matches before us, someone bladed like hell. That wasn't just color. It looked like a damn transfusion gone wrong. It looked like somebody chained up a dead deer and cleaned it right in the ring. There was blood all over the place. Fresh blood. I wanted to puke.

"Geesh," Sarah Stock said, taking it all in. "I don't want to roll around in that."

"Shit," I said. "We'll catch hepatitis or something."

Taylor Wilde's natural resting babyface smile changed to a look of puzzlement.

"What do we do then?"

"Don't bump in the pile of blood," I said. "Stay away from it."

Once our match got underway, the blood didn't matter anymore. We stepped over it like dog shit in a park. That part was easy. However, a new threat immediately became evident. What mattered more to me was the brutey chicks were throwing potatoes at my girls.

"Yeow!" I said grabbing my chest.

That one is going to leave a mark!

The Lucha girls were stiffing the living shit out of my nuggs. They weren't just chopping me, either. Those bitches were throwing straight up closed fists to the tits.

I tagged out to get a breather, and threw Taylor to the wolves.

Is there some kind language barrier going on? Is something being lost in translation?

I uploaded the information before me into the giant super computer in my head to try to find the disconnect.

There was some kind of user error going on, some kind of malfunction happening and I needed results, quickly.

I watched a little more, and I saw poor Taylor getting her ass handed to her and served up on a plate.

That did not compute.

For Lucha being from a style that glorified more technical and flashy moves than its American counterpart, the girls we were facing were acting like they were in the Ultimate Fighting Championship (UFC).

This wasn't a style clash. This wasn't the difference between American-style wrestling and Luchadorism. Those right hands landed like they were trying to make a statement and that statement was, "these are our spots, and this is our country. So, go the fuck home."

They just want to kick some American ass.

"Taylor, tag me in NOW," I said. I had bought some time, and now it was time for the receipt.

Taylor happily obliged.

When I finally tagged in, one of the brutes popped me hard. Then, I returned the favor ten-fold.

SMACK!

I hit her so hard, I heard something crack. At that moment, I thought I broke a finger, but secretly I was also hoping I broke a bone in her face.

My opponent immediately drew me outside of the ring and started to throw shit at me.

I dodged a chair and a trashcan with actual garbage in it. Then, it was my turn.

"Oh, yeah?" I said. "Two can play that."

I reached over to a fan who was minding his own business and enjoying an adult beverage. I grabbed the beer out of his hands and nodded at him. Then, I held it up over my head and poured it down into my mouth in one long stream like a saké bomb from a hibachi restaurant chef.

I chipmunked as much of it as I could before I grabbed that bitch by the throat.

Now you get to drink from the fire hose!

I hosed that bitch down. I mean, I spit beer all over her. She rubbed the burning alcohol out of her eyes. And when she was ready to come back up for air thinking I was all out, I grabbed another whole cup and launched it at her.

The crowd popped.

When she came to thinking she was going to throw another chair at me yet a second time, I pulled it out of her hands and punched her in one of her boobs like she had done to me. I did it so hard, however, I think a fan in the rafters held up a baseball mitt and caught her nipple flying by.

Well, whatever I did, it worked. I did what they taught me in Wrestling Class 101.

I handed some brute shit right back to her.

After that, the rest of the match went as smooth as hell. They respected me, and in turn, they had to respect my partners. We had a number of matches with the same girls after that in a big Mexican loop, but they never fucked with us again.

I had heard this advice before, but learned it was real in Mexico, first hand. Sometimes, you just have to give it back and then you are "in."

TNA CONTRACT

When I got back to the states, I still needed to stall. I didn't know what to do about TNA. Terry Taylor was not all that intimidating to talk to, but the whole idea of taking a deal and getting locked in was.

As far as Terry Taylor was concerned, he was a wrestler that worked for every major promotion from 1979-1996. Essentially, he was one of the boys and knew the deal, so he wasn't all that difficult to talk to. After his wrestling career came to an end, he made a new career for himself outside of the ring working as a road agent, trainer, interviewer, and also director of talent relations.

He bounced in and out of promotions. Taylor was working for WCW back when I started wrestling in 1999. Then, he went to WWE and worked for them until 2003. After that, he made his way over to TNA.

Having been around the block, Taylor knew that when he was offering me a contract for the reboot of the women's division and rebranding it as "Knockouts," it was a big opportunity. He also knew that it was a big decision for me to make, so he gave me a few days to sleep on it. There would be no sleep, however.

I am so going to lose sleep over this one.

I had to call him back, and was just dreading it. You know when you have to make a big decision and just didn't know if you were making the right one? It wasn't a lot of money, but it was an opportunity for exposure. It was an opportunity to get seen.

Even though Triple H recommended I take it, I still wasn't sure what I was getting into. So, I called Terry Taylor back looking for even more clarification.

"I think I want to take it!" I said quickly after exchanging pleasantries once again.

"That's great to hear," Taylor replied.

"I just need a copy of the contract for my lawyer to look at," I said.

He obliged, and in a few days I had it for review.

I brought it to my new legal advisor, Al Snow.

Attorney Al Snow, Esquire of Counsel, looked it over and shook his head. "It is a big whopping contract," he advised, sarcastically.

Basically, I was being offered $300 an appearance. If I was just booked once a week that would be the drizzling shits. However, after another call I heard that wasn't the case.

I was looking at TV tapings and scheduled to work a lot of house shows, so quite often I would actually make about $1200 a weekend; that wasn't all that bad. TNA would also book us out to other promoters who would call them and keep a percentage. But the verbiage on my contract let me accept independent bookings on my own. (Some talent that were exclusive to TNA had weird contracts where they had to give a percentage of indy paydays that they found back to the company. Fortunately for me, that was not the case).

Al Snow and I talked some more and he convinced me to take the deal. I had nothing else on the table, and it could only help me for the moment. Since there was nothing else out there, I had to take it.

I was still in Louisville at time, but I knew I would have to leave. TNA wasn't going to be a lot of money, but it was going to be more than I was making in OVW with no fast track to WWE.

On paper, it showed I was going to make roughly $70,000 a year. After hotel and transportation, I realized that I used to make more money bartending back home in

Minnesota. But this, for the moment, wasn't about the money. It was about believing and investing in myself. It was about exposure. It was about being seen.

I knew that sometimes you have to take a few steps backward before you can move forward.

Come the end of the year, I lined everything up to move back home to Minnesota as TNA promised to fly me in for TV tapings. Yes, working for TNA meant I was going to be hanging out again down in my old Disney stomping grounds, Orlando.

With my days off, I took up a side hustle. I decided to become a bartender there. This would help pay the bills and make things a little easier.

KNOCKOUTS

By this point, the whole "Miss TNA" concept had come and gone. There was a year or so where not much attention was placed on the girls.

In a big departure to TNA's former packaging of their female talent as eye candy and literally "T&A," per the ridiculous bad-pun name of the company, the new emphasis of "The Knockouts" was going to be on athleticism and wrestling ability. This turnabout in how the women would be showcased came around the same time the WWE Divas moniker went away. The shift from models to fitness models and athletic performers was happening in wrestling everywhere. It was a good thing.

TNA's new women's division emphasized serious wrestling competition, the same as its male counterparts. It was envisioned to have sex appeal and comedy, as well as giving us real credibility as athletes.

The official debut of the new women's division came a little before I got there at *Final Resolution* in 2007. TNA initiated the new approach building up a feud between Gail Kim and Jacqueline Moore.

The first TNA Women's Knockout champion was crowned on October 14, 2007 at *Bound for Glory* in a 10-Knockout gauntlet match which Kim won. Around this time, TNA booked several additional female wrestlers for that particular match, but the match wasn't the only reason. Bringing a bunch of the girls in was also instrumental in letting the powers that be get a chance to see them, and see if they potentially wanted to sign them.

I was in that 10-women gauntlet match along with Gail Kim, Awesome Kong, Angel Williams, Christy Hemme, Jackie Moore, Traci Brooks, Roxxi Laveaux, Shelly Martinez and Talia Madison. For this match, happening at the annual TNA PPV, *Bound for Glory*, I made my re-debut. I was eliminated by Laveaux, and the match was eventually won by Kim.

Even though I was booked to be one of the main villains in the women's division, fans immediately liked what I was doing with my new full-time character, ODB. Instead of the rock-n-roller Poison chick, I went with more of a drunken biker bar babe after a couple of drinks. I had a different look and brought the character to life into the ring with my new drunken style. Showing decent wrestling skills while being buzzed seemed to catch on immediately.

Also filling out the new division, TNA had Salinas, Angelina Love, and Velvet Sky. They also booked Alexa Jade to be used as TNA enhancement talent to make the girls look stronger.

The Knockouts also filled out the card with supporting female roles. Karen Angle (now Karen Jarrett) was working as a valet, and a new backstage interviewer named Crystal Louthan started conducting interviews.

Right away, things felt good. It was about time. We weren't just juicy body parts anymore. Women were actually being featured as real athletes. It almost seemed too good to be true. When Gail Kim was crowned as the first Knockouts champ, we wondered if the push would all go away, and everything before that was just a gimmick for a PPV. That was not the case, however. The next feature was immediately put into place on TV, with TNA putting a spotlight on a program between Christy Hemme and Roxxi Laveaux.

The girls as a whole were getting a push. Finally!

With the creation of an actual official women's championship title belt, matches and segments involving The Knockouts, new fans took interest. The additional storylines became well received. Fans seemed to care more and ratings for *Impact!* increased.

As far as my contract working out, it did. I was bartending during the week and also able to take on independent bookings. My television exposure helped me get seen and this exposure increased my ability to find work outside of TNA, and subsequently raise my indy prices to some degree with supply and demand. Because there are only so many Saturdays in a month, I could charge more when I had to travel farther from home when I was getting an offer for a bullshit show in East Bufu, Nevada.

I got all kinds of offers outside of TNA and it was great. I did, however, from time to time get some weird offers.

I remember one particular call I received from some clowns...

JUGGALO CHAMPIONSHIT WRESTLING
Whoop! Whoop!

Yes, the phone call from the clowns was from the Insane Clown Posse (ICP). Now, when the ICP calls you for a booking for their Juggalo Championshit Wrestling (JCW), you know you have made it.

For those of you who are not down with the clowns, the ICP is a hardcore Detroit rap group. This terrible twosome is comprised of Joseph Bruce and Joseph Utsler who go by the alter clown egos of "Violent J" and "Shaggy 2 Dope."

Those two guys are a trip. They are huge wrestling fans themselves, so their music (and everything they do) is often larger-than-life and very gimmicky.

Because of their fame, they put together an annual gathering, a festival for their fans that is like a hybrid between a big concert and circus event with all kinds of weird sideshows and attractions. To go along with this "Gathering of the Juggalos" they even have their own wrestling promotion, which is beyond fucked up. (By the way, ICP calls their fans "Juggalos." The Juggalos come from all walks of life and are typically body-modified misfits, who paint their faces and take on their own rule-breaking clown persona gimmicks.)

Because of their loyal die-hard fan support from all of their Juggalos and Juggalettes, The Gathering of The Juggalos has since become an annual week-long getaway (where they take over an entire campground or park) complete with a few stages for huge musical acts to perform on. This yearly gathering is like an evil Woodstock. Picture spring break with clowns and midgets, and an occasional appearance by someone random like David Hasselhoff. It is loaded with music, weirdness, and all kinds of debauchery.

Some of its happenings include standup comedy, random celebrity appearances, wet t-shirt contests, autograph sessions, karaoke jams, and seminars with artists. There is also the "Life-Threatening Bonfire" where you can get a really nice tan, and the *Inflatable Games* where you can fight other Juggalos in blow-up sumo-style costumes or giant boxing gloves, all on a waterslide.

Their wrestling show, JCW, is now a tradition and one of the Juggalos' most favorite happenings at the event.

When I showed up to wrestle for my first JCW event, the Juggalos blew my mind.

As we pulled into the Hogrock Campgrounds at Cave-In-Rock, Illinois, I immediately saw tits. They were a far cry from "The Beautiful Ones" Angelina Love had flashed at me, but I still did a double take. I just wasn't expecting to see painted puppies. The nipple art I saw was something like a cross between the band Kiss and the late wrestler Kamala.

As we drove on, we went passed the "magic bridge." There, I was informed by the driver was where you could go to get "whatever kind of medicine you needed."

Before the show, I walked around to try and take it all in. Everyone was drinking that sugary Faygo soda shit, which was the clown drink of choice apparently, and some wrestling fans recognized me and offered me some.

Normally, I'm not one to turn down a free drink. However, Faygo itself is super-loaded with lethal amounts of sugar and caffeine. That alone probably could fuck me up, let alone whatever the Juggalos were spiking it with.

"No thanks," I said politely declining.

I walked down the path. In addition to open drinking, there was also ganja smoke blowing, people doing blow, and I think I also saw a public blow job line by a bush.

I am in fucking Sodom and Gomorrah.

As I continued, I made my way toward one of the stages and heard some kind of crazy rap going on. This year's musical line up featured tons of rap acts that I never heard of, all aligned with the ICP. The actual headliners included Three 6 Mafia, Ice-T, 2 Live Crew, and Afroman who incidentally was supposed to play an extra-long set, but then he got high.

When I made it to the stage, I saw that there was an act already in session. All of a sudden a pregnant Juggalette jumped on stage and pulled out yet another boob. How do I know she was pregnant? Well, one red flag was that she sprayed down the first row of Juggalos with breast milk.

Creamy.

I didn't think I was lactose intolerant, but I didn't want to find out so I headed quickly to the wrestling event pavilion. In the few minutes that I was out and about there, I saw all kinds of nonsense and had enough.

I looked like a low-key Juggalo so I was probably safe, but playing it safe wasn't a bad idea in looking at all the shit that was going down. Only a few years after this at another gathering, Tila Tequila would show up and act all diva-ish towards the crowd. That was a bad move. They didn't like it at all. They responded by throwing a watermelon filled with piss and dogshit at her head, then chased her off the stage. In the end, some crazy Juggalettes cornered her and put the boots to her, hard. From what I've heard, they fucked her up good.

When I showed up to the venue, where the wrestling show dubbed as *Bloodymania II* was set to take place, I went backstage. Some of the wrestlers and other people producing the show were already there and it was a big party scene. They didn't give a fuck what was going on. People were right there shooting heroin in the back. They were all very generous with their gimmicks. Many offered me booger sugar and all kinds of mean nasty ugly things. But that stuff just wasn't my cup of tea, so I also declined their offerings.

Anyone that knows me knows that my cup of tea was not actually tea – *it is booze.*

"I don't want any of that shit, but fuck it. When in Rome, act like the Romans. Can I have a beer?"

And just like that, I had a beer.

After that, my opponent for the evening showed up: Mickie "The Moose" Knuckles.

I had worked her a handful of times before, even some in TNA. She was around a lot early on and thought she was tough, back in our indy days. However, I never had a problem with her. This time, however, something was different. Knuckles got in the ring with me, and right off the bat something had changed.

The match started out like any other. We locked up and the first minute or so was traditional cookie-cutter shit, but it eventually came to blows as we had planned.

Whappp!

"Lighten up, girl," I said, after taking a fairly stiff shot.

She said nothing. We continued on, then I got hit with another bad one.

Whappp!!!

"I said, lighten up, girl!" I repeated, after taking yet another potato.

Again, she said nothing, but kept on working. She was playing up how hardcore she was to the fans and ignoring what we had planned.

What in the hell? I don't know why, but I think she is shooting on me.

It didn't take long to realize what exactly what was happening. Moose was marking out to herself and felt like I should just job to her. She started stiffing me some more, and I got pissed, so I pulled her in tight with a headlock.

"What the hell, Moose?!"

She wriggled free and jumped out of the ring. Then, randomly she started throwing shit at me like ECW New Jack, acting like she was all hardcore.

As you know, I cannot just take a whooping and not give something back. Doing that would mean being a mark, a glutton for punishment, or just an overall pussy. Just as I had learned in Mexico, when someone shoots on you, YOU HAVE TO GIVE IT BACK. If you don't, you lose respect and/or they keep on doing it.

Don't get me wrong. Wrestling isn't ballet and sometimes it hurts. You can take a shot or two, and then say something. But when you see the bullshit is continuing full force, the rule is you give back a return receipt for the crap you did not order. You lay something in and see if it stops. Nine times out of ten, it stops.

The Moose continued to shit on me. She winged a chair at me. She threw a wrench at me. She tossed a trash can at me. My guess is she just wanted to look impressive to the bloodthirsty fans at *Bloodymania*, but her mistake was that she was trying to do this at my expense without any sort of care in the world. You have to take care of your opponent, and she was doing none of that launching crap right at me.

Moose jumped out of the ring and looked for more weapons. Without finding anything, she came back in the ring with a chair, and swung it at my face.

THUMP!

That sound wasn't me getting hit, however, but rather me kicking the chair out of her hand, and then kicking her as hard as I could in her Jabba the Hutt gut.

Okay. That's it you juicy fucker. You have now crossed the line.

She was a hot mess, and I was not having it. It was time for me to throw some trash right back at her, ODB style.

ODB computer activate! I need a game plan.

If it isn't already obvious, Moose was called "Moose" for a reason. She was big – very big. Now, if she had been a guy I had to slow down, I would have just kicked her in the nuts. The problem was, under all that glorious FUPA, (you can Google that term yourself) I knew there was still likely no balls to be found.

From my experience, I knew one pelvic punt precisely planted to the penial proximity (aka testicular region) could take any man down, big or small. I had conducted a number of such scientific experiments on Daivari many times and the results were always the same. However, my findings showed that a dick-kick to this big mama wasn't going to have quite the same results. I surmised that a calculated "cunt punt," while painful, would only just piss her off. So, I rather decided to adjust my go-to "nutsack attack" to the closest female equivalence; the two dangling targets that girls have.

Going for the jugular, I grabbed at her giant jugs.

You see my highly advanced ODB computer brain calculated the first part of the equation. My calculations determined that if I ripped her shirt, the odds of Moose slowing down were high. This slow-down technique, of course would not be one created out of pain, but perhaps out of modestly.

If she has no shirt on, what is she going to do? Fight me with those fun bags swinging?

My hypothesis was solid. Nobody wanted to see that and she would have to cover up, right?

Banking on any ounce of human decency and humility that Moose had under all that flubber, I grabbed her white trash wife beater shirt and ripped it like Hulk Hogan.

Floppp! Floppp!

Moose covered her moose milkies right up. I tugged the fabric some more, and then I finally ripped her tank top right off of her body. This practically exposed her jugs to all the Juggalos. Holy cow! All she was left wearing was an UDDERLY sheer, see-thru bra. Very pepperoni.

Talk about putting lipstick on a pig.

The audience stopped dead in their tracks.

You could hear a pin drop along with all of their jaws. In the dead of the silence, everything started to move in super slow motion.

Once everyone realized what they were looking at, those fucked up Juggalos jumped out of their seats. Their eyes were bugging out of their painted heads. They popped even though NOBODY really wanted to see that shit.

Moose looked down to see what had happened, taking full mammary inventory. As she was distracted, I heaved her hefty frame over to the corner.

In the absence of sound, I think I heard the *Titanic* theme song start playing off somewhere in the distance, but maybe it was only in my head.

Then, I did what any respecting individual would do... I chopped the living shit out of her boobs.

SMACK! SMACK! SMACK!

Hamburger meat. Chopped liver. Cube steak.

The clowns couldn't believe what was happening.

Now, this was perhaps an even worse titty-butcher job than the one I did to Anderson's torso in the ring after he cheated on me. When I was done, Moose's chest looked like minced meat. She was teary eyed and squinty, and I think I saw one of her pepperoni nipples twist and fall off and roll down the steps. Moose looked at me a mess.

"Really?"

"Yep," I said.

The audience finally went nuts as I made my exit. They stood on top of their seats screaming and shouting.

I was down with the clowns.

When I got back to the locker room, the boys were marking out. Whenever there is a shoot in the ring, there is usually a full house at the curtain. Dudes were marking out as I made my way to my dressing room. I didn't put up with her shit, and they knew it.

Moose was nowhere to be found. She was either off repenting her sins, or trying to Sabu-superglue her hooters back together. I don't know.

The ICP themselves were dying. They came by and high fived me, along with more of the wrestlers. I got cleaned up and left the magical land, and never looked back.

There was one guy though who I don't think liked my massacre of Moose's mammaries: Ian Rotten.

If you are not familiar with him, Rotten was by all definitions a match to the word "carnie." He was a rough-around-the-edges former wrestler who worked some for Global Force Wrestling (GFW) and even for Extreme Championship Wrestling (ECW). He was also that promoter running IWA: Mid-South who didn't like to pay me, and had a history of making controversial decisions. He was the contact who brought me into that show, and he was also the one who contacted my boss at TNA after it.

I don't know if he had a thing for Knuckles or what, but he wasn't happy with how I chose to handle the situation I found myself in. He made it very clear that he didn't appreciate my masterpiece in the ring, and subsequently he decided to stooge me out.

The prick.

I didn't know it at the time, but Ian Rotten called my boss, Scott D'Amore, to complain about me.

Now, Scott began working with TNA as a road agent back in 2003. Eventually, he took on more of an onscreen role as the manager of Team Canada. Somewhere along the way, he also began working backstage as a creative team member and trainer, operating the TNA Academy along with Terry Taylor. But by May 2005, D'Amore was appointed head of the TNA booking team.

When I showed up for a taping after that whole JCW Gathering thing, Scott D'Amore pulled me off to the side.

"Hey, Jess," he said. "We have a little concern."

"What's that, Scott?" I asked.

"Well, we had you set to work some here with Moose, but we heard about what happened at The Gathering."

I tightened my face, but didn't reply.

"For one, we decided to change what would have been some singles matches between you and her into tag matches, just to be careful."

"That's not necessary." I said. "But if she's just going to go right back into shooting on me again, the same as I would any wrestler, I'm going to have to give it back."

"And I wouldn't ask you not to," he said. D'Amore was a trained wrestler. I think he was even trained by Al Snow. He knew the deal. "However, what we are more concerned with is that you were drinking before the match."

My face turned red. It was probably more red than Moose's chest was after that match.

"My drinking?" I asked. "Who told you that? Ian?"

He didn't reply.

"Scott, there were wresters shooting up in the back, and you are complaining about a beer I had before the show?"

"I'm not complaining, but I was told this is what initiated the aggression from Mickie. No?"

I walked away. I wasn't going to dignify that with an answer. It was ridiculous, and he knew it.

Fuck it. If they want to let me out of my contract before I even start because of this, then I don't want to be here.

Fortunately, that wasn't the case. After that, I never heard about the incident again.

I did have to do some more business with the Moose, though. It was probably a good idea to let us work in tags. Having others around kept things more cool.

Roxxi Laveaux and I ended up working with Mickie Knuckles a lot. There weren't any further incidents. Either Moose realized that she was in the wrong about the whole thing, or decided not to stir the pot anymore. Either way, she was gone from TNA in a few months after that.

Incidentally, she apologized to me about the whole thing later on. We are cool now. It's good to let go and let go of heat. Holding on to negative feelings is a bad thing to do.

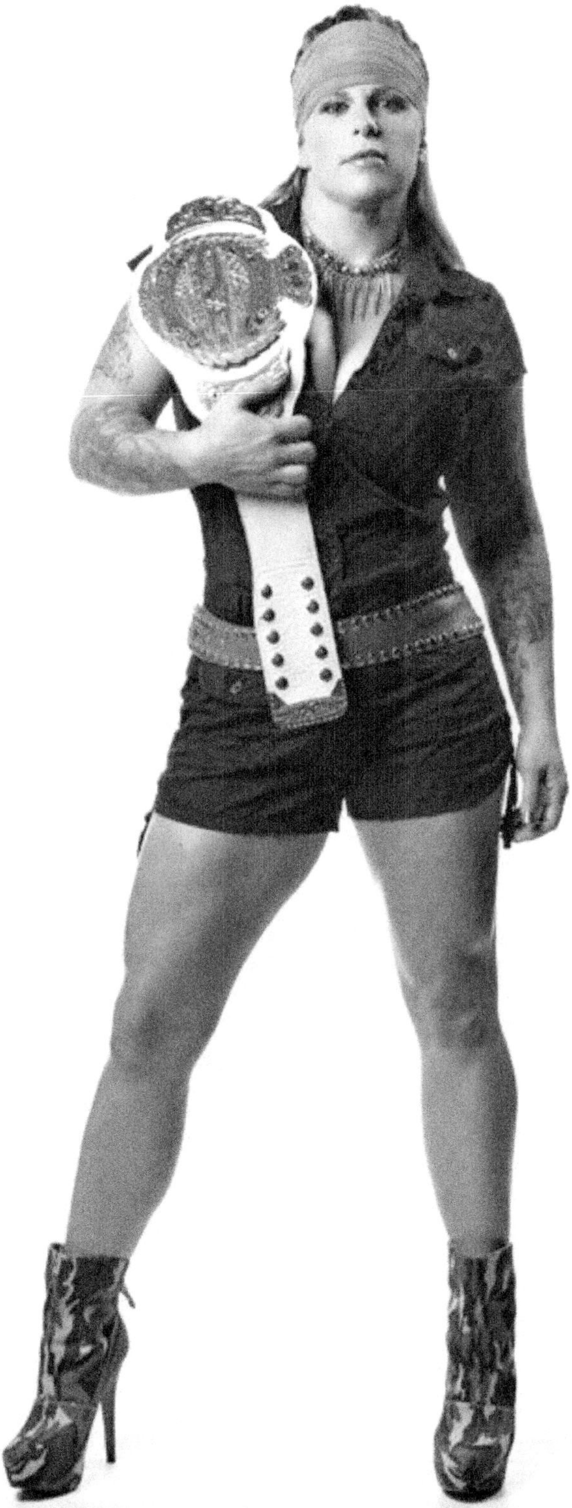

CHAPTER 7 – KNOCKOUT CHAMPION

After debuting for TNA in 2007 as part of the company building The Knockouts division, all of my first appearances were me as a villainess. The idea was to make me a brash, ass-kicking mold-breaking bitch who beat up the pretty girls. So… I did just that.

On top of this, I figured using my size was not heel enough, so I used a booze flask as a trademark weapon to defeat babyfaces like Gail Kim.

However, just like other heels in wrestling history, I guess I did my job a little too well. Due to the bloodthirsty fans' positive response to my different persona, it was evident that I was becoming an "anti-hero" in their eyes. Some gave me the massive compliment of calling me a female Stone Cold Steve Austin. Whatever they called me, by the cheers I was getting, the office knew that I had to quickly become a babyface.

As a face, I continued to wrestle almost exactly the same way as I did as a heel. The only thing that changed was the fan reaction. It became even louder than before! Once I officially turned face, I did something that really turned heads in the office; I sold more shirts. This spike in merchandise meant I was valuable to the company.

PITCHING

The office figured I must be doing something right. I continued to pitch and offer good ideas for ODB, and they continued to use a lot of it.

One very important thing I learned from my time in OVW that I took with me to TNA again came from Al Snow. He said that "the writers aren't always thinking of you." He told me that one of the best ways to make my character work was to pitch my own ideas for it. After all, who could write the best stuff for your character other than yourself? You are the one who knows how you talk. You are the one who knows what you can do. Being your own writer is ideal. I know this isn't the case in WWE now. However, it doesn't hurt to ask and I do know that they appreciate creativity. Showing creativity does create more creative license.

I told this thought about pitching to both Dutch Mantel and Vince Russo to see what they thought. They both totally agreed. They believed in me and told me to feel free to pitch my stuff to any and all of the writers.

So, whenever I had time, I wrote. I filled notebooks with little quotes and pieces of promos. I even started to write entire storylines up with full week-to-week plots. Once I had some decent stuff, I decided to drop off my ideas with no fears at all about pitching stuff for my own character.

I didn't make demands. I didn't act unprofessional. I wasn't a diva. I just offered some ideas, and it seemed that, nine times out of ten, the writers loved it. For one, the writers had all kinds of stuff going on. Giving them more material to work with gave them a starting point and a template they could play with. Without this, I was a blank chapter that probably would have stayed blank. My ideas gave them a push in the right direction and that helped us all.

Al Snow was right again. If I didn't do some of my own writing or offer some of my own ideas as pitches, I know that I wouldn't have had what I had. Creating with the team over my career instead of waiting for them to come up with something for me was the best advice I could have ever taken. I gave my ideas and some eventually even worked into the men's division. That gave me even more exposure.

Having writing that was naturally truer to my character did me well. The fans recognized it and started popping for me, even when I wasn't on the card. The first time I heard that, I knew I was really getting over.

I remember one night somewhere in the beginning of 2008, I was in the back watching a Knockout match. Out of nowhere and for no reason at all, everyone in the audience were chanting, "ODB! ODB! ODB!"

The ideas I had been bringing to the table for my character were paying off.

ODB! ...ODB!

I was laughing when I heard it. I had absolutely nothing to do with anything going on in the ring, but apparently the fans wanted me to. I rushed over to the curtains like a kid in a candy shop to see what the cause of it was. I figured maybe one of the wresters was mocking me or something, but I was wrong. As far as the cause for the chant, *there wasn't one*. It was just a message coming from the crowd that they wanted to see me.

Fan approval!

As I was looking out at the audience, Dixie Carter came up behind me.

"Wow," she said, knowing there was no way to ignore what she was hearing. "They sure do love you."

"Oh, yeah. About that," I said, jokingly. "Actually, I pay them to do that."

Dixie for whatever reason decided to piss on my parade. Rather than being complimentary to my work, she shook her head.

"Oh honey, we don't pay you that much," she replied.

Then, she walked away, like she had done a mic drop or something.

What a bitch.

You would think she would have seen money in me and been happy to work with me, but that just wasn't the case. She was the elite owner of the promotion, and I was just white trash in her eyes. However, I didn't let her perception of me bother me.

TAKING OFF

Throughout 2008, as my weird random pops continued, TNA continued to expand The Knockout roster. They knew they had a good thing and were essentially throwing a bunch more stuff against the wall to see what would stick. Mickie Knuckles was back in one of these talent search trial runs along with Payton Banks, Raisha Saeed, Sharmell, and Rhaka Khan.

In the spring of 2008, the heel focus started to shift onto Knockout champion, Awesome Kong. What happened was, I started to get a babyface response; it didn't matter what I did. People liked my drinking gimmick, and I could almost do no wrong.

Kong held a $25,000 fan challenge where she put her title and $25,000 on the line against any fan in the building. This was a neat way to bring in even more women to see who would be a good fit for a spot with TNA in the expanding division.

The challenge was eventually won by Taylor Wilde, and featured tryout matches for Daffney and Josie Robinson (later renamed Sojournor Bolt), both of whom later became full-time wrestlers in The Knockout division. Other participants in the challenge included Serena Deeb, Melissa Wolfram, Leva Bates, Amber O'Neal, Becky Bayless, and TNA ring girl Kimberly also volunteered to wrestle Kong, but were not selected as challengers. Mercedes Steele appeared as a jobber against Kong, while Portia Perez and Mercedes Martinez both received tryout matches with TNA. I do think the promotion really was trying to better the division.

Rhaka, incidentally was being favored at the time. (This is what happens when you date a main eventer.) A lot of the girls didn't think she was very good, so they didn't like the fact that she was getting used. One of them, Velvet Sky, was very vocal about this. She told some of the agents that Rhaka was the drizzling shits and didn't deserve the push she was getting.

After that happened, and she said what the rest of us were thinking, Velvet got some heat for a while.

That's called politics, folks.

AWESOME KONG

When the first Knockout Champ was being crowned, I forgot to mention, Kong went up over the top and her top came down for all to see. She ran to the back, crying. It sucked. After that it was double-sided tape for all, and the main rule for everyone became always help someone if a tit comes out. (One time it happened with Angelina who was in the middle of cutting a promo so I cut her off before she was done hitting her. She was clueless until I said, "Fix 'yer nip!")

Speaking of Kong, I continued to be creative and do the very best that I could. As a kid, I remembered when two giants would finally collide in the ring it was always a big deal. While I was very aware I was nowhere near the size or fame of an Andre the Giant, Bundy, or Big John Studd, I did know that I was perceived by the fans as "being larger than life" when it came to the other Knockouts. Therefore, I wanted to face TNA's best monster of the ring... AWESOME KONG.

Now, the awesome one was intense and scary as hell. The person playing her, Kia Stevens, is just great. She is super talented and plays the part perfectly. She recently appeared as "Welfare Queen" in the Netflix series "GLOW," based on the Gorgeous Ladies of Wrestling promotion and series that ran in the '80s.

Our pairing, in my mind, would be epic and make great television. Some would imagine it would be like pitting two kaijus together on a creature double feature – like a Godzilla versus Mothra type situation.

I asked to work with her and, at first, TNA wanted nothing to do with it. I think the powers that be didn't like the idea, but eventually that changed. (I nagged Vince Russo enough, I think, and he gave in due to my persistence.)

To start, we worked a number of house shows together to see what we could do. Immediately we knew we had chemistry. Working with her was like a night off, and the crowd loved it. We did a lot of old school "big man" Memphis spots, you know, like the "work hard and finally knock your opponent of their feet" kind of thing. It was super basic, but the old stuff works. We got a huge response.

During our trial for what we both had hoped could turn into a good money run, there was only one night when things didn't turn out as well as they could have. This had nothing to do with anything being shitty in the ring, however. Or did it?

The day began like any other. I got to the arena early and heard a gurgle. I didn't really feel sick, but thought maybe I had eaten some bad sushi. Either way, my stomach was talking to me and it was telling me to be careful.

"If you bump wrong," my stomach said, "your ass is going to unload."

I yelled at my stomach for stooging on my asshole, but I knew it was right.

GURGLE!

The noises got worse and worse.

I ducked into the closest bathroom, but realized it was too close to the other girls. *They might hear me blow it up!*

I couldn't risk it. I ran down the hall as a courtesy to the others and not to out myself for possibly destroying the place. I needed to find a nice solo stall for some quality alone dumping time, and was happy when I found a handicap accessible lockable bathroom.

I closed the door, dead bolted it, and immediately dropped to the bowl with a nuclear green apple splatter. It burned on the way out, and I got the sweats. I had that spicy diarrhea that stung my bunghole. The spice was not nice. It felt like I had just been let out of Mexican prison.

Then something else hit me.

Holy shit. This, and I have to work Kong tonight?

As I walked cautiously back to the dressing room area, I knew it wasn't over. There were a few steps that felt like a close call, and I had to clench my butt checks together to stop a repeat performance.

Exhale. I sat down and took it easy.

When Kong finally showed up, I pulled her off to the side trying to figure out the most professional way to say it. I had to tell her what was up and that we had to subsequently work our match "differently" and "with caution."

I never wanted to take the easy way out, but was afraid my poo was going to take the easy way out of me, if I didn't.

"Oh my god. Girl, you too?" she rubbed her stomach and laughed after a possible bad meal at a rest stop. "Maybe it's in the water!"

It was funny. We hadn't eaten the same food, but Kong also had the Hershey squirts and had no qualms about saying it.

Because we couldn't call in a double sick day as that would eliminate a match from the card, we figured we would just take it easy out there – as to not hose the audience down with liquid shit.

Once we agreed, we knew we needed to tell someone we were breaking our norm. D'Lo Brown was actually the agent for our match, so we pulled him off to the side to give him a heads up on our *shitty situation*.

"Listen, D'Lo," Kong said. "I know I am going over, but I need to do it with something else, okay?"

"Something else?" he asked.

"No powerbomb," I clarified. "Just for today."

"No, no, no," he said. "We need to see the powerbomb. That's Kong's move."

"Listen, man. You don't get it," I tried to clarify. "A powerbomb might cause a power shit."

"We both got the runs," Kong laughed.

"Say what?" D'Lo Brown asked.

"You heard us right. Bad sushi and gas station chili."

There was a long dramatic pause. D'Lo swallowed hard. We giggled knowing we put him in an awkward position.

"Sorry, girls," he said after some time to think. He wrinkled up his nose and walked away, appalled at the idea of both of us having the runs. "Can't change the finish. You all are going to have to figure it out."

When the bell rang, we worked the simplest, lightest match we could put together with practically no bumps. It was going to be all big-man spots, and practically nothing else this time. It had to be, or else someone would be leaving leaking hot cocoa.

Do you know the weeble-wobble spot? Where like Hacksaw Jim Duggan would hit Kamala five times off the ropes with a shoulder tackle, with the Ugandan Giant wobbling more and more before he finally went down? We planned that spot for pretty much our whole match, but the difference was Kong took the tackle attempt 20 times instead of just a handful before going down.

It was awesome. Kong played it off just perfectly, waving her arms more and more after each point of impact until she finally got knocked off her feet.

The giant went down!

When it happened, the fans jumped to their feet. She had only bumped once the whole match, but the buildup was everything, and that was all we needed.

That wobble spot saved us. It was genius. I covered Kong to a standing ovation (thank you), and then the swerve. She kicked out and cut me off with invisible brass knuckles, super old school. It was probably the easiest match I have ever been in. Somehow, we made it through right to the end without any poop on us, and the finish was upon us.

"You ready?" Kong asked.

She kicked me in the gut. I bent over to take the powerbomb. I sucked in my stomach and puckered my B-hole as hard as I could.

Up, up, up and... down!
POW!

I hit the mat, and fortunately for me no turds hit my underwear.

1-2-3.

After that, I stood up slowly; to sell the move, and also to check inventory.

Still no poop. Creamy rim at most.

The kick to the midsection woke up my insides, however. I felt the return of the gurgle.

Feets don't fail me now!

After that, I rolled out of the ring and ran back to the locker room.

Kong saw me bolt and knew what was up. She felt sympathy squirts and didn't stick around to hear her name, either. She wasn't far behind me, sprinting back up that aisle.

When I pushed passed the curtain, I realized that something had changed. The gurgle became a burp. It was then I realized that my dump instead decided to take a detour, and headed north. I felt nauseous.

I had to vomit.

Kong rushed through the curtain just in time to see me gagging and looking for a place to put it. That hacking motion became contagious. Kong cupped her hands over her mouth. Her eyes bugged out of her head. She then had to puke, too.

Almost in unison, we stuck our heads in the closest garbage can we could find.

After letting the bad stuff in us know it was not coming out of our assholes during the match, it decided to recalculate and change route to find another way out of us – all at the exact same moment.

The chunks won.

We laughed as we bonded, barfing together, side by side. You know how sometimes it comes out your nose?

It was disgusting.

The sickest part about the whole scene was we were right in public where all in the back could see us. Some fan ran over to us as we were still heaving. He immediately started snapping pictures of our synchronized yack session probably with visions of selling it to a magazine or something.

"Fuck that," I said trying to hide my face.

Kong saw what was going down and wasn't having it.

"Oh, hell no…"

Kong jumped up from our safe haven. She pie-faced the kid, knocked the camera out of his hand, and broke it, all in one swoop. Then, she grabbed him by the collar and had him kicked him out of the locker room. When she was done taking out the trash, she came right over to her spot at the can and continued to toss her cookies.

After that, all was just fine. Our matches were great, and we proved what we had to. Word got back to us that we were going to get our televised angle after all.

At *TNA: Genesis*, they had me score the pinfall in a six-women tag team match. I won a shot at Kong's Knockout championship. To build up for our TV feud, I was going to have to get through Kong's new posse this time – which they were calling "Kongtourage."

Kong's new group was Raisha Saeed (Cheerleader Melissa under a veil), Sojournor Bolt, and Rhaka Khan. If you asked how well that went, well, Rhaka Khan (the actual Queen of Shits) was in the mix, so that should set your expectations right there.

It was a good little program that culminated at *TNA: Against All Odds*, where I unsuccessfully challenged Kong for the championship.

That wasn't the end of my chance at the Knockout title, however. That was just the start.

CHAMPIONSHIP GOLD

When the TNA Knockout title was first debuted, Gail Kim started out with the strap. She eventually passed it over to Awesome Kong, who lost it to Taylor Wilde, but then Kong got it back. While I feuded with Kong for a bit, I didn't take the belt, and then Kong dropped it to Angelina Love.

Angelina went on to drop the title to Tara (aka WWE's Victoria,) before winning it back. Angelina was on fire with her whole Beautiful People gimmick. She was the exact opposite of me; she was a sexy, prim and proper, model-like wrestler. I was a rough, defiant brawler who liked to drink. Therefore, Angelina was the perfect foil for me. I had been practically turned babyface by the fans because I was a relatable anti-hero at this point, and I needed an enemy. I felt it was maybe time for the Knockout title belt to be held by someone who was even more dirty and more bitchy than ever before. But I didn't want to lobby for a shot with it without talking to the current champ.

Angelina and I were cool, so one day I just asked. I told her it was a personal goal of mine, and I asked her what she thought about giving me a whack at it next, before I pitched any kind of self-serving idea.

I said I only wanted to make a plea for a run with the belt for myself with her permission, and of course, she was down. Angelina was fine with it.

To her credit, she was always unselfish and wanted the best for the product. She had held the title twice already, and knew I was hot with the fans. If I was going to ever have a chance at winning the championship, now made sense to her. It was as good a time as any, she suggested.

I didn't want just a match. That was too easy. Working with the writers, I pitched in with the idea of an ODB Dating Game that would lead to an eventual title change.

People sent in videos which were totally ridiculous and worse than the worst you could probably find on Tinder today. We did this promo about letting one lucky guy spend the night with me, which could sound like a date, but of course also mean something else. At *Destination X*, the announcers called three contestants out. I remember one of the commentators said something like, "there is not enough Cialis in the world to satisfy ODB." I laughed at that comment.

Anyhow, much like most reality competitions on TV today, yes it was all a work. The chosen contestants were workers and in on the gag. For the story, I took on a guy by the name of Cody Deaner to be my date and ultimately he became my manager. He was actually a Canadian wrestler who before that went by the name Cody Steele.

Deaner was a good dude. He was from up north and he worked in similar circles as me on the independents for a time. We had mutual friends. He worked with guys I knew like Shawn Spears up in Ontario before this and was ready to go. Working with him was a no-brainer.

This whole love interest angle ultimately led up to an intergender tag match on August 16, 2009 at *Hard Justice*. It was The Beautiful People (Angelina Love & Velvet Sky) vs. ODB and my manager, Cody Deaner. However, it wasn't just a tag match, the Women's title was also on the line.

In the end, Deaner pinned Velvet Sky to win the Knockout championship. I claimed the title as my own and we pulled a gimmick where there was confusion as to whether or not I should be the champion. I held the title for only 11 days before it was vacated. Commissioner Mick Foley vacated the belt because Deaner argued he had rightfully won the title.

That ultimately led to an ODB versus Deaner match for the vacated strap. In the end, of course, I became the undisputed winner and the new Knockout champion.

It's not every day that you achieve a childhood dream.

Even though it was a storyline, that night I went back to my hotel room and stared at the title in my hands. I don't know how long I stared at it, but it truly meant something to me. It wasn't just a prop. It meant that a major promotion put their trust in me and believed in me. That was everything.

How did I play a part in making this happen? Was it all hard work in the ring? Was it a good pitch? Was it the art of persuasion? Being a team player? Offering ideas to a team of writers that wanted ideas? Being the right person in the right place at the right time?

Maybe it was a little bit of all of that.

DRINKS ON DIXIE!

The writers loved me. I was a team player and contributed. However, not everybody was a fan of the ODB.

Dixie Carter was a weird one. There were all kinds of rumors about her backstage being a bitch and being fake. Some went as far as to call her a whore. Some of the rumors pegged her for being a bit of a swinger or something, I don't know, and I can't say that I ever saw any of that directly, but I heard shit.

Fortunately for me, ODB pops from the crowd kept happening and couldn't be ignored. That gave me credibility whether one "See you next Tuesday" liked it or not. I know that Dixie Carter didn't like it, nor understand it. I wasn't the eye candy she normally looked for, and I also wasn't the big monster. I was me – rough around the edges and didn't fit in her cookie cutter expectations. This is probably why the fans liked me, but Dixie Carter just didn't get that.

There was a rumor out there developing that Dixie Carter was a cougar on the prowl. Some say she was such a mark for wrestling that she was willing to chip away at her father's fortune just to hang with the boys. Others say that fandom went hand and hand with actually partying with the boys to get over with them.

Whenever there was new blood in the locker room, it seemed like Dixie was all over it. She would mark right out.

It's also ironic that she did that boyfriend storyline on TV with AJ Styles. From what people were saying in the locker room, if Carter took a liking to one of the boys, it was never one of the obvious clean-cut boy-toy ones like AJ. The boys were accusing her of having crushes on the bigger, nastier rugged ones. They said she liked the bad boys. The rumor was if she had a type, it would be more like Bruiser Brody and less like AJ. The bigger the better.

To be clear, I never saw any of this. The boys liked to make up shit about their boss, the same as anyone does at any job. Hell, you know the deal. For years, wrestlers said Vince McMahon was gay and "gayfabed" about how he pushed his penis onto his wrestlers in exchange for a push. There is no evidence of any of that with him, so similar rumors against Carter could and should be viewed exactly the same way.

However, the mark rumors were true for sure. Dixie did go way out of her way to impress some of the workers for sure, sparing no expense.

I remember one time, there was a Tennessee Titans show with a smaller group of them stopping by. For no real reason at all other than to look good with the boys, she threw a giant and super expensive private party after the event.

There was absolutely no reason to waste all that money other than to show off.

As a side note at that very party, we were all playing pool when Dixie's man came by all rubbing elbows with me, despite the fact he was with Dixie. It sure looked like he wanted a piece of the ODB. Yep, that's Serg for you.

Now, I don't think this wasn't the first time he hit on me, either. Flirty Serg used to hit on me all the time. The difference at this party was he was openly coming on to me in front of everyone, almost like he didn't care.

It was at this moment that I wondered if Dixie and her silly husband were in some kind of gross open relationship, because he probably would have made out with me right there if I had let him.

He made a dumb joke about wanting to take me out for a test ride, or something lame about my headlights.

"I'm sorry, Serg," I said. "I'm more of a Wrangler girl, and you are a Mini Cooper."

"Wait, what did you say?"

"You're just not my type, little man!"

The boys around me popped at my dick joke.

These show-off parties were Carter's show ponies, but some could argue that they were just extensions of her growing ego. Some of the talent suggested that she used these events to remind everyone that she was something special and she was the only reason we had jobs.

This is probably why if a wrestler didn't go to her party, she was personally offended. It was almost like she was a stubborn old math teacher taking attendance at each and every one of these parties. If she didn't see you there, she would ask others where you were.

Not everyone liked to feed into her ego bullshit. The Hebners, for one, were like me and were also my drinking buddies. We preferred drinking in our rooms and didn't want to be part of those Dixie festivities.

We figured out early on that we had to go to these parties even though we didn't want to endorse them, or she would go out of her way to bury us. So we decided to play her game, but only on our terms. The trick was to get in and out. We would show up just long enough for mother Dixie to see us, then head for the hills. Eventually, we even got smart and learned how to get Dixie to pay for our own after-show drinking habits with the drive-by party appearances at her parties. Yes, it was two birds with one stone!

What we would do is appear at these parties fashionably late and intentionally go out of our way to have the bosses see our faces. Then, before magically disappearing ourselves, we would find the booze supply and smuggle as much of it out of the building as possible.

Legit, we had it all down to a science. Sometimes we would shamelessly pull the rental right up to the back door and pop the trunk. Then, we would fill a giant cooler with as many drinks as we could before our disappearing act, back to the hotel for our own after-after party.

"Drinks on Dixie," we would say.

WRITING

Eventually, Dixie Carter started marking out for herself too much as many promoters do. She started to believe her own shit and wrote herself into all the storylines out of ego.

She would literally push girls out of the makeup chair so she could get made up and go out and hog the spotlight.

She did that to all the girls.

After that, the Carter heat on me continued. Before shows, we would often sit around in an open space to go over ideas for TV. A lot of times, the showrunners had a card figured out, but would then go into the possibilities of promos and other non-ring type shots to help get over the storylines.

The wrestlers often sat around and ate something during these meetings. Some would chime in some ideas when their match was read off. Others listened for instructions.

Before these meetings, I often submitted more writing to the writers. More often than not, my very words were read back to me. It seems the writers took my stuff, frequently loved it, and expanded on the possibilities. Usually, a lot of my stuff would fly but there were times that Dixie Carter would come along after the fact, just to make sure to shit on me.

One example of this involved a word.

"Hey, Jess," Vince Russo said in his thick New York accent. "When you do your promos for now on, we got a word we want you to stay away from if you can."

"What is that, Vince?" I asked for clarification.

"Well, Dixie just doesn't like you calling The Knockouts whores," he said.

"Well, isn't that kind of ironic?" I asked.

Russo smiled but no-sold my joke.

"Good one," he said, clearly understanding that I was talking more about Carter and her weird relationships with talent, rather than the idea that The Knockouts were whores.

"While I got you on the hook," he said. "I need to talk about how you, um, um, handle your girls."

"The girls? Why? Is one of them complaining, again?"

"Not the girls," he corrected me with a giggle. He looked and nodded. "YOUR girls."

"Oh, the double D's?" I went right into character and made Russo feel uncomfortable. I grabbed my boobs and jiggled them for all they were worth, and he ran away.

There was, however, a pertinent issue growing of just how long I should "touch myself." At another show, Russo pulled me aside again where none of the boys could see.

"So, Jess," he said. "Listen, bro. I need to talk to you a second."

I was not a bro, but he called everyone that so I didn't take offense.

"On the boob-grabs," he said.

"Can't do that anymore?"

"No, no, you can do that," he said. "But it's better to do it in the second hour."

I thought about it for a second.

"Okay, so it's kind of like swearing," I asked. "Like you can get away with more later at night?

"Yes, exactly. Exactly."

So, I went out there and did my thing and grabbed the double D's somewhere around 9:30pm. It got the usual fan appreciation that it always got, but when I came back to the dressing room, Russo was waiting by the curtain.

"Was that okay, Vince?"

"Beautiful, beautiful," he said. "But just a little clarification. And you know it's not coming from me, you know. Because you know I love what you do."

"Okay."

"When you do the boob grab thing, can you just keep it down to three seconds?"

"Three seconds?"

"If you do it longer, they say it borders on being salacious."

In Russo's defense, I didn't believe it was him asking for the three-second time limit on the boob grabbing. Hell, I am not sure if Russo even knew what the word "salacious" meant.

LOCKER ROOM

A lot of people have often wondered what it must have been like being in The Knockouts' locker room. Being a fly on the wall probably would have been interesting to many fans, but I have to tell you, it wasn't all that exciting.

There weren't pillow fights and naked chicks walking around, nor girls scrubbing each other's backs in the showers.

I will say this however; *we were pretty foul.*

When we talked about guys or whatever, we went way, way, way into detail. You didn't just say "we kissed." You got a full detailed diatribe of the lips and breath and the wetness and whatever onions you could smell left over from their lunch. Yes, it was always that detailed.

I remember one of the girls who will remain nameless went out on a date. The next day, we were all up in her face asking for details.

"Did he open the door for you?"

"Did he kiss you good night?"

"Did he tell you how pretty you looked?"

Those were the common questions being asked.

"No."

"Well, was there any dirt?

"Only the dirt between my toes."

We were all startled to hear what came next. I guess he weirdly offered to rub her feet. She obliged. Then, one thing led to another and other body parts became involved. However, this is not going where you think.

She went on a daunting, descript, and disgusting diatribe of how he stopped using his hand on her feet, and changed it up to his mouth. Yes, he started sucking her toes like they were candy.

The funny thing about our girl talk deep inside the sanctum of the TNA locker room was that it was always all about the gruesome details.

I mean, yes, she could have just said he sucked her toes like Mel Philips (Google "WWE ring boy scandal") and called it a day. But no, that would not be the TNA Knockout way.

We heard all the juicy details about how his wet, warm tongue circled each toe, and licked the arch of each toe pit, then massaged the ball of her stinky foot.

So, again, when asked what our locker room was like, I always say it is the attention to fine detail that defined us.

DIRTY LAUNDRY

In 2008, Karen Angle filed for divorce from her husband Kurt Angle. Kurt was in a rough place at the time, so this wasn't a huge surprise. The surprise, however, was that the writers eventually wanted to use their situation as inspiration for a storyline. Talk about bad taste?

The break up was real but dirty laundry was soon to air out on live television, after Karen moved on from Kurt and fell in love with Jeff Jarrett.

This touchy situation wasn't just a mention in some quick promo to pop the boys in the back. It started on TV late in 2009 after Jeff was suspended a few months for lying to Dixie. It became over a full year long storyline between Jeff, Karen, and Kurt on TNA television! In 2010, Jeff Jarrett and Karen got married for real, thus playing into the realism.

I remember a lot of wrestlers were walking on eggshells whenever the topic came up. Even the writers including Eric Bischoff knew the whole thing was delicate and I think he did his best to avoid it every chance he could backstage. However, I didn't like it at all, and I think they could have done without such a personal storyline.

Promoters have made quite a business off of taking real-life situations and turning it into a work. Yes, the obvious one that did well in recent years back then was the nWo as I have stated before, but you also have the backstage heat between Bret Hart and Shawn Michaels leading to a huge match in the ring. There was also heat between The Blue Meanie and JBL that lead to a match on TV. You had Kevin Sullivan booked against Chris Benoit with discord over Nancy (Woman) leaving Sullivan and starting a relationship with Benoit, which as we all know actually ended up really happening. When information leaked that two of our guys had issues, it only made sense to turn those very real emotions into an angle and get the smart fans to buy into it.

I don't know how to describe just how uncomfortable the whole thing was in real life and don't even know today how they were able to build that whole thing into a storyline. It was totally insane.

From what I understand, the three of them were very professional. They met together and tried to squash whatever heat there was the best that they could in order to make money. Truth be told, they did find ways to tell a great story, but I don't know if I could have done that. The breakup was still fresh and they just pulled the Band-Aid off of that son of a bitch and ran with it.

There was also a super cringey storyline playing out a few years later at *Against All Odds* (2011) where if Kurt won, he would receive custody of his and Karen's kids. Ick!

"Oh boy," I remember saying when I first heard about that stipulation. That stipulation was just unbelievable to me.

In the end, they were professionals and the blow off match was still good. Kurt was always a natural. He couldn't have a bad match if he tried. Jeff and Karen also did a great job. If I were writing it, I probably wouldn't have gone there.

BEAUTIFUL PEOPLE

Just before I won the title is when I began feuding with The Beautiful People, and what better fit could I have had? I was the antithesis of the cookie-cutter Knockout, so our storyline only made sense.

There have been a number of great stables in TNA. The Main Event Mafia, Fortune, The Latin American Xchange (LAX), Aces & Eights, Christian's Coalition, Team Canada, The World Elite… the list goes on and on. However, when it comes to which faction has had more success over their tenure, it's hard to argue that The Beautiful People weren't right up there with the best – and with Angelina Love and Velvet Sky at the helm, you couldn't have asked for two girls to play the role better.

The idea of taking two attractive girls and having them bully their way through the women's division was one that many people could relate to. The concept of the group was a fairly simple one following an archetype that everyone can recognize. You have seen it, I am sure, first hand. The mean girl culture was huge back then in pop culture with movies and television shows all taking advantage of the idea. So, it only made sense to have TNA's version of mean girls picking fights with those they felt didn't meet their beauty standards.

A number of other people would join the faction over the years, and I often worked with them. Of course, Sky and Love were the core of The Beautiful People, but others would trickle in and out. At various points, other members to wear the beautiful hat included Madison Rayne, Lacey Von Erich, and even Cute Kip (a beautiful rendition of Billy Gunn!)

Like most pro wrestling factions, the group eventually would break up and reform again several times in various forms. They were a great opposition for me, nonetheless.

RETURN OF DAIVARI

Things were taking off for me, so when Shawn Daivari called me to check up on things in TNA as he often did, I told him he should come down and we should get the band back together. After doing a bang-up job in WWE with both Muhammad Hassan and then with The Great Khali in the summer of 2008, it was announced that he had joined the TNA roster under the new name of Sheik Abdul Bashir, with a similar anti-American gimmick.

Bert Prentice used to use both of us when we first started out during TNA's weekly PPV days, so Daivari had an in with at least that part of management – the same as I did. Also having history with Scott D'Amore helped. He just met with Terry Taylor and a few weeks later he was in!

He showed up in TNA mid-2008 for a good year and a half run. They first decided to film some vignettes with him in Houston. Daivari was in full gear at some power plant. He was cutting promos and doing the whole anti-USA thing, when a siren went off somewhere in the distance.

"Cut," the director said. "Wait a second, and we will go again after they drive by."

The problem was, the siren didn't fade away – it got louder and louder.

All of the sudden, the police came speeding up on the scene. Someone had called law enforcement and Homeland Security arrived.

When they saw Daivari standing there all dressed up in a turban, they put their hands on their guns and everything.

The Spike TV crew laughed a little and showed them their press passes, but the cops were not amused. They told them that everyone had to leave.

It was fun to travel again like the old days. Daivari was there in 2009 when I won the title and was the proudest I had ever seen him. He was so happy for me. I'll never forget it.

One time, we were on a plane flying back from some house shows to Orlando for a taping. Daivari called over a flight attendant, and I knew he was up to no good. He knew Gunn was obsessed with looks and wanting to stay youthful, so when they announced over the loudspeaker that it was Gunn's 65th birthday and sang to him, Gunn was pissed.

When we finally got to our TV taping, the rib was reversed. When Daivari walked into the venue, the other wrestlers grabbed him and held a wrestler's court. This was a very fraternity-like thing to do and only wrestlers were allowed. (Russo tried to enter the festivities, but the big bad "Bailiff" Road Dogg threw him out.)

Sometimes these locker room meetings were used to squash heat, but mostly wrestler's court was just some bullshit the boys would do out of boredom. With so much downtime during the tapings and the whole "hurry up and wait" atmosphere, the wrestlers would stage a whole courtroom, pull a dude in and just roast the fuck out of a guy.

For this wrestler's court case, Daivari was a good sport and ended up taking a plea bargain, which was to buy a case of beer for the locker room.

After court adjourned, the show started. Daivari went out to film the first match of that taping, then he immediately left the building. Nobody noticed.

People had all but forgotten the beer thing, and had no idea that he was over at Walmart loading up on so much adult beverages that the sheer amount was pretty much a rib.

When he came back from his shopping spree, he called me out to help. Then, we went over to a corner of the locker room and started to build an elaborate bar with all the trimmings. There was beer and booze from a package store he found nearby. When we were done, there were bottles of Grey Goose and beers on ice. It was quite the spread. Daivari put the finishing touches on his display of penance with signs that read "Talent Only."

We all had quite a party that night.

The funny thing is, that locker room bar was up for about a full year, until Universal Studios made us tear it down.

Politics in TNA eventually did Daivari in. Once Russo became the head of creative, there was some kind of heat. As is common in pro wrestling, sometimes people's gimmicks are just not everybody's cup of tea. Daivari found himself getting less of a TV push after that. He was only getting booked on house shows under Russo, and barely making any money off of those payoffs. Daivari felt some of the writers/bookers didn't like his act and started to strip away pieces of it.

One night I think he flipped out on management over something money related, and got heat. He was supposed to sign a two-year extension with Jeff Jarrett (who he liked) as his boss, but that fell through so he resigned. It's too bad too, because he was super talented. I loved working with him.

LISA MARIE

I continued to ride with Traci Brooks when I could, but that didn't always work out because of conflicts in our schedules. I found riding with Brian Hebner seemed to work out better, so we drove together quite a bit.

However, when WWE's Victoria showed up to TNA as "Tara," we also clicked. Lisa Marie Varon creeped her way into my car like the spider girl that she was and became another one of my regular copilots on the road.

We rode together a lot, and we were trouble when we got together! Because of this, her husband, Lee Varon, called her a lot to check up on us.

Together, they were pretty smart. They owned a lot of restaurants together. In Louisville, they owned a pizza joint and some custom motorcycle shop. When they moved to Chicago, they also bought some bar and renamed it The Squared Circle Pub. It was a cool sports bar with a wrestling theme. Sometimes we would go over there and hang out. Her husband was the cook there, and it was fun to go and watch all the other PPVs pulling in the customers. If we were off and I was around, we would show up to see anything from ROH to WWE. Lisa Marie and I would even bartend together some and have fun with the fans.

When we were on the road travelling together, we liked to go out. One time I remember well was when we went out looking to get a drink and ended up walking into a real random biker bar in Georgia.

When we walked in, it was like the needle on a record scratched suddenly. There were all these old school bikers sitting around, and these two big jacked chicks walked in. We cased the joint, and we were the only girls in the place. On top of that, we were bigger than everybody.

"Maybe we should try again," I said under my breath, trying to not move my lips, because all eyes were on us.

"No, no," she said. "This is going to rock."

Lisa Marie was more outgoing than me. She looked over to the corner and saw some karaoke gimmick. We waited a minute and there was some old George Burns-looking motherfucker who went up to sing. He sang Bon Jovi's "Livin' on a Prayer," and people loved it.

I just wanted to drink, but yep, you guessed it. Lisa Marie dragged me up to the mic.

After that, I realized I had just been enlisted to sing Sheryl Crow and Kid Rock's duet, "Picture." Our performance would soon be what international music critics would call "one of the most moving renditions of this classic ever performed at any hole-in-the-wall in the entire world."

And I, of course, naturally sang the Kid Rock part.

We used to travel for days and days on the road sometimes. Speaking of karaoke, it felt like we were living the lyrics to that Bob Seger song, "Turn The Page." I will admit, that we would often stop and get a 24-pack of Lite beer and the one in the back would partake on the down-low. We were smart about it, however, and never got pulled over for DWI and knew not to do it. It was the passenger who would mostly be the one drinking along the way. Because of this, the drunken passenger on our rides was almost never any help in the navigator role (which was usually the role for passengers on the road) because something about a 24-pack and reading a road map didn't mix.

One day we were travelling in uncharted territory. We were out in the middle of nowhere, making our way to an *Impact!* show. We were driving and having a good old time singing along with the radio for what seemed like days. There was nothing around but trees, and we got a little lost.

As we pulled around a bend, we finally saw our first sign of civilization, as uncivilized as it may have seemed. It was a huge painted sign.

"Do you think Dixie has us performing there tonight?" I asked.

The sign read "strip club" and looked like whoever had painted it had done so with their left hand, if you know what I am saying. Maybe their other fingers were full at the time? I don't know. It just looked super shady. We both laughed.

Now, many fans sexualize the women wrestlers; it goes with the territory. The business has always had a bit of inappropriateness regarding both sex and race. But no matter how much fans wanted to pretend that all their favorite female wrestlers were strippers, for the majority of us, this was the furthest thing from the truth.

We both discovered that we were in the same boat. We had never been inside a strip club before.

"I've always been curious what they look like, like for real," Lisa Marie said. "I mean, you see what they look like on TV and in the movies and all, but they can't look like that. Can they?"

"There's only one way to find out," I said.

"Are you thinking what I'm thinking?" Lisa Marie asked. "We are early. Let's go."

"Oh boy." I said.

We drove off the road and down what looked more like a dirt ditch than an actual street. We pulled into a gravel parking lot that didn't have many cars at all. It was around dinner time, maybe that was a little bit too early for the nocturnal wildlife to come out.

We got out of the car and walked up a long ramp into a log cabin like structure. When we opened the creaky door, it snapped behind us. It almost made us feel like we were being locked in.

When we looked around, the place was pretty much a ghost town. There were no dancers. There were no customers. There were no people sitting at the benches. There was just a bar with an old man sitting at it, nursing a drink with his back to us.

We decided to dive into the dive bar. We looked across the dining area and there was a stage with a greasy looking stripper pole. Lisa Marie grabbed my hand and pulled me straight for it.

"There is where all the action goes down," I said.

"I dare you to go jump on that pole up there," she said. "Spin around. Look sexy."

"Ew. No way."

"Twenty dollars?" she bribed.

"Ew, gross," I said. "No way."

"What, too cheap? You've done worse for a slice of pizza," she said, elbowing me.

As we laughed, we were startled by the bartender.

"Hello ladies, and what brings you here today?"

"Well," I said. "We were just looking to support a local business."

"Two Red Bulls, please," Lisa Marie ordered.

The drinks turned into appetizers, and the apps turned into food. Realizing that the bill was on its way, Lisa was just being Lisa, doing what she used to do everywhere to see if she could get a deal: *she name dropped wrestling.*

"Oh geesh," I said, rolling my eyes knowing her gimmick. I knew her, and I knew the deal. I knew exactly where she was going with all this. Her plan always was, if she could play off any amount of fame we had to get a free meal, that is what she was going to do.

Somehow, word got to the back. At this, and I am not sure why, but a handful of the establishment's talent came out to see what was going on. Lisa Marie smelled wrestling fans so she hammed it up. I was embarrassed, but had to play along.

"Are you a wrestler, too?" one of the girls asked.

"Yup," I said. "That's right."

Now with guys who are fans, they will almost give you the shirts off of their backs if you ask. However, it was not every day that one of the TNA Knockouts could work other girls to get free stuff, so Lisa Marie, of course, was more than up for the challenge.

She put on the charm. She put on the sweetness. She used all the tricks in the book. One thing she used to do was something she said that she learned at college: when you say the person's name, they connect to you and they are more apt to give you what they want. Therefore, she went right down the line and asked all the girls their names first and the whole deal. Once she did, she exclaimed that she had presents for all of them. Then, she disappeared to the car, and returned with cheap 8x10s and made them out to each one, personalized.

We took pictures with the girls, gave free tickets to the bartenders, and yes in the end, we used our charm to our advantage.

"How much do we owe?" I asked.

"Oh, your money is no good here," the tallest of the dancers said. "Right, Bob."

"The least we can do," the bartender replied, winking.

"Thanks girls," Lisa Maria said. "See you next time."

We walked back out to the lot, and I looked at her and shook my head.

"What?" she asked, laughing.

"We couldn't have just paid?"

"TNA budget cuts are real," she said. "Times are tough, right?"

I got in the car.

"A girl's gotta earn a living," she said.

Anyhow, before we had left, we had posed with the girls out by their "fancy" strip joint sign. Before we took off, Lisa Marie tapped through her phone to find the picture.

She was quickly becoming a social media whore come late 2009, and I knew exactly what she was doing, but decided to ask anyhow.

"What are you doing?" I asked.

"I'm gonna put that picture on Twitter," she replied.

"Wait, what? Us with a bunch of strippers?" I laughed. "For what? What did you write?"

She didn't say. She kayfabed the shit out of me. She quickly put her phone in her bag.

"Come on you bitch," I said, not driving away and demanding to see what she had done with her phone.

Still no dice.

Eventually, I took off. There was no way I was going to make her show me.

Being a former bodybuilder with big arms and all, I often got gay heat from the audience. I wanted no part of a post that depicted me as checking out the chicks at a titty bar, and she knew it.

When she finally showed me the post, I realized that it was a different kind of heat that I needed to worry about in this case.

The post mentioned that "budget cuts were legit." It implied that we were so broke that we had to share a room and resort to stripping to make ends meet.

"What the hell, girl?!" I said. "Dixie is going to just love that... take it down."

"Don't worry," she said. "I'll take all the blame. I promise."

We kept driving until we made it to our hotel, and to where our shared room was.

When we got there, I knew better. I just stayed in the car.

"You coming?" she asked, looking back at me in full strategic mode.

"No, not yet. I'll be in, in a few," I said, pretending to do something on my own phone.

"Wait, why not?"

"I'm good. You just go and check us in," I said. "I don't want any part of you trying to pay for the rooms in free wrestling tickets."

Another time, I remember we were off to a show together somewhere. As part of Lisa Marie's new gimmick, she had a pet tarantula that she would use to intimidate her opponents with. However, we were off to a show somewhere and she was told that she couldn't bring her spider on the plane.

When we finally got there, instead of hitting up a strip bar, this time we stopped at a dollar store.

I thought nothing of it, at first. She came out eating a snack, and that was that. It just so happened that she learned she was going to be working with me, and had a trick up her sleeve.

That night at the show, the dollar store visit was way out of my head. When we finally walked down to the ring, everything was normal. However, when Lisa Marie finally went to lock up with me, she stopped the match immediately.

"Wait, wait, wait!" she yelled, holding her hands up in the air.

Then, she stuck her hands down into her tights, and pulled out a fistful of plastic spiders.

"What in the fuck?"

She reached down the crotch of her tights again, and pulled out the last one or two stragglers, then threw the whole handful at me.

What could I do but sell it?

I jumped out of the ring and I started thinking about how the audience up in the cheap seats must have thought that Lisa Marie Varon had got a bad case of the crabs or something, or was maybe throwing pubes at me.

Inside the ring, the ref, Brian Hebner, started laughing. It was contagious apparently, and then Lisa started.

I started to laugh too.

I almost never broke character, but the whole thing was ridiculous. She got me good.

I walked around the ring trying to compose myself, trying my best not to laugh. When I finally got back into the ring, I looked down at the fistful of fake arachnids, and lost it.

I wasn't experiencing arachnophobia, but I had caught a bad case of the giggles.

I rolled back out of the ring to contain myself. I attempted to heel on a fan or something, but it just didn't work. Then it hit me. I needed time.

I went over to the timekeeper and jaw jacked him and waited. I was feeling unsuspected amount of pressure.

I need a time out!

"What are you doing?" Jeremy Borash asked me, leaning over the table.

"I need to take a minute," I replied biting my lip. "Stall."

"Huh?"

More like bathroom stall. "I almost peed my pants!"

Then Borash started laughing. I think he could see the yellow in my eyes. I really thought I was about to piss myself.

I walked around the ring a second, still cracking up at the pile of fake bugs laying there in the ring.

I was dying, and I felt like just a little bit of pee was about to make a run-in on our match.

I stopped, took a few short breaths and finally rolled into the ring. When I did, I went right back into the lockup.

"We gotta take it home," I said with my face down towards the mat. "I'm about to piss myself."

Lisa Marie asked if I was serious about having to use the bathroom, and I confirmed.

She had me do a quick school boy for the finish, then I rolled out of the ring and tiptoed back to the locker room with my legs crossed.

LATE 2009

By late in 2009, I was the Knockout Champion and our division was getting hot. The TNA Knockouts were getting all kinds of side work from our new exposure. The list of non-wrestling bookings just grew longer and longer.

Some TNA Knockouts were beginning to develop what could become "life after wrestling" television and movie careers outside of TNA. Backstage interviewer Lauren Brooke hosts *Top Ten* and *Golf Destination* on the Golf Channel. SoCal Val started showing up on television commercials for Morphoplex. Christy Hemme started a music career by featuring her singles on social media and picked up roles in *Bloodstained Memoirs*, *Fallen Angels*, and *Bubba's Chili Parlor*.

Alissa Flash would appear in a documentary called *False Finish*. Former backstage interviewer Leticia Cline appeared in the fifth season of the reality series *Beauty and the Geek*, and a reality series called *Bowling Beauties*.

Taylor Wilde and The Beautiful People (Angelina Love and Velvet Sky) appeared on an MTV reality show. Love and Sky also got featured on the cover of the December 2009 issue of *Muscle & Fitness* magazine, (which also included photos of Lauren Brooke and SoCal Val!) Angelina Love appeared in a film entitled *Good Intentions* starring country music star LeAnn Rimes and (my *90210* boyfriend) Luke Perry. Love also appeared in an episode of the reality series *Kenny vs. Penny* with Traci Brooks.

Traci Brooks also had an uber cheesy role in an uber cheesy B-film called *Zombie Beach Party*. After that, she went on to be the first TNA Knockout under contract to pose for *Playboy*. (Christy Hemme posed for the magazine prior to joining TNA.)

SIDE BOOB HUSTLE

Come the end of 2009, all my girls were working side hustles making extra loot, and I was worried about whether or not I had boob insurance.

As I mentioned at the start of this book, I had all of those matches at TNA's *New Year's Knockout Eve* and along the way, I popped a tire.

It didn't just pop like a balloon at a kid's birthday party. It was more like a slow leak. I didn't even know it had happened at the time.

TNA's *New Year's Knockout Eve* PPV was the last show of 2009. It was a tournament for the number one contender. The winner would get a title match the next week for the TNA Knockouts title on the first live show of 2010. At the PPV, however, I had not one, not two, but three matches I had to work on.

I got there early to prepare. There was no last-minute driving in a storm or anything for me this time. We were in sunny Florida, and I was going to win that tournament, so that meant I was in for a really long night. I had a lot of planning to do, but I didn't leave any room for potential injuries. The pressure was on, despite the fact that one of my girls was going to lose pressure in the process, whether I liked it or not.

To start the night, I had to work with Traci Brooks. Now, for those of you who have ever seen her, you know she really knows how to fill out a card, as well as a T-shirt. We had a pretty physical match. I took a spear and some stiff chops that could have both led to the tenderizing of my left implant. I don't know exactly when it happened, but it did.

I moved on to the next bracket in the tournament and had to take on Awesome Kong. Now, if I already had some air leaking out of "my tire" at this point, or not, I don't know. But taking on Kong surely wouldn't help the matter. On top of the chops I received from Brooks, Kong started in with some more chops of her own. If you have ever been chopped by Kong, you would know that she is a wrestler that follows through. Add her throwing me into the ring steps before the match even started, and then the possibility of my implant failure then increases.

When you are in a match, adrenaline kicks in. That shit is like full-body Novocain. When adrenaline hits just right, there is very little pain (unlike the usual stiff hits from Kong which actually hurt and do the opposite.) I knew that my adrenaline was going to elevate my stock at this PPV. When you are as hyped up as I was going into this event, the rush can make you feel almost nothing. That is where I was. I was in the zone.

I put on a pretty good show in this match with a ton of offense, so I'm not putting Kong (or anyone, for that matter) to blame for the not-so-fun thing that happened to my fun bag. I was running around like crazy that night. It is even quite possible that when I hit Kong with The Bronco Muncher, I may have even clipped my nip on my own, slamming into the second rope. I don't know. I did take a number of clotheslines from Kong that would have made Stan Hansen blush, before I beat her to move on to the third and final match of the tournament. It is entirely possible that around this point in the night that I may have hurt one of my girls. Now, some women can take on a whole football team and that to me would seem painful, but I would argue that a handful of pro wrestling chops could be worse. Those hurt no matter how you take them! There was some stinging. I was slightly sore, but that was normal wrestler pain.

My boobie hurts.

We went out to drink after the show, and I kept rubbing it but never thought to look at it. It was sore, but so was my back so I thought nothing of it. I got to my hotel, and got ready for bed. When I went in the bathroom and got undressed, I stood in front of the mirror.

I looked trippier than an uneven sidewalk.

Holy shit! How did I not notice that?

It had dropped from 700 cc's of saline. There was nothing much left than just an empty bag.

I wanted to call someone, but it was late. I knew that would do no good. I went to bed wearing a sad face emoji.

The next morning, I called Terry Taylor right away practically at sunrise.

"I have a secret to tell you," I said to probably the worst person you could share a secret with in this business.

"Shoot."

"My left titty is gone," I chuckled. "Do you cover this?"

"Gone?! Like popped, gone?"

"Exactly," I said. "And thanks for listening, I am happy to get that off my chest." (Insert a drumroll sound here!)

Knowing it was okay to laugh because I was making jokes about it, Taylor made some joke back (that I don't remember) to lighten the mood and then said, "Okay, though. Seriously, I'll look into this, but I really don't think so."

I continued to make some calls, and then Taylor called back and said, "No."

Fortunately for me, in the end, I had boob insurance and just didn't know it.

It was kind of traumatic at first to look at my chest in the mirror, but I knew I could get it fixed. I wasn't the first person to have this happen. I just used an old school remedy, a sock, and continued to work shows before I could get in for the procedure and nobody was the wiser.

Right after New Year's Knockout Eve, however, Traci got married. She was my girl so I of course was going to get all dolled up minus a boob and make an appearance.

At Traci's wedding to the love of her life Frankie Kazarian, I showed up with my freshly busted breast implant courtesy of that PPV. I probably shouldn't have been there being injured and all, but I wouldn't have missed it for the world. I didn't hide my deflated boob, either. Just like our days on the road, I roughed it to make everything work. I just taped my tit up. It hurt, but I gangster'ed through it.

Traci thought it was funny. "That is just who she is," she would say to one of her guests asking who the girl with one boobie was. By the end of the night, all the guests knew I had a broken boob, and it was great.

A few days later, I went back to the "fix a flat" plastic surgeon to see if I could get a refill. There I found out they were going to have to actually remove the bag and give me a brand new implant because it was too damaged to fix from all of the wrestling I was doing.

My only regret is that after they removed the bag, they threw it out. I should have asked to keep it.

...I could have made a fortune off of that shit on eBay.

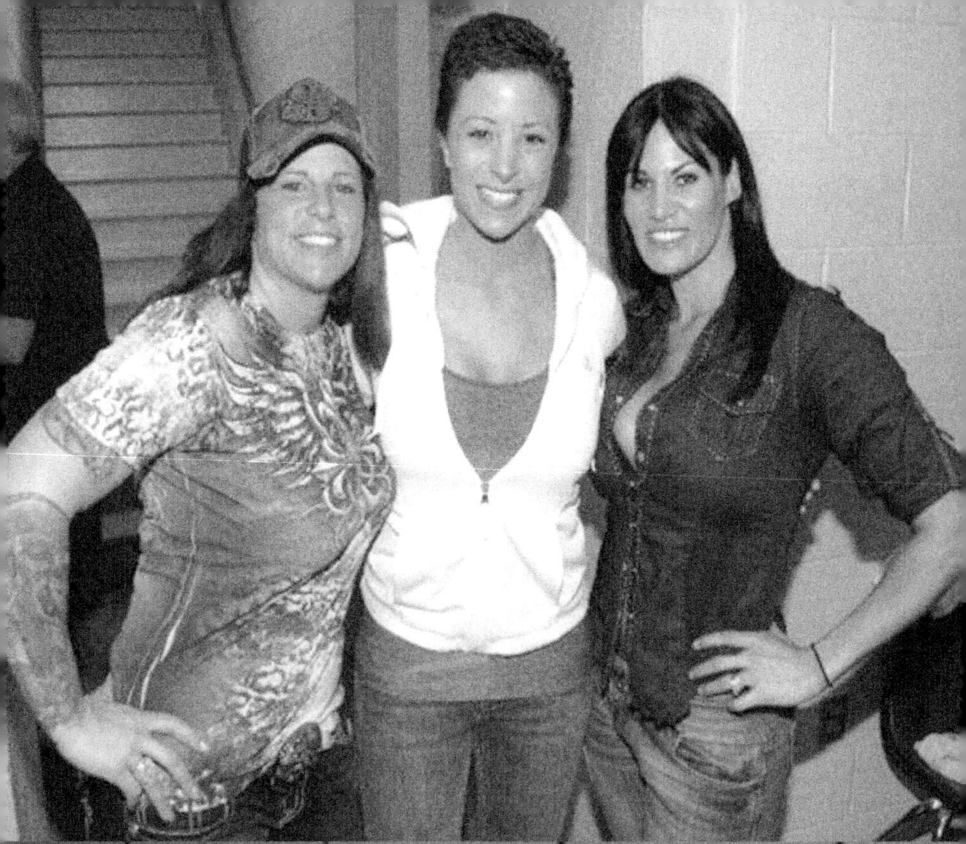

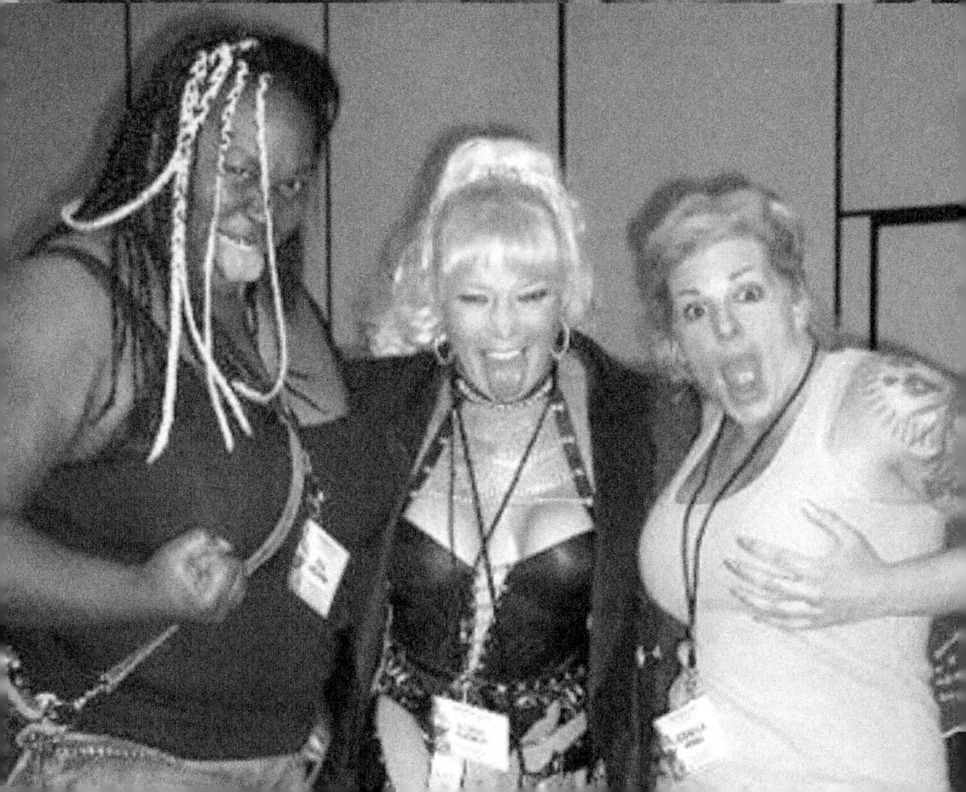

CHAPTER 8 – HOGAN & BISCHOFF'S IMPACT

    Since Panda took over, there was word on the street that TNA was now willing to pay out big to ex-WWE talent. This meant they had money. Come October 2009, Eric Bischoff smelled some of that cash. He came along and helped negotiate a deal that would bring in the one name that could potentially boost ratings in the eyes of executives everywhere: Hulk Hogan.

    By January 4, 2010, Hogan came in as talent with Bischoff by his side. With Hogan's official TNA debut, Hulkamaniacs were witnessing his first real appearance on a wrestling program after over two years away from the business. This was huge.

    The main event of the episode had AJ Styles successfully defending his TNA World championship against Kurt Angle. This match was deliberately placed in an attempt to keep all the passers-byers who were tuning in just to see Hogan. It worked. That first Hogan appearance was a solid show, and subsequently, there was a buzz around the promotion like never before.

    The one big thing that Hogan and Bischoff accomplished on day one was getting the promotion's name out there. Yes, they immediately raised TNA's awareness. Many fans who had never heard of TNA before, now sure did. Others who had heard of TNA, but had never tuned in before, also did. That live show brought a level of importance to the promotion that we never had before.

    Along with the many new eyes that came with this new duo for the company, other intricacies would also follow. Talent and what you would see on camera wasn't the only dynamic with the Hogan/Bischoff debut. There would also be the added impact of what they meant to how TNA operated in order to rebuild the franchise.

    Behind the scenes, Bischoff was also appointed as an executive producer. Part of this made sense, as he had done so well with the creation of the nWo and his success with WCW in the Monday Night Wars. Part of this could have also just been Dixie not knowing what the fuck she was doing and

CHAPTER 8 – Hogan & Bischoff's Impact   203

marking out, because she put Bischoff into a role where she had to answer some to him.

Hogan was also signed as a consultant and part of the creative team from 2010-2013. This meant more room for his buddies when a spot was open, and more room for old school – which many felt was not what an X Division (cruiserweight-like) heavy TNA was all about.

Bischoff supported Hogan in the new push to appeal to older wrestling fans. This direction was a total turnaround from everything that happened in the promotion historically before them. No more trying to be "the alternative."

Now, even though I liked the heels as a kid, I guess I was maybe a closet Hogan fan from my childhood days. I was sure I was being perceived as to be of no threat to him or the spotlight he needed, so for me, I was cool with him showing up. I was actually kind of excited. However, there were a number of people who felt that he would usher out the alternative wrestling fan base demographic that they thrived off of and thus TNA would turn into "WWE-Lite."

Immediately people saw TNA's stock rise, but many wondered if this was a temporary peak in the market. Others believed that the organization was in trouble as Hogan's presence could be the kiss of death. While it was true that both Hogan and Bischoff had done wonders for the wrestling business, they also had been around when the wrestling business was bad.

Either way, TNA made its biggest move in history and, at the start, people were finally talking about the promotion.

The first noticeable thing to happen under Hogan and Bischoff's tenures was right there on paper. TNA re-branded its flagship program to a less suggestive name; IMPACT Wrestling. They also reintroduced the four-sided ring to look more like their competition.

The final glove was tossed when they decided to move our TV show to Monday nights opposite *WWE Raw*.

A NEW MONDAY NIGHT WAR

On March 8, 2010, IMPACT's move to Mondays would be first time two major wrestling promotions would go head to head again since the launch of *WCW Monday Nitro* in 1995.

The locker room was scared, but it certainly did create an intensity of excitement that we didn't have before this.

For that episode, I remember showing up to the locker room and thinking I was in the wrong building. When I got there, I saw Jeff Hardy, Scott Hall, Sean Waltman and when I walked around the corner, there was Ric Flair.

In the spirit of WCW, Bischoff opened the purse strings and it worked. TNA broke all of its own company records, including highest TV ratings ever (1.5) and highest viewership (2.2 million).

Many knew that robbing the WWE locker room technique didn't pay off in the long run. They knew what had happened with WCW. However, most agreed this move was a great way to kick off a new era for TNA.

For the first time since 2001, WWE was finally challenged. Spike TV decided to keep our original Thursday night slot open as well to replay our new Monday night shows. To keep the ball rolling, Bischoff brought in as many high-profile former WWE wrestlers that he could including Rob Van Dam, and even an old friend of mine...

THE RETURN OF THE ASSHOLE

I remember showing up and walking into the girl's locker room and everyone was acting weird.

You know how people are talking some and you hear it, but the moment you walk into the room, everything goes quiet. My bitches did that to me, and I was pissed.

"Um, hello?" I said wheeling in my gear bag.

"Hi, Jess," Angelina Love said.

I looked at her like I just sniffed a shit.

"What?" Angelina said looking guilty.

"What? I should be asking you what. What was that?"

"What do you mean?" she said.

The other girls laughed, uncomfortably.

"Okay, if you won't talk, someone will." I said, before turning around to immediately to ask Traci Brooks what was going on.

"Sooo..."

"So?" Traci repeated.

"You motherfuckers were just talking about me," I said. "Now if one of you has a problem with me, you better say it to my face."

"Look," Traci said. "Okay, I'll say it."

"Say what?" I laughed.

"They hired Ken (Anderson)," Traci said. "He's actually already here."

I paused. All the girls leaned in to see how I would sell the news that my ex-boyfriend was in the same building as me, and would continue to be for who knew how long? The bitches moved in closer, as if to be my support for some massive emotional breakdown or something.

My response: I laughed.

"Come on," I said. "That's it?"

"That's it." Angelina said.

"Figured ya'll knew me better than that," I said.

Now, Traci had been with me since day one. She knew that I got to chop the shit out of Ken in that match after our breakup, so I figured she knew I was over him. But I guess they all just needed to hear it.

"When I am done with you, I AM DONE WITH YOU!"

The words I said might have been tough for some of those girls to understand, and yes, it was tough when we first broke up. But creating a clear division after that was key for me to move on. For some of the girls in the locker room who would go back and hookup with their exes after bad breakups, they maybe never fully got over those guys – and maybe that is what they were projecting onto me.

I knew from experience that these things could become a minefield of bad feelings. This distraction is something that I wanted no part of. This is why I always made a conscious effort to never keep the door open, as some of the other Knockouts perhaps did.

You see, one problem that many girls have is not being able to completely cut someone off and let "the end" be the end. This can be a real problem for many, especially in wrestling where we roll with the same circle day in and day out. In my opinion, if you don't completely cut off an ex-boyfriend or girlfriend when it is over for good reason, you confuse your own brain. If you try to stay friends with them during the break up, this can easily lead to what some call retro-sexual relationships.

You all know a retro-sexual. I have known many girls who were lonely and went back to their exes for one-night stands and friends with benefits type situations. In their minds, it's better than hooking up with someone they don't know. However, I won't engage in retro-sexuality, nor do I recommend it. What happens is it blurs the lines in a relationship and makes it so that it is hard for girls to get over guys in many cases.

If I can offer any advice to any of the girls in the wrestling business or even those in other professions, I would suggest trying to find that place in your head where you can compartmentalize your ex-boyfriend/girlfriend once you have broken up, if you still have to see them on a regular basis. Whether it is in a working relationship, or a shared custody type situation, if you go back to them for simply physical needs, it complicates situations.

Fortunately for me, with Anderson and other relationships I have had, I have had no problem with focusing on moving on and never looking back. But I can see why the girls didn't understand my mindset.

Wrestling is pretty up close and in your face. As a wrestler, could you imagine sharing a ring with a former fling? Would the idea of having to physically wrestle with your ex mess you up in the head? Working with an ex sucks, but it's better when you have accepted that they are your ex.

Things happen like this everywhere. People find themselves in weird working situations all the time and don't know how to make it work, however, it doesn't have to be that way. I knew this at the moment I heard Anderson was back.

Why do these girls care more than I do? I am totally over him.

When a relationship in the locker room (or work) does turn sour though, it can be very bad. You can't get away from the person and quite often the promoter smells money and puts you with them all the more. (Those bastards!) This happened in TNA when Karen Angle left Kurt for Jeff Jarrett, and then they wrote it into a storyline.

The whole idea of having to deal with an ex is difficult. Some single moms out there, or divorcees, can probably relate to this. When a kid is in the mix, the exes are around for a long time and you just have to deal with him. The same thing happens in wrestling except instead of sharing a child, you are sharing the locker room and sometimes a match. You have to rise to the occasion and look passed the past.

However, this level of understanding and cooperation is something that a lot of younger people do not have. I don't think that most of the girls that I worked with at TNA at this time understood my mentality and how I looked at Anderson. I meant exactly what I said, when I said, "when I am done with you, I am done with you." I guess in that respect, I am kind of like a guy. I learned the importance of and how to move on from Anderson, and I didn't give it much of a second thought when I heard that I was going to have to work with him soon.

When my girls told me Anderson was coming back to TNA, I honestly didn't have any hard feelings, and I honestly didn't care. The more I thought about it, the more I realized that I was actually kind of happy for him. I don't know if that was some real higher-level Gandhi-like thinking, but a few of the girls just didn't get it. They continued to think there had to be drama, and I was just no-selling it. They thought that since he cheated on me, I should be pissed he was around and he should ultimately get what was coming to him.

I can't stress this enough. *There was no more heat whatsoever.*

If there are any girls in wrestling, or women in general who need help in this area, I guess I do have some advice.

I've already warned you: DO NOT GO RETRO-SEXUAL.

When you are done, you are done. No taking a step backward. Going back for a one-and-done, or whatever you are going to call it prolongs getting over him and prevents the closure you need to move on. So, in my opinion, fuck that.

When I saw Anderson in the locker room, it wasn't like we hadn't talked before. We kept in touch a little when he left for WWF to do his whole son of Vince McMahon angle. I talked to him about work a few times, one because I figured I may go there one day, and two, because I did care about him as a person, still. There just was no number three, however. We were done.

A lot of people were impressed with how I handled seeing him in TNA, or rather should I say, how there was no real tension or anything. It's almost like the other wrestlers wanted to see some sort of conflict that truly wasn't there. Others, however, would ask me how I managed to be so professional.

So, how do you go back into looking at an ex as just a regular person you have to work with? Yes, it can be extremely awkward to work with someone after a breakup. After all, you are going from being the most important people in each other's lives to seeing them by the copy machine once in a while. Most people want to avoid their exes at all costs after a breakup, right? But if you work together, this can't happen. Maybe that is why the retro-sexual thing becomes such a thing with some chicks, I don't know. But when you have to deal with someone you want out of your life because it is your job, you can't pretend they never existed.

To make matters worse, if you are a wrestler, you will probably hear more details about your ex than you want to. Ever hear of "telephone – tell a wrestler?" Wrestlers travel with each other so there is a whole hell of a lot of talking and gossiping going on. Hearing about your ex's post-breakup dating life can and does suck.

I know it sounds touchy-feely, but if you are going to work with an ex, you have to release the negativity if you are going to survive. You have to realize that your ex is an ex for a reason. You have to realize that they went away for a reason. If you can do this, if you can reprogram your mind in a positive sense, then that bit of jealousy or whatever you are feeling will go away more easily.

When your ex is still a part of your everyday life, rewiring your brain on how you think of them is a tough one. The new programming has to lesson your focus on the end of a romantic relationship, and instead prioritize having a professional one.

ODB'S WORK & RELATIONSHIP TIPS

To the new girls just starting out, I guess I can throw you a list of what I have both done and learned over the years:

1) **SHOP IN DIFFERENT STORES** – Try to keep business and pleasure separate whenever you can. Yeah, the wrestlers you work with may look attractive and easy to pick up because they are right there. It is a cosmetic sport after all, but you might do better shopping elsewhere if you catch my drift. If you find that connection at work, that's great, but you have to keep in mind that there is always the possibility of a breakup and then you're working with your ex.

2) **BE A PROFESSIONAL** – Awkward circumstances or any sort of personal drama can screw up your job. If you do have an ex in the locker room, stay away from drama. Not only will conducting yourself professionally after a breakup make your relationship with your ex easier, but the less you draw attention to it, the more quickly others will forget you ever dated.

3) **FOCUS ON YOUR WORK ETHIC** – When you are at work, it should always be "work first." Don't accept mediocrity. Always ask yourself, "how can I do my very best?" Worrying about a relationship (or an ex) takes you off your game. Concentrate on doing the very best you can do. You have to ask yourself, if you want to let a relationship fuck up you career.

4) **THINK ABOUT THE FUTURE** – What you do now can come back to haunt you later on. Especially this is true in the cyclical world of wrestling. Sometimes you get fired, and then they think about hiring you back. This happened to me many times in the business. When you are being reconsidered, you want to be remembered for your work ethic, not who you have banged and your contributions to any shit-talking, thereafter. A reputation can take a professional lifetime to build and five minutes to destroy. Keep that in mind before you choose who to date, or before you gossip/badmouth an ex. Anybody could end up being your boss one day.

5) **SQUASH THE HEAT** – If you and your ex work with the same people, make a real effort to put your coworkers at ease regardless of how things ended. Maybe have a quick talk with your ex about how you are going to mutually coexist for the good of everyone. Try to compliment your ex when possible, and avoid the breakup details if someone asks about them – no matter how tempting it might be to dish or vent. Letting people know you are okay with each other, is key.

6) **KEEP THE DRAMA OFF THE CLOCK** – Any unfinished business or breakup related conversations should take place after hours. Do not talk about your breakup or vent to any of your coworkers if that would keep the heat going.

7) **ALWAYS TAKE THE HIGH ROAD** – Even though you can't control your ex's actions, you can control yours. Fortunately for me, it was relatively easy working with Anderson. But my girls have stressed that in other cases taking the high road is the only way to drive. This is huge!

8) **FAKE IT UNTIL YOU MAKE IT** – If you just can not do all the stuff that I've advised above, do what wrestlers do best. Work it. Pretending to be able to get passed all the bullshit actually makes your brain picture what it would actually be like in that happy place. Faking it can result into really positive sentiments. It can dump the negativity you still feel and give you the closure you need.

TNA 2010

TNA grew quite a bit in 2010. The company reached a level where it had never been before. Record numbers were reached on both the Monday and Thursday night shows. Also, TNA was doing well on the road and breaking house show records at particular venues.

The company started to develop depth. More stars found their way to TNA including Shannon Moore, Mickie James, Tommy Dreamer and more.

With the good came the bad. It appeared that the X Division wasn't high on Bischoff and Hogan's list of priorities. With all the names coming into TNA, there was less emphasis on the X Division and their focus shifted onto the matches involving said names. Pro wrestling seemed to be evolving into more fast-paced action to cater to the younger fans. TNA brought that mindset to the table with the X Division, but started to turn its back some on this successful formula. Some would argue that the X Division was what set us apart from WWE programming altogether, and the new focus and direction in booking made us more like them. "TNA was starting to look like a cheap imitation of our main competitor."

There also appeared to be some unnecessary spending going on that mirrored what went on in WCW. Some of the wrestlers didn't like how TNA was becoming a network of "good old boys," seeing that a number of people from the Hogan regime were finding a lucrative pay window sponsored by Panda. These names included the signing of The Nasty Boys and Bubba the Love Sponge.

PILLOW FIGHTING WHORES

We were encouraged to blur the lines of realism wherever we could. Bischoff firmly believed that there was money to be made on working the "smart marks." He did that with the nWo in WCW, often working behind-the-scene scenarios into storylines wherever he could. Using the pro wrestling "dirt sheets" as a means to create interest was definitely part of his formula for success. Fans wanted to believe, and this was a perfect means to make them think some of what was happening on the screen was in fact real.

With social media starting to make an impact in the world, many of us decided to jump on the bandwagon. It was a great way to develop your character when the cameras went black.

Taking a little bit of realism and mixing it with your character could create interest and some good heat at times. Fans would read these bits online and really eat it up.

ODB was taking off as a character more than ever before. I truly believed in the idea of treating female wrestlers like our male counterparts, and we were moving in the right direction. However, with the push to be more mainstream, there was beginning to be more and more tits-and-ass diva-type content bleeding back into the mix.

One night, I was feeling kind of bummed about what I was seeing on TNA programming. I was playing with my cellphone and thought to myself, what would ODB say about a bunch of Knockouts in their underwear on TV. Therefore, I clicked on the little bird icon and tweeted a masterpiece:

"WTF is happening to the Knockout Division? You got whores pillow fighting and washing cars in bikinis in the back! Who knows what else?!"

After that, things moved quickly. I guess I was a trendsetter, or maybe I became what some would call a social media influencer before this term existed. My post predated Roseanne Barr getting fired from her own show for what she said on social media. However, it got pretty much the same results from my employer.

Wrestling fans saw my post and replied/shit on about what they too didn't like about TNA. They probably took it a bit too far, however, and I was going to get the shrapnel.

Someone higher up didn't like what I had said, and it wasn't long before I was fired. When I asked what was behind all this, I was told it certainly was because of my pillow fight comment on Twitter. I couldn't get a confirmation on just who was behind the decision. Those days, TNA had "too many chiefs and not enough Indians." Whenever a decision was made, nobody knew which manager, director, booker, agent, or owner was behind it. There was also a lot of examples of the right hand not knowing what the left hand was doing. So just the same in this case as many others, I didn't know who had pulled the plug on me. However, I am sure you can guess who I was blaming in my head.

I bet it was Dixie Carter.

I didn't bother to object. I didn't bother to make a plea bargain with the court. I figured if that bitch was the one behind my ousting, I wasn't going to give her the satisfaction of groveling to get my job back.

She can go fuck herself.

I was out for a few months. After that, I came back for a one-spot. They booked me as a surprise, and fortunately, I got a big pop that couldn't be ignored.

Bischoff was standing at the curtain when the fans went wild for me, and when I made my way back to the locker room, it was obvious. He knew they had left money on the table with me, and it had been all over something silly I said in character on the internet.

"Hey Jess," he said. "Let's get you your job back."

"Sounds good to me."

RETURN OF THE BITCH

Bischoff is the man. He pulled some strings for me backstage and made good with his promise. So eventually, TNA called again and I was back for a new run.

Because the smart fan internet wrestling community was becoming more and more of a target for storylines, they figured working even more realism into the storylines was the best way to go. The internet community was getting bigger and bigger and they all knew I had been fired, so we decided to make my firing part of the angle. We had seen these realism stories work with Shawn Michaels and Bret Hart. We had seen them work with the nWo, and in many other instances over history. Ultimately, they decided to give me a leaked realism storyline.

My appearance in the May 19th episode of the newly christened, *IMPACT Wrestling* would have me attacking Velvet Sky. The story was that after I had gotten fired, I was pissed at the "pillow fighting whores" who were left behind.

The commentators explained that I was not under contract with TNA. To make my showing up "unexpectedly" for TV even more real, they had me make my entrance through the crowd with no entrance music.

They had me work a program with Velvet Sky for the next few months. She was my nemesis. I was the Lex Luthor to her Superman. I attacked her whenever I could and even made her lose matches – just to be one dirty bitch.

Eventually our feud evolved into Sky and Miss Tessmacher (aka Brooke Adams) against me and my new partner, Jacqueline Moore.

Moore was just awesome, by the way, so I need to go off on another tangent right now and say more about her.

JACKIE MOORE

Let's back up a little and talk about Jackie.

Back around the time I started to first make an impact on *TNA Impact!*, another woman was also being impactful. Back in November 2004, Jacqueline Moore made her debut in TNA as a fan favorite.

She was used quite a bit as a singles competitor in the women's division, but by this point in her career she had done it all. That's why when she acted as a referee, or even wrestled in some of the men's matches, nobody questioned whether something was going to work or not. She knew how to do everything.

Jackie Moore grew up a wrestling fan out of Dallas, Texas where she would watch the Von Erichs, who were known for their very "snug" wrestling style. She was a fighting-sports athlete herself, training in kickboxing, taekwondo, and other martial arts. So, it came as no surprise to anyone that she would eventually make the transition over to try out professional wrestling for herself.

Still a teenager, she saw an advertisement one day in a magazine for a wrestling tryout at a local gym. There, she met legendary manager General Skandor Akbar.

Much like myself, Jackie Moore found herself in a man's sport. She was the only woman in Akbar's wrestling school, and not unlike myself, she had no choice but to train with and against men.

"Jess," she said one day when we were comparing notes. "The boys didn't take it easy on me. They tossed me around like I was one of the guys!"

"Been there done that," I commiserated.

Jackie Moore's hard work and dedication did her well. In 1988, Jackie debuted for World Class Championship Wrestling (WCCW) as Sweet Georgia Brown. The promotion had been so popular at the time that it opened many doors for her early on. She went and wrestled in Japan over the following three years and people started to take notice.

After that in 1991, she showed up in Memphis, under the new name Miss Texas. Jackie Moore became the first USWA (Memphis version) Women's champion.

Through the WWF's partnership with the USWA, she showed up on WWF programming under the name Wynonna in vignettes for Jeff Jarrett. With more years of experience under her belt, she ended up on WCW television in 1997, as the heel manager of Kevin Sullivan. Finally, in 1998, Jackie Moore made her way back to WWF and defeated Sable for the vacated WWF Women's championship, becoming the first African American woman to hold that title.

Once she made it to TNA, I always hit her up for any information I could to tap her great mind for the business. She was tough, and I wanted to be tough like her.

I remember one of her toughest TNA moments had to be when she was booked working steel cage matches and street fights against Gail Kim. In one of those bouts, Moore was slammed into a metal garbage can and got her clocked cleaned by a broomstick.

"I looked down and saw my teeth on the mat," she said, recalling the match where she lost her smile in a much worse fashion than when Shawn Michaels said he lost his during his infamous promo. "Instead of freaking out... I just continued to wrestle. I didn't roll out of the ring and say, 'I can't continue.'"

The show must go on, right?

After that match, Jackie had to get a root canal and dental implants that would stick with her for life.

That's just who she was.

Before being moved backstage to eventually work as an agent for TNA, she had another run in her and she was set to work with me. Before that would happen, we would first have to team together to make things even more heated.

Going back to my storyline, I was not under contract with TNA and making my entrances in matches through the crowd with no entrance music. During the summer of that year, Jackie Moore and I were directed to jump the girls and beat the shit out of them... so we did. At one point we were called into the office to take it down a notch.

I remember going in and seeing Bruce Prichard who just shook his head.

"Okay, girls," he said. "I know we wanted rough, but do you really have to tear some of the other girl's weaves out of their freakin' heads?"

Jackie Moore looked at me and we both laughed.

After several weeks that summer of working as babyfaces against the establishment, ODB and Jackie Moore "officially signed contracts" back in the mix on TV.

MORE TWITTER TROUBLE

Lisa Marie Varon and myself weren't the only ones who would catch heat for posting something unliked by the office on Twitter. There was also a tweet that went out from one of the announcers that had Kong fuming.

Now, first of all, I want to go on record to say that working with Kong was always easy. She was great to work with and a sweetheart in the locker room. Just like any other wrestler, we all have had our bad days. And I would argue that Kong had no more than anyone else.

There was an issue at one point, however, I think between her and Matt Hardy's wife, Reby Sky. Kong felt Sky didn't belong in the locker room, so she picked up her bags and put them out in the hallway. I think they had words over this, and since then, Kong has referred to Reby Sky by some choice words. That's about all I can tell you on that one.

The bigger thing people remember about Kong's time with TNA was right after there was a horrible earthquake in Haiti. TNA had just brought in a new interviewer who was coincidentally good friends with the Hogan regime. The idea was, if you were the mouthpiece of a large national platform, you could mention TNA on your other show and thus bring even more eyes to the product. This is one reason why TNA decided to bring in radio shock jock Bubba the Love Sponge.

Bubba was a radio personality known for his lack of political correctness. Much like Howard Stern, he was into gross humor, dick jokes, liquid ass fart spray gags, and burying whoever he had to bury as part of his shtick. He was mostly a heel on the airwaves, and coming from an indy wrestling background himself, he used carnie references on his radio show. Therefore, he was a good, edgy fit for TNA.

After the earthquake that destroyed most of Haiti, Bubba took the conservative viewpoint and didn't want massive tax dollars headed in that direction. Therefore, he tweeted, "I say fuck Haiti. Why do we have to take care of everybody? Our country is in shambles. – Bubba."

I guess his thought was that New Orleans was still a mess with storm damage from Hurricane Katrina. To his defense, that storm was then only four years old in the history books and there was still a lot to repair. However, that didn't excuse the mess that was happening in Haiti.

I am no political genius. I am not the person to talk to about how to spend government money or anything of the sort. However, maybe if Bubba wanted to say something like that, he could have done it in a better way.

Bubba took heat from the fans. He eventually gave in and released an apology, but it came off as too little too late.

Before the Monday night taping, after Bubba had made that tweet, the girls saw Kong in the locker room. She said she was going to kill him when she saw him and we figured she was just messing around. What we didn't realize at the time was that Kong had raised over $5,000 for Haiti relief and she felt personally insulted by Bubba.

Anyhow, to make a long story short, Kong did find Bubba during the taping. She speared him the very first chance she got. Then, she got up and punched him directly in the face.

"Haiti!" she screeched. "That is for Haiti!"

I was part of the pull apart group. Angelina Love and I pulled Kong out to the parking lot and calmed her down.

Both Bubba and Kong were sent home to cool off.

After that, there wasn't as much heat backstage on Kong as there was heat on Bubba. Either way, both of them ended up leaving the promotion pretty much right after that happened.

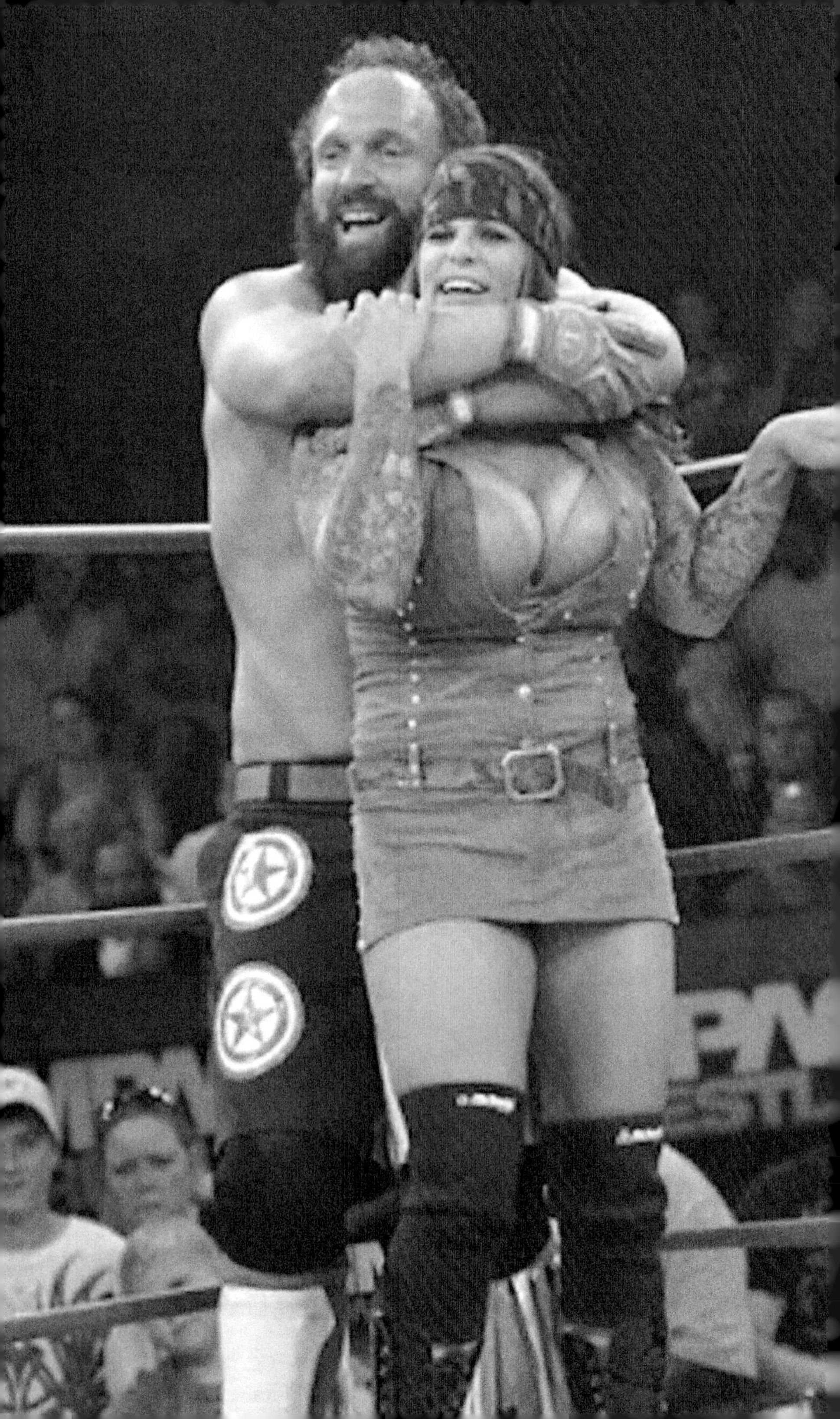

CHAPTER 9 - WORK HUSBAND

Earlier on, I talked about me having a work wife in the likes of Traci. However, many remember me for an ongoing angle I did with my "work husband," Eric Young.

"EY" as I called him was an awesome partner to have.

After graduating from high school, EY went right into training. He learned his craft from Waldo Von Erich up in Cambridge, Ontario Canada. After training for about 10 weeks, he had his first match in Benton Harbor, Michigan, against his friend "Suicide" Sean Ball in 1998.

After that, he kept trying to learn more and perfect his craft. He took on more training from Scott D'Amore and Chris Kanyon. Then he went to work on the independent circuit.

The independents just don't pay the bills when you are starting out. They don't even come close. It is not until you get some kind of television exposure from one of the major promotions that you can even dare ask for some kind of monetary payoff over $50. Sad, I know, but all the money goes to the name talent.

Like me, EY took on side hustles. Maybe that is an understatement. EY was a workaholic for sure. While I was bartending, EY was working in a pizza parlor, manufacturing brass horse harnesses, and sand casting. During his time in the Ontario independent scene, EY also set up his own wrestling camp, Wrestleplex, out of Cambridge. That gym would go on to produce Jake O'Reilly, Crazzy Steve, and also Shawn Spears.

Eventually through Scott D'Amore, EY showed up in TNA, where he would wrestle from 2004-2016. He immediately became a staple of the X Division. He would do a few years in his Canadian gimmick, move onto a feud with Bobby Roode, and then do some stuff with The Main Event Mafia. After that he worked some with Kevin Nash and X-Pac, then TNA decided to change his gimmick and made him turn nuts.

As the new TNA Television champion, EY's mental state led him to believe that the TV title meant he should only be defending against television stars. Therefore, he wrestled an *American Gladiator* (alum Matt Morgan) and also defended against TNA producer/former cast member of *The*

Wonder Years, Jason Hervey. After that, he went on a several-week- long trip to ultra-exotic land of Hollywood to find and eventually wrestle the great Scott Baio.

Seeing his comedy chops, it only made sense that he would end up working with me in some capacity. He had everything he needed to ride with ODB, after all, he was funny AND mentally unstable.

Come December 22, 2011, TNA randomly teamed me up with EY in a wild card tournament. After that pairing, TNA decided to have my character take on an on-screen relationship with EY. It led to a courtship and an eventual wedding ceremony!

The wedding itself was in a steel cage and was a very long segment. We had hoochie mamas come out and try to tempt EY away from me, but he wasn't having it. In the end, we both were in our underwear (a nod to pillow fighting whores) and even had the preacher disrobe. It was a crazy thing to see, but the fans loved it. Still today, that is one of my most favorite interview segments ever.

When I got to the back, incidentally, one of the first people to come over and congratulate me was the Hulkster.

"That was just great, brother!" he said complimenting me. "You guys nailed it!"

Coming from him, that meant a lot. Here he was, one of the biggest names of all time, taking time out to tell me he enjoyed my work.

Despite the little girl in me who didn't like Hulk, I gave him a big hug with tears in my eyes. (It might have been awkward for the Hulkster because I was still in my bra and panties, but who the hell cares.)

Working with EY was fun. I know a lot of times they would give us some bullet points that they wanted to get accomplished for promos and just let us have at it. EY liked to improv, as did I. He also didn't give a shit about anything. We had both been there a while and were confident in our abilities. Therefore, when they would ask us to do a promo on the fly, they knew we could.

I do know, however, that sometimes we would just be ridiculous. We would shoot a promo, acting so crazy that the writers would shake their heads.

"Okay, do it again," they would laugh. "One more time."

Sometimes that "one more time" would end up being 10 or 12 takes and we would never know which version of the promo they would end up using. We did know, however, that whatever they picked was going to be slightly insane because all of it was.

EY was super gifted, and other people noticed. The Animal Planet channel contacted him and offered him a deal. They were ready to shoot an American reality television series that would make him an even bigger star and give him exposure to an entirely different demographic. He accepted, and the show turned into him traveling out each week to meet and fish with the most unusual fishermen that he could find.

EY then took on two schedules that were pretty conflicting. TNA was great about letting him go off and film his own show, *Off the Hook: Extreme Catches*. It was twice as much work as he thought it was going to be, but he told me it was worth it.

I was happy for him. He had an amazing experience, and it was something I knew he should be super proud of. During this time, around mid-2012, EY was gone from TNA a lot doing his thing. His pairing with me kept his name alive, and I would just fill in a lot in his absence. Most of the time that he was gone, he was not in the same state or sometimes not even the same country. But TNA knew that his absence was worth it in order to let him cross promote. It was a good thing for TNA, Spike TV, and Animal Planet. That little fishing show brought extra eyes to TNA, and vice versa.

CHOKED UP IN ERIC'S ABSENCE

Before one particular TNA show, I remember coming into the arena early to get ready to figure out what I was doing for the night. EY had "gone fishing" as they say, still out shooting episodes of his show for Animal Planet.

I went over to a white board where they had all the matches mapped out and were putting together the card, before going over it with the wrestlers.

It read: Tara & Gail Kim vs. Miss Tessmacher & ODB

I had worked with them a bunch so I knew it would be good. I started running over some ideas quickly in my head when I was interrupted from someone behind me.

"I just saw our boy on TMZ!" a familiar voice said.

I didn't need to turn around. It was Ken Anderson, and he didn't need to specify who he was talking about.

"Did you say TMZ?"

"Yes, I did."

"Shawn?"

"Yeah!" he said laughing. "I guess some guy was fucking around, making death threats to passengers on a train up in Minnesota. He choked the motherfucker out."

"No way!"

"Way."

"Holy shit."

With my current partner, EY, out and about making waves outside the wrestling world, it seemed my older partner and arguable first work husband, Shawn Daivari, was doing the same thing. The difference was that Daivari wasn't on a reality show, he was on something even more real than that – the freakin' news!

Headlines were breaking everywhere about my previous "work husband."

I found links to the story online and even the actual video on YouTube!

"Shawn Daivari, who has worked for WWE and TNA, brought the scripted world of pro wrestling into the real world when he choked out a man threatening to kill another passenger on a Minnesota train."

The security footage showed good old Daivari just sitting there, minding his own business when some drunk guy named Levin Blair got into the railcar.

The drunk guy is clearly out of it, and Daivari is just watching the shit show before him with a front row seat when another guy gets on the train. The new passenger tries to put his bike on a rack, and Blair threatened him. Shit goes sideways, and another passenger tries to calm everyone down, asking Blair to sit down.

The drunk guy threatens to kill him, so they hit the security call button. The problem was, the passengers were still mid-route with the train moving, and nobody was able to come save them.

The drunken Blair dude then got up in the passenger's face and was about to make things violent. Daivari got up, summoning all the strength of The Iron Sheik that he could, to "make Blair humble."

He immediately put the bastard into a rear naked choke that would make Samoa Joe proud. The assailant spilled out onto the floor, and that wasn't the only thing spilling.

Pissssss...

When Daivari took him down, he apparently body-scissored the guy so hard that he made him pee! Yes, you can't make this shit up. In all the coverage, it was reported that the man's bladder gave, or in other words, the motherfucker pissed himself.

Daivari squeezed the juice right out of him like he was an orange.

The footage is great. It even shows the finish. We see the train pull up to the next stop with Daivari throwing the guy out onto the deck for officials to deal with.

If you haven't seen this on YouTube, you should look it up right now.

I will wait...

It's awesome, right?

Daivari is the man.

In some cases, the newscasters laughed a little over the idea of a wrestler having to do some real "fighting" in their delivery, but for the most part they were positive about the story. A neat little message was being reported on an international platform about wrestlers. From what I was seeing, the gist of things was very positive for pro wrestling.

Most of the journalists were reporting that wrestlers were in fact badass and not to be taken lightly.

"What people don't know is that these wrestlers are legitimate athletes," one said.

"They have had real trainers if they have been employed for a wrestling company," another said. "You don't want to mess around with any of them."

"These guys have like MMA and fighting backgrounds," another reported. "Even though they get paid to perform what some think is fake fighting, they really know how to fight."

Everything seemed to portray Daivari and the business in a positive light. This was a good thing.

Unfortunately for Daivari, it was a non-title match, so Blair retained his Minnesota Piss-Drunk championship belt.

THE BREAK UP

Come the next year or so, EY thanked me for putting him over so hard when he wasn't around on TNA programming. I always made it a point to work his name in whenever he wasn't around if I had mic time, and he appreciated me for this.

His gratitude was manifested in inviting me onto his show as a guest for the June 23, 2013, episode.

When I asked permission from the TNA officials to go and shoot the show with him, there were no issues and they let me go do it. However, strangely enough, there was some foul play and politics after the fact in which I will discuss more in detail in the next chapter.

Dixie Carter at it again.

It didn't matter. I always made sure my work was so good they couldn't deny me my due. I went on to hold the women's title four times, whether Dixie liked it or not. I can't stress enough the importance of a good work ethic. Hard work pays off.

EY out of the picture was a missing piece of the puzzle, however. It was not EY's fault, but I was sometimes booked on the back burner when he was away.

I remember one time, they flew me into Texas for *Lockdown*, but when I got there, I saw the card and my name was nowhere to be found. I soon learned that they had no intention of using me.

"What are you doing here?" one of the guys backstage said when they saw me.

It was another clear case of the people in charge not communicating with each other.

Eventually, EY's athletic ability was beyond evident to everyone and they started to fizzle out our angle together. They figured they were wasting him by putting him with me, and maybe they were right.

CHAPTER 9 – Work Husband

When EY finally won the TNA championship in Orlando, I asked one of the agents backstage, "should I go out to celebrate? I am his wife, right?"

They agreed, but the writing was on the wall for one of my most memorable angles. When EY went serious, they scrapped our connection for the most part.

Eventually, I do want to work on a divorce angle at *IMPACT!* if we are ever both on the same card, for the fans. I think that would be funny, but the opportunity where it would make sense just hasn't happened yet.

In a recent interview, EY had this to say about his time working with his work wife:

"On working with ODB, she is easily the most interesting piece of the puzzle. Yeah, that's for sure. I mean she's just awesome, man. An absolute pro. The most popular woman wrestler, I've ever seen. Everywhere we go, I can't wrestle without the fans still chanting her name. And she's not even there. She's not even wrestling! So, she's one of my really good friends in the business. Awesome to work with. And an absolute pro. She is the greatest."

Thanks, EY!

CHAPTER 10 - FISHING FOR A FUTURE

Wrestling and acting quite often go hand-in-hand, so when I was asked if I wanted to go shoot a horror movie with a bunch of wrestlers in it, I was all over it.

Death from Above is a 2011 horror film that was put together by director Bruce Koehler. The film featured professional wrestling stars Kurt Angle, Sid Eudy, Rhyno, James Storm, Matt Morgan, and yours truly.

I would say that *Death from Above* was a low budget film, but that would be an insult to low budget films. To many, it probably looked like someone just walked into a TNA locker room and started handing out scripts to the first people they ran into. It was bad quality and bad writing, but I figured you have to start somewhere.

The story was a little tough to follow. There was an ancient Druid on a quest to rule the world. Kurt Angle's character becomes possessed and is looking for these magic necklaces. He randomly kills people in order to steal their motorcycles, cars, or trucks to continue his search. He does so by stabbing the shit out of anyone who gets in his way. Psycho Sid finally shows up at the end to take the demon guy back to whatever realm he came from. He chokes the guy out and it ends. If you love pro wrestling and monster trucks, then *Death from Above* is the movie is for you. For me, it was pretty much unmemorable, and didn't make me crave more gigs from the acting world.

I wasn't exactly bit by the acting bug.

Soon after that, however, I appeared on EY's show. As I wrote in the last chapter, I appeared on the June 23, 2013, episode of Animal Planet's *Off the Hook: Extreme Catches* which was head over heels a better production than the horror flick I had just done.

That show had the potential to put EY on the map. EY's stumbling into Hollywood was inspiring. He is the one who convinced me to keep my eyes open, and made me believe that a wrestler could take on other performing roles that didn't include zombies.

I did know this – *a plan B is essential*. I had seen the washed-up guys come through the TNA locker room, and even worse, the ones on the independent scene who had to continue to wrestle even though their bodies were falling apart. I knew that wrestling was a gig you could only do for just so long as a performer. At some point, your body just can't take it anymore, we all know this. I'm a durable person. My body is built to get beat up, to be honest, but eventually I knew it was going to break and I had to start thinking of doing something else.

At this point, I didn't know what my next move was.

EY also knew the deal. Wrestling could only last so long. You can't do this forever. Nobody is built to be a pro wrestler forever. It's a very physical profession. To travel, to take the bumps and bruises, to put in all the long hours – it's all a very grueling and unnatural thing to put your body through.

I guess one of EY's friends was doing some work in production for Animal Planet, and one day she saw a job opening. She knew he wanted to move over to something else on TV other than wrestling if the opportunity arose. This one particular posting stuck out. It said they were looking for a host for a fishing show and wanted someone funny who was comfortable in front of the camera. She sent them a link of EY on YouTube and just like that… he was hired.

He was a natural. Even though he was a fish out of water, he didn't need to be a professional fisherman to do well. The situations they put him into did that for him. He went from catching sharks from a paddleboard to scuba spearfishing under an oil rig. He got to meet all these crazy characters, maniacs that would fish 20 hours straight with no sleep. All of the funny stuff that would happen on the show came easy to EY who was great at improv.

MY FISHING TRIP

So question: what does it look like when a former wrestler jumps out of the ring and into the ocean. Answer: Wet. (And cold!)

"So what will the show be like?" I asked Eric.

"It might not be the biggest show on the planet, but it will bring you a new audience," he said. "People who don't know you. That's always good. That's the goal, right, to get known by more people after we are done."

"Yeah?" I asked.

"I get stopped now in the airport, but now by young kids that don't watch wrestling. Boys who like to fish. Also like their sisters, girls like 12 saying they watch the show and they love it. They don't like fishing because fish are 'gross', but they say it's funny and a fun show to watch."

He was right. *Unlikely fans broaden your brand.*

Eric was throwing all kinds or weird stunts into his show (like unusual and often dangerous fishing methods) to get ratings. He was getting hunter-types, as well as people who liked comedy, and the whole Jackass stunt type of demographic to tune in. One episode had him scuba-diving in pantyhose trying to catch a sand shark and succeeding!

Part of the fun, apparently, was keeping it edgy but not dirty with EY's filthy mouth. He was smart. He knew that Animal Planet was not a huge fan of his colorful choice of words at times, but his approach would make the show stand out from the rest on the channel. He also knew kids watched his shows. Therefore, he would cuss and get bleeped, but just wouldn't talk with too much racy content, or anything. He just pushed it the right amount.

For my episode, we were off to an ice festival in sunny Minnesota. It is funny because in all the hype they billed me as EY's actual wife. The press picked up on this so we stayed kayfabe. I played off the whole idea I didn't like him leaving home for long periods of time to go on fishing trips, and I also didn't much care for the cold myself.

Minnesota has a yearly shindig – a huge ice fishing tournament/party called the *Eelpout Festival*. It is held on a frozen lake and attracts sometimes more than 10,000 partygoers. Our episode was perfect for me, a native of the state, born and raised, of course.

It is explained in the opening credits of the show that EY is an extreme adrenaline junkie ready to fish with some help from the craziest extreme experts in the world. So I showed up to the festival on ice with Animal Planet to help him with what I do best – *party!*

Eric started the "cold open" (pardon the pun) by saying, "My beard is freezing, and I'm risking frost bite." Then he cannonballed into the water! I mean, it was the middle of freaking winter. He just came back from a stop at Garrison in Minnesota where he did some ice biking, and I don't think he was even thawed out yet. (Yes, 80 miles per hour dirt biking on ice. Did I also mention he's nuts?)

For our segment, however, I wasn't there to help with the fishing. I was there to help with the biggest ice party on the planet part.

Now, Eelpout is a rare fish that only spawn in the winter. They have some weird fetish, I guess. They like to do it right under the ice, literally. So the best time is also the coldest time in Minnesota, and that is the only real time you can catch those suckers.

Eelpout is not actually an eel. It is a cod family, and it's good eatin' fish so vendors crowd the place with their foods, frying up fish all over the place like a county fair.

Like most television shows, this one was shot out of sequence. Before the polar plunge, we started drinking beers with the locals, sitting on house furniture and couches in front of an ice fishing holes. We visited bonfires, and joined in the fun making frozen smores on fishing poles, while some of them were fishing and waiting for a bite.

Soon after that, Animal Planet took us off to a tent to warm up, before being whisked off to the "Bikini Ice Fishing Team" which I thought was ridiculous. Here I was, freaking freezing like hell, and these girls practically had their tits out like they were in Miami.

For that segment, anyhow, Eric was basically surrounded by a bunch of hot whores showing him how to drill with some big green ice-driller that looked like a weed whacker.

I watched all of this unfold in front of me thinking all I could about the situation: "Damn, it is cold."

For the week event, they said it got to be 50 below with wind chill. It was 5 degrees out (a heat wave) when Eric actually jumped in the water for the plunge spot. Animal Planet knew that would cramp things up, so they got a ton of other footage in first knowing he would be a frozen mess.

They were right, too. Right after he climbed out of the water, he said it felt like jumping into broken glass and was off to bundle up for an hour or so.

"Serious shrinkage," he said. "But $500 for charity."

After that, there was a spring break-like bikini contest on our side of the lake which I stayed around for, almost like a news correspondent to that part of the show. However, when Eric finally melted, he was back off to business – to the other side of the lake to film the fishing part of the show with pro fisher Jeff Anderson, who pulled up on a snow mobile.

They picked a sweet spot with the hopes to compete in "the biggest fish" category of the contest rather than catching the most. Eric caught a 4-pounder within like the first five minutes, a juicy yellow slimy one, but then nothing after that for hours. Not even a nibble. We continued to get updates in our area from a producer who was getting calls from the camera man shooting EY. After that, I'm glad I continued to shoot where I was at the party end of things. There was plenty of warmth there where I was stationed, but it dropped to -18 by nightfall on EY's side of the lake.

He had beard icicles.

Finally, a second bite came. The final fish EY caught was 8.10 pounds and that got him into the official contest. In the end, he ultimately came in 11th place. However, everything was fun and that wasn't the worst part of the whole thing, by far.

The worst part was TNA decided that they didn't want my segment airing on the actual show on the channel.

What the hell?

TNA requested to use my footage to promote the show as part of the agreement they had with Animal Planet. Rather than to plug the show during *Impact!*, they wanted to just jack my footage and show my segments as their own content. When Animal Planet resisted this idea, I am told that TNA threatened to make things difficult with EY's availability.

So despite the fact that I was advertised on all the promotional stuff for the actual episode, they pulled the footage and just aired my segments on TNA television. If you go to Amazon Prime now to watch the episode, you won't see me, despite my name being in the credits.

That's right, something smelled fishy then and still does today.

Dixie you bitch!

Once again, the grizzled ring vet in me knows that Dixie didn't like me. I saw evidence of this countless times and even heard it from another of people she confided in. She thought I didn't look like the "hot and sexy" girl division they wanted to promote so she didn't let me get my character out to a bigger and different audience. We can't show the world that TNA had women who looked like me on their programming, after all. Guys won't tune in.

That's typical Dixie for you.

PAYING BILLS

It's true. I didn't play the sexy bitch at TNA. I played the anti-sexy bitch. I was good at it, too.

I am not really into some of the aspects of where the business is evolving. While women are being treated more as equals now to some degree, and there are less bra and panty matches and sexualization going on as a whole, there is further evidence that the future of the industry is going in a direction that I don't like. To put it bluntly, sometimes it is just plain gross.

When some people come out to see me at an appearance, sometimes they ask, "why don't you wrestle anymore?" Currently, I'm pretty busy with plan B and the next chapter of my life which I will discuss further in the next chapter of this book. But there are also a few things happening in pro wrestling that I am not a big fan of.

As much as you might think I am crazy and outspoken from what you see on television, I am pretty shy at heart. To each their own, but I don't agree with milking fans into buying me gifts off of an Amazon Wishlist, and some of the shit that Sunny does like showing her tits and spreading her bum bum on OnlyFans. It is fine if you disagree, but I will call a spade a spade. That's not wrestling. If I can see your chocolate starfish, that's a porno.

Wrestling merchandise is one thing. That goes hand-in-hand with being a part of a wrestler's income. I know there are collectors out there who like wrestling memorabilia. There are some who collect autographs, action figures, and wrestling belts. When you have someone who maybe wants a ring-worn costume, I'm sort of okay with that. However, one time, Angelina Love had a fan who wanted to buy a pair of her tights for a very high amount. However, after the offer, he went on to tell her matter-of-factly that they be heavily worn, and specifically "not washed."

Not washed? You sick, sick, motherfucker.

Some of the girls sell their panties online, and get even more money when they are "heavily worn." Gag! This kind of thing, in my opinion, is crossing a line. It's also kind of sketchy when you go out to a show and see fans, and one comes up to you and thanks you for selling them your panties. Again, to each their own, but if we are out there saying we want equal rights with the guys, the seller shouldn't enable the smeller.

AGENTS

Some guys are doing a great job these days living off of their limited run on TV. If you got any sort of play by one of the bigger promotions, you can walk right into comic-cons and toy fairs and make a whole living off of signing pictures.

What has happened is wrestlers have found a whole life after the ring where they can sign autographs to make a living. There are public signings and personal ones in hotel rooms and even live ones streaming online these days. These are all fine and dandy, but I think most wrestlers would agree that it does suck to charge fans money for an autograph. A solution for this over the years is for wrestlers to hire an agent.

An agent will find the booking, or create a venue for the signing. They will promote it. They will pay the wrestler ahead of time and usually work out the transportation. The wrester gets some kind of guarantee usually, like a flat rate. And then sometimes they get a piece of the action, like a percentage of the sales. This formula on paper is good because then the wrestler doesn't have to be put into the uncomfortable position of asking a fan for $20 when they take a picture with someone or sign an autograph. The agent does all of that. They are literally the money man.

The problem is, however, anyone can and will call themselves an agent. There is no training for this. There is no certificate or license. Because of this, the agent direction the business is going in is one of the things I don't often care for because it is sometimes bad for business.

There is this whole thing now where hardcore fans call themselves agents just so they can pay to be with a wrestler. They book wrestlers to do these shitty appearances and want to drive you around in their car for the weekend like they own you. Think of this as a live in-person Cameo video that never stops for them.

No thank you.

I want to make it very clear: some agents are legit and do a great job and make money for everyone, but some of these "agents" are not agents, or promoters or anything of the sort at all. They are fans, or egomaniacs. They also can be real assholes that treat wrestlers like shit.

I don't want to get into a shitty car that smells like cheese and armpits. I do not want to go out to eat with you and your friends while you show me off like you own me. I do not want to do a loop with you sitting by my side and making me feel weird for hours on end enduring your pent up whatever and mommy issues.

Tell me where to go, and I will show up. I will do the appearance, but that's it.

Some of these guys want you on the clock for three days solid, 24-hours a day legit.

These days, getting into those cars with one of these agents who is wearing dirty sweatpants and smells like fish piss is hell. That is not my idea of a good means of income. I would rather take a shift at White Castle's to be perfectly honest with you than to be a sideshow attraction for one of these weird ringleaders.

So "F.U." to all you weird wannabe agents. You know who you are.

Because of these weirdos, when my full-time status with TNA came to an end in 2014, I knew I needed to plan for a future outside the ring.

Who knew my plan B would spawn out of a trailer park, a pile of food, and a former boy band singer?

SLOTH & CHUNK'S
Rocky Roooaaad?

AIRSTREAM
KEEP CALM AND CHIVE ON

CHAPTER 11 – BOY BANDS & FAMILY RECIPES

      I didn't know where I was going to end up in a life after wrestling world. One thing I did know, however, is that I wanted to live off of my savings and travel. I didn't know where I was heading and figured that some of that finding out would come from the journey. My thought was when wrestling dried up for me, I would go where life would book me, no matter what the road. In order to do this, I needed just the right wheels.

      Somewhere around this time, I decided to go old school. All the best old wrestlers practiced being cheap bastards the best they could to survive. With the same mentality as my OVW days, I decided to start saving the money I made. Since a wrestler spent a shitload on hotels, I decided to practice using my own accommodations to get by. Therefore, in 2013, I bought a sexy 1978 International Airstream.

      That beast was a 30-foot mobile house on wheels.

      That purchase was an investment. It was like having a bunch of hotel rooms paid for up front. After it was all paid off, I figured everything would be gravy. I was right, but I just didn't know that it would be gravy and beef perhaps at the same time.

      Once I got my mobile home, I would wrestle and then I would sleep right in the Airstream. I would just pull right up to the TNA show, do my gig, and walk out to the lot for bed!

      I wasn't one of Bob Ryder's boys that he owned. I didn't have the deal where I had to throw some of my indy paydays back to the company after they found a higher paying gig for me somewhere to go wrestle for in the name of TNA. I could just go wherever I wanted and keep all the money for myself. I also didn't tell them, just in case.

      I started doing higher paying independent gigs and they would always pay me extra for hotel and transportation. I would often wrestle and then pull up to a Walmart somewhere and go to sleep.

      Now that I have outed myself in the "not telling TNA about my independent gigs" department and giving them a piece of a gig that I put together as an independent contractor, I only have one thing left to say on the topic: *Screw you Dixie! XOXO*

TIME TO EAT

One time, I was at a TNA show. It was a few hours before they needed me, so I was in my Airstream getting ready for a photo shoot. I jumped out of my mobile home to grab something to eat. They had a little spread set aside for the wrestlers. It wasn't like the big deal that WWE used to do, but when I came around a corner, I did a full on double take. I was walking down the hall, just minding my own business and playing with my phone. I wasn't paying attention for like five seconds and ended up bumping into someone.

My eyes bugged out of my head.

"What in the world?"

No, I hadn't walked in on Dixie Carter in a filthy five-way with four midgets. I was standing shoulder-to-shoulder with one fifth of NSYNC. Yes, the very boy band that provided the soundtrack as I traveled with Traci Brooks high and low and to practically every doldrum across America. I felt like I already knew him.

"Joey Fatone?" I asked, trying my absolute hardest not to mark out.

"Um, yes?"

Of course, it was him. Fatone was from Orlando. I guess he had found his way backstage before, just not on my watch unfortunately. I would soon find out that he was a big wrestling fan and had since stayed in contact and befriended some of the TNA guys. I just hadn't heard about any of this before.

Fortunately for me, I just came out of makeup. Quite often I would run around in sweats and just wear whatever, but out of the grace of God, I was all dazzled up for some kind of shoot that they were doing. I stopped and there he was. For once, I was so happy that I didn't look like shit.

I will be the first one to admit that most wrestlers don't mark out for other wrestlers as much as they do for people that are famous in other fields of entertainment. We work with wrestlers every day, but it isn't often that we get to hang out with big name actors, or musicians. This is why when you do come across someone famous outside of your field of study, you hope to make a decent impression more so than with wrestlers who have smelled your bad breath or body odor so many times before.

"Oh, shit. You're Joey Fatone," I said.

"It's gonna be me," he said. (Okay, he didn't really say that, but never let the truth get in the way of a good story.)

I went on to introduce myself.

"I know you," he said. "I like your stuff with Eric Young."

I was impressed. He knew pro wrestling, and not just WWE!

We clicked. We talked for a good 10 minutes about the similarities between the wrestling world and the music industry. He was a super nice guy.

Later that night before the show started, I was about to get ready for my match when an unfamiliar face approached me. I figured it was some kind of employee or something who just wanted a picture.

"Hey, ODB?" he asked.

"Yeah?"

"I'm Joe's manager," he said.

I looked him over quickly, trying to figure out who he meant by Joe, or who he even was.

No, I don't know him. He probably wants a selfie.

When he said "manager," my mind immediately went to the concept of "wrestling manager" and thought this was someone new I was going to have to work with in the future.

"Samoa Joe?"

"I wish," he said. "No, Joey... Fatone."

"Oh, OH!" I laughed. "Joey's awesome."

"Sorry to bug you before your match," he said. "But I saw you talking with him before."

"Oh, yeah. He's cool. No problem."

"He asked me to go find out," he said. "Joey was wondering if you like to hang out and get drinks, like after the show?"

"Drink? Us? Ha, yes, of course!" I said, joking. "We're pro wrestlers. That's like part of the job description."

"That's what he figured."

"Do you guys want to come with us?"

"Yes, I think that would be fun," he said. "Joey's a big fan and would love the invite."

And fun it was. After the show, we all went out to some bar, and Fatone fit right in. It was like he was one of the boys. He ordered some rounds, and was doing shots. He was telling stories about Justin Timberlake. It was all cool.

Before we said "Bye Bye Bye," we asked him to come to the PPV next week.

"You have to come," EY said.

"Maybe we can get you on the show," I said. "Do you have any boots?"

Joey Fatone looked at his manager, almost for permission. His manager fumbled through a calendar on his phone and nodded. And to our surprise, a week later he did just that. Joey Fatone was in the IMPACT ZONE.

Joey knew the deal. He got to the PPV early enough that we were able to both pitch the idea to the writers and also write him into a storyline. He was ecstatic, like the proverbial kid in a candy store.

What we did was we made a little angle where EY was all pissed off, and he was being very jealous of Joey Fatone. It was pretty funny, and Joey played the role great.

After that, I stayed in touch with him, and he came to a few more of our shows. Then one day he called me up out of the blue.

"Listen, Jessie," he said. "Now I did your show, so you have to do mine."

He pitched me the idea this time.

"Hmmm," I said playing hard to get. "I don't know."

"Come on!" he said. "It will be fun."

"Honestly," I said, waiting a beat to make him nervous. "I probably would have done it either way with the pitch or without."

So, it was set.

The dirt sheets read, "TNA Knockout ODB is scheduled to appear on former NSYNC member Joey Fatone's *My Family Recipe Rocks* television show, on the Live Well Network. The episode featuring ODB is to be taped next week!"

FAMILY RECIPE

My Family Recipe Rocks was a 30-minute television cooking show produced for the Live Well Network in Fresno, California and hosted by Joey Fatone. Running for three seasons, starting back in 2012, it featured people of all walks of life from Carrot Top to Carnie Wilson. For my episode, just like the flavor of the whole show, Joey wanted it to look different than the typical cooking show set in a professional kitchen. I had just the right idea for what they were looking for that would also compliment my character well.

Joey grew up around a big Italian family. He prided himself on knowing about home-cooked meals and the point of the show was to tap into the dishes that different people's relatives had passed down from generation to generation. The show's concept was to have him travel the world and find some of the best cooks out there, and find their secrets, right in their own domains. For this episode of *My Family Recipe Rocks*, I continued to play hard to get and in the spirit of the show, I made Joey come to my stomping grounds, north of the Twin Cities to Clear Lake, Minnesota.

I knew I had my new '78 Airstream and that it would look really badass on TV, so I suggested we shoot the episode in my mobile home! To go along with my wrestling persona, I figured we should film the episode on location from a real-life trailer park, but not just any trailer park. We chose a thematically particular, high-end Airstream-only trailer park that only allowed vintage Airstreams through their gates.

My whole family was invited to give the episode that homey feel that Joey was looking for. We played up on the camping aesthetic by having everyone circle around a fire. Joey had never really been camping before, so it was perfect.

The show did a pretty cool bio on me, explaining to a new audience who I was and where I came from. After that, it was all up to me to provide content.

I didn't have any sort of formal cooking background. I bartended some, for sure. I mean, behind the bar, I was a natural. It only made sense from all the hours I spent sitting in front of a bar that some of this knowledge would be absorbed and thus I could handle the action on the other side. At the time of this episode, I was bartending at a place called Courtside Bar & Grill in Anoka, Minnesota. But I have to admit, I wasn't really a cook at all. I was more of a drink specialist. I did, however, have certain things I liked to cook for camping trips, so I decided to just roll with my little dishes and share what I was comfortable with: *comfort food!*

Around the campfire, I got my menu together for the show. I booked the card to include Bean Dip, Wacko Taco, Campfire Cone, and Bloody Marys (with the card subject to change.)

We started with the Bloody Mary. I had a friend and fellow bartender, Lynn Jerentosky, come to pass down her original Bloody Mary recipe to start my segment. We had known each other for a long time and I mentioned how we played bar BINGO together and also ran meat raffles as a side hustle. After that, we explained how I adopted her recipe adding my own custom ODB garnish to the drink.
This included an olive (O), a deviled egg (D), and a piece of bacon (B) on a skewer.

Very creative, and very delicious, *I know. So* was everything else. The idea was to make some Minnesota rough-it life-hack recipes that you could throw together at a campground and just grub.

Here are some other throw-together white trash recipes from the *My Family Recipes Rock* show...

One Dirty Bean Dip
1 Can of refried beans
1 Block of cream cheese
1 Package of Velveeta cheese
1 Can of Hormel chili

COOK: Put it in your crock pot and let that shit stew. When it bubbles, time to shut it off. BAM – you are done.

Campfire Cones
1 Package of ice cream cones
1 Bag of marshmallows
1 Bag of chocolate chips

COOK: Fill the damn cone with marshmallows and chocolate chips to your heart's content. Then, wrap the son-of-a-bitch up in tin foil. Finally, throw that shit in your bonfire for a few.

Taco in a Bag
1 Small Doritos bag
1 Bowl of ground beef
1 Container of salsa
1 Tub of sour cream
ADD: Cheese, lettuce, diced tomatoes

DISCLAIMER: Now, this is as trashy as it gets. It is a Minnesota thing. You open the Doritos bag very carefully on the top and pour in all the contents on top of the chips to taste. If you like it hot, slap some hot sauce in there too. Then, once it is nice and full, close the bag and crunch it all up. Bam! Taco in a bag. Now you can walk and talk and eat… and not worry about dropping your food.

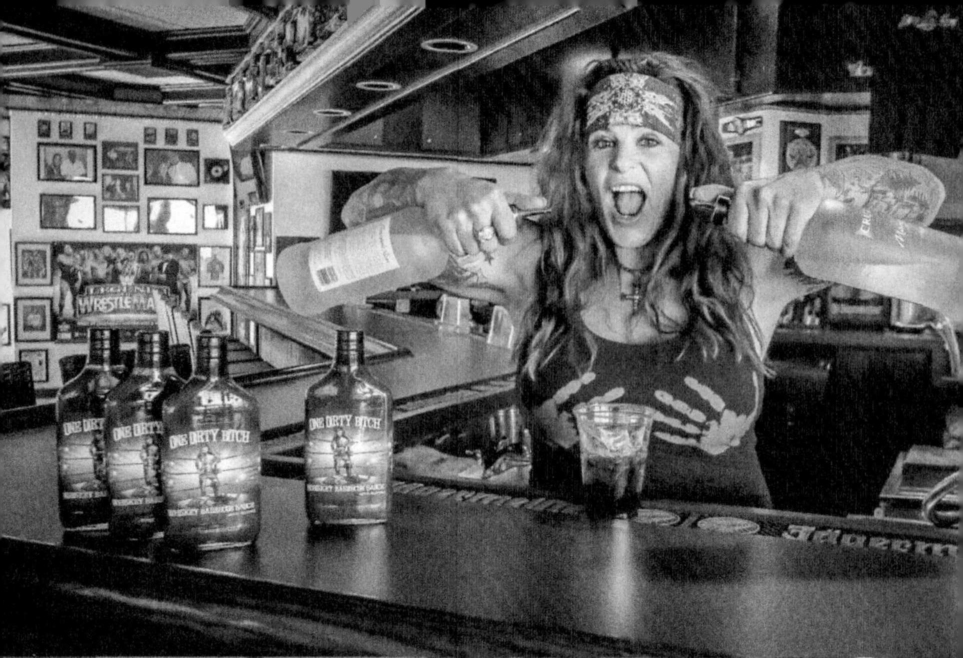
ONE DIRTY BITCH

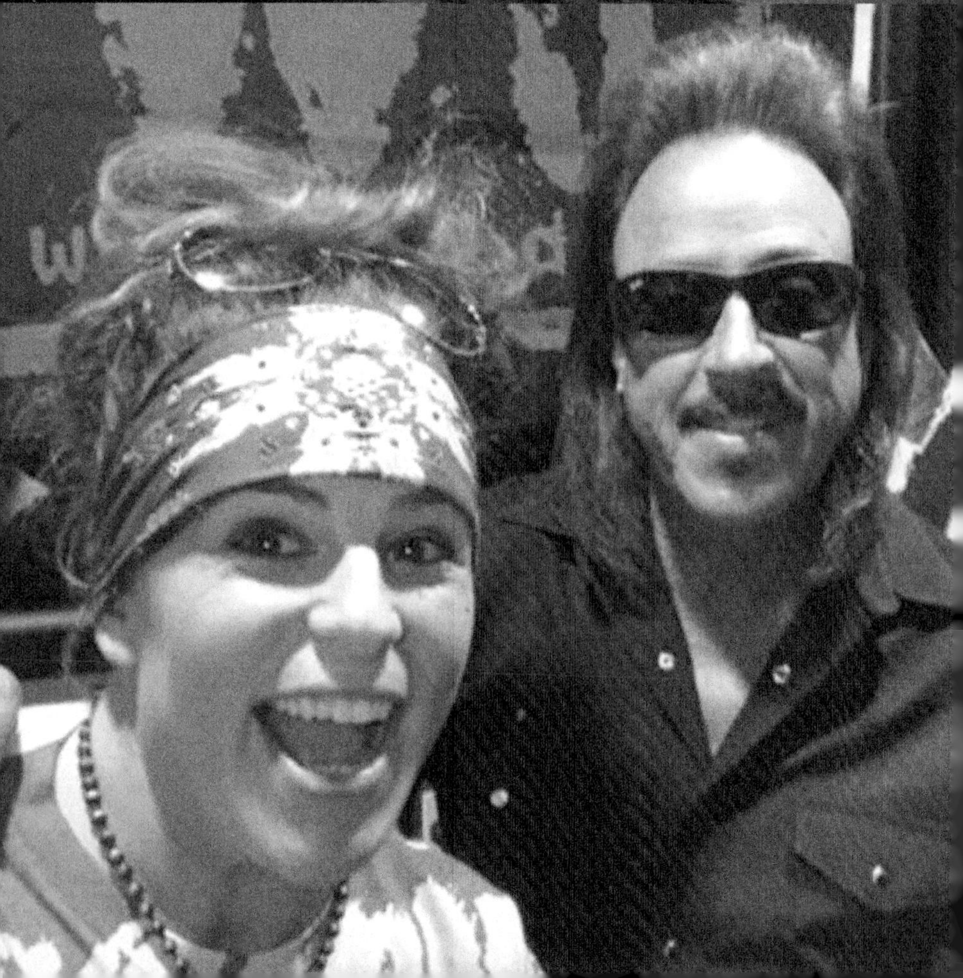

CHAPTER 12 – ONE DIRTY BARTENDER

Eventually, I saw a glimmer of light at the end of the tunnel. I didn't know what it was. It was distant at first. It was far away and blurry. But every passing year, I was walking down that dark unknown hall toward my future, step by step, reaching closer to the end of all I really knew. Over time, I could see it was coming closer and closer.

I knew my full-time wrestling career was near the end.

Is there life after wrestling?

This is a question that countless professional wrestlers ask themselves in the twilight of their careers.

After doing EY's show and seeing how Joey Fatone reinvented himself to the world, I knew I could do the same. I could reinvent myself, just like they did. I could transition into something else. I just wasn't sure exactly where my new world was going to be. I stayed positive, however. I knew I just needed to keep my feelers out there and listen.

I was a hustler. I developed a universal skill craved by many, and that was my work ethic. That is what I knew.

When my spot aired on Fatone's recipe show, I got a call. It was from a company called Pepper Palace. They asked me if I wanted to change up my brand a little and sell my own barbecue sauce.

The gears started spinning a little.

"Hmm. Well," I replied to the faceless voice on the other end of the phone. "As an ODB sauce, I suppose we would need whiskey in it, if I did."

I didn't know it but that was the beginning of plan B.

Food.

Pepper Palace figured out how to make my whiskey sauce happen, but the rest was up to me. The end of the tunnel was blurry and still hard to see, but I could smell it. Something told me, my journey was going to be food-related.

Switching from sports entertainment to food entertainment wasn't going to be easy though. I suspected that the long road ahead was going to be a food fight.

I knew I had to reinvent myself from being a wrestler, to being a wrestler backing food. I needed to invest in myself and make a brand.

I knew I could sell my product online to wrestling fans, but I figured why limit myself to that? People like barbeque sauce, why not expand to everyone else beyond wrestling?

Doing a little research, I came to find out that just like the comic-cons that a lot of wrestlers find a second income at from doing appearances, there were also food-cons, so to speak. There were food industry events and tradeshows happening all over the nation, I just didn't know anything about that world.

In order to reach an even bigger demographic than the wrestling fans, I knew I needed my own sauce on hand, for wherever I might be and whomever I might meet. Yes, it probably would be cheaper to print on demand so to speak, but physically having the product in front of me felt like the way to go. I didn't want to hand a potential customer, or God forbid, a potential grocery store product buyer, a business card or flyer with my website on it. I wanted to give them a show, and then give them a taste to get hooked.

Listening to my gut, I stocked up on my own supply and decided to go explore the food convention world.

I found contacts and began to register as a vendor.

At first, I made some mistakes. I booked tables at some conventions that were a bad match and a total disaster both in selling product and making connections.

One of my early best ones was for an event called Zest Fest in Dallas, Texas. I signed up for a hot sauce convention, and then had Pepper Palace hook me up with the product. When that big event arrived, I wasn't used to the protocol. When I pulled up to the convention center downtown with my Airstream, I didn't know where to go. So, I parked right out front, only a few steps away from the main entrance. Little did I know (or maybe I did but played stupid) that the logo on my truck was going to act as an advertisement for everyone walking in. My ride became a portable billboard! When people came in, I was one of the first tables they saw.

Now, I don't know how many of you know Virgil, but he is one of the biggest hustlers in the game. He sets up his merch table anywhere he can to make a buck. My man will even set up in the subway if he thinks he is going to get enough traffic to work someone for a $20 picture. Anyhow, he once said that if you set up your table right after the ticket table, you hit the fans first. That means if they only have $20, you have the first crack at it. You don't risk them walking around all the booths and spending their pocket money before they get to you. Hell, Virgil is such a worker, he sets up his table in front of the ticket booth out in the hall (or even on the street) so that he can milk fans before they can spend their money to even get into the event!

Boy was he right. On that day, my table was right inside the doorway; it was like one of the first things people saw when they came through the doors. And seeing how they just saw my Airstream, I sold product hand over fist that day. That was just great because it gave me even more capital to invest in my own product.

After that, I decided to explore my options even more. I traveled to a bunch of biker conventions, including the big one at Sturgis that you might remember WCW doing their *Hog Wild* events. I figured bikers needed to eat too, and my product might be a good match.

I was right. I think the very first one I did was in 2015 which promised to be a huge one – like the 75th anniversary. Man, did it cost me a lot of fucking money. The premium spots were right on Main street. It was $2500 for the whole weekend. In the end, I had chosen wisely. I had no clue what I would need to bring with me to sell, so I loaded up my ride to the roof. I made money for sure. In the end, it was enough to pay for all the product that moved and to pay for my spot. I came close to only breaking even, maybe a little more which paid for the trip, but that's all I wanted out of it – exposure.

Not having to compete with tons of other people like me, I found a little niche and got my product picked up by some shop owners. Still though, travel expenses costed money. Even though I was finding some moderate success, it was like starting over on the indies as a brand new wrestler. In the world of professional food vendors, I knew I needed to build my name.

I was still taking some wrestling bookings because I was between contracts at TNA, but also thinking how to keep my face out there to push a future in the food industry.

ROH WRESTLING
Keep on trucking.

I kept at what Chavo suggested and that was to always be seen whenever and wherever possible. Ring of Honor was huge with the diehard fans and those were a target demographic. Putting your brand in many places to get more eyeballs on it is always a good move for business, so that is just what I did.

On a quick break from TNA in 2015, I made a call and picked up a spot working with the Briscoe Brothers in their feud with The Kingdom (Michael Bennett, Matt Taven and Maria Kanellis). Soon after that, I was on the ROH PPV celebrating their 13th Anniversary. I also got to work with Maria Kanellis – who was just great.

I don't have a whole lot of stories to tell from there, though some fans may have seen me on their program from time to time and remember me there. However, I really only had a handful of gigs before I was back over to *Impact!* gracing them with my pretty face. I do get questioned about my time at ROH a lot, which means people appreciated my cameos. I appreciated them having me.

I did get to work with guys like Jay Lethal and Truth Martini who were also just awesome.

"Absolutely loved her," Brutal Bob Evans says looking back at my honorable time there. "All the boys did. She was probably there a dozen times or so, back when we really didn't have any women. She was so good. It was really great what she brought to the table!"

RAISING THE BAR

Now, all throughout my wrestling career and even before I was thinking about getting into the food service industry more of late, I found time to make some money bartending during the week when I wasn't wrestling.

As far back as 2010 when I left TNA the first time, I was bartending at a place called Courtside in 2010 in Anoka, Minnesota. Anoka was known as the Halloween capital of the world. Because of that, we made all kinds of weird custom drinks that all sounded deadly. Ghosts and ghouls and any kind of monster you could think of. The tourists ate it up like zombies eating brains, and they tipped pretty well.

It was pretty fun. I would often work the customers, and throw in entertaining crap along the way that I learned from wrestling. I would cut promos on patrons, turn heel on people, and sometimes throw worked punches at guys who needed it. Eventually, I started to work my way back into TNA, but kept my bartending job. It was the smart thing to do, knowing that bitch Dixie Carter was still at the helm. I became a moonlighter.

Because TNA would record some shows ahead of time, there were times that I would be behind the bar pouring a beer and also up on the screen bodyslamming a mofo at the same time. Guys would rubberneck. They would do a double take and look at the TV and then back at me before shaking their heads.

The first time I remember seeing this double-dipping revelation happen in front of me, I saw the back and forth of an older face. This one regular would look at me, then look up at the wall, then back at me. There was an ah-ha moment, then he laughed.

"Geesh," Fredrick said. "I think I really must have had a little too much."

"Why do you say that?" I asked, knowing he must have figured me out. "I mean it's probably true, all the drinking you have been doing that you have had a little too much. But still, you look confused."

"I am. That girl beating the shit out of everyone there on the TV," he said slurring his words, "she looks an awful lot like you."

The older gentleman took off his glasses. He huffed some sour breath on them and then wiped the lenses off on his shirt sleeve for emphasis.

"Because it is her, you blind old geezer!" another regular laughed, smartening him up. "You didn't know?"

"Well, no," Fredrick said. "I was thinking these drinks she made really packed a punch, not her, literally."

"Look at the guns! It's her," his friend laughed.

"Is it true?" he asked.

I laughed and flexed.

The room popped.

"But why in the world would you come here and bartend while you have a career beating up girls on TV?"

"Beating up girls is my job," I said. "But coming here is what I like to do."

I continued both my wrestling career and bartending at Courtside for five years probably, and it was an excellent way to supplement a wrestler's income. At the same time, I would go on the road with TNA, and also do a lot of independent bookings. We never ignored the wrestling stuff. In fact, we played off of it whenever we could. We even threw an ODB bachelorette party when the character was getting married to EY, just so we could have an event to offer drink specials at.

I was good at juggling both jobs, so much so that they often called me employee of month at the bar.

I would legit get on a plane for TNA, wrestle all weekend in Germany, and then be walking off the jet into the airport when I would get a text from the bar.

Hey, Jess can you work tonight?

Yeah, okay.

CHAPTER 12 – One Dirty Bartender

Then, an hour later, fresh with jetlag and time zone sickness, I would be rushing into Courtside.

"Here's your white Russian sir. By the way, I was right near Russia only a few hours ago. Funny, thing," I'd say.

Even though my Courtside gig ended, bartending kept going. I just changed the place and the faces.

I started spinning bottles at my best friend Melissa Hudy's place not too far away from the old one at a little place aptly called "The Lil' Bar." My big bartending experience followed me, as did my connection to wrestling.

At The Lil' Bar of Champlin, Minnesota, the other employees had put up various pictures of wrestlers on the walls, and we developed a little fan following because of my wrestling connection. The bar sold my sauce, and it was a good little arrangement for both of us.

I continued my larger-than-life character behind the counter there and worked half in the ODB persona. I would work the people whenever I could and do all kinds of silly stuff I had picked up in the ring. Just like at Courtside, people would tell me that I was missing my calling. Other guys there would look at me after headbutting a block of ice or something, and ask why I would be wasting my time in such a little hole in the wall. It was very much like they expected me to belt out some lyrics to Billy Joel's "Piano Man," or something.

But my response there was the same deal; I liked bartending and wrestling was just something different I brought to the table.

Quite often, I would bartend at The Lil' Bar on Thursday nights and the moment I would walk in, the vibe would immediately change. As I would walk in, it was like someone changed the channel. Everyone would drop whatever they were doing and it was time for wrestling. For one, the channel changing analogy was literal. They would take one look at me and immediately put TNA up on the big screen TV, no matter what was on and who was watching.

As I have said before, wrestling fans are loyal. Wrestling connects people of all different walks of life together and makes them feel connected. From time to time, new customers would walk into the bar and would see the action in the ring on the screen and loved it. Their connection to the sport made them become instant regulars under my watch, which was great for the company.

Being that we were in Minnesota, the regulars who were wrestling fans would switch gears on my shift. They would out themselves for their fandom and would tell stories about how they got to drink with other local wrestlers, like Mr. Perfect and The Road Warriors. Just a few moments with those guys and you knew that you were listening to stories they had been telling their whole lives. It was funny to think that by me being there with them, I was going to be added to their legends as a new chapter.

Eventually, one day, a woman came into the bar. She was looking at me up and down all weird. I didn't give it much thought. I am totally straight but sometimes gay chicks checked me out because of my big arms or whatever.

To each their own.

Anyhow, this chick continued to stare. It was starting to get strange. I turned my back when she didn't approach the bar for service, but watched her through the mirror. I pretended to clean some spots off of some of the martini glasses and realized that she was kind of sizing me up. This is something other wrestlers might empathize with. She was giving me a vibe that she maybe wanted to fight me.

This happens a lot in the wrestling world, or pretty much any fighting world for that matter. Fighters often have some ego in them and want to be the best. Often, jealousy floods a person's brain when they see an accomplished fighter who has perhaps made it further in the sport than they ever could. Then your spidey sense goes off and you recognize that look they give you. That look usually means that they want to prove to themselves and the whole world around them that they can actually beat you.

Shit. Am I gonna have to fight this bitch?

This throw down ESPN ESP shit is real. Then, to make matters worse, when you add a little alcohol to the mix and people start wondering if they can take out the fighter in you, the risk of an actual confrontation happening increases. It can easily go from just a look to an actual, you are not so tough moment.

When I saw that look on her face, I thought I recognized it and got ready for the worst.

After a few more minutes of being burnt by her laser eyes, I had had enough. It was put up or shut up time.

"What's up?" I said to the fixated face across the glasses burning a hole into mine. I would have added "bitch" to the end of that sentence, but she cut me off.

"Not much," she said.

"Can I help you with something?" I chose my words, as to not provoke a situation.

"Yeah. Just wondering. Are you a pro wrestler?"

There it is.

Now after that, usually they would follow up with an autograph request or throwing the gauntlet down. If the latter, then there would be some kind of personal diss right before the inevitable fight challenge.

However, this was not the case. She smiled.

"I knew I recognized you."

It turned out she didn't want to fight at all. She was Mr. Perfect's widow.

After that, she too became a regular out of her love for wrestling. She came in quite a bit and fell in love with the place. Maybe it felt like home. She was with her people. Sometimes her and his kids would come in, too. His daughter, in particular, was so much like her father that she would get drunk and get into fights with the other regulars. I would be washing a glass and look up to see her throwing the contents of hers into someone's face.

"Oh boy," I would say. "Another perfect evening at The Lil' Bar."

BROKEN MOONLIGHTING

I continued to work two jobs – bartending and wrestling. I was on again, off again in TNA. The promotion was hurting from the open checkbook "WCW strategy" that they had used for so long. Dixie money was dumped into it over and over again from her father's fuel company.

Come later 2015, Billy Corgan showed up. Yes, from The Smashing Pumpkins! He threw some money into the promotion and was mainstream enough to get more eyes.

On top of this, the Hardys were coming into their own. Jeff started doing his Willow gimmick, and then out of nowhere, Matt became "Broken." He started doing this foil act to his brother's monster-like creature. It was very reminiscent of *Frankenstein*, with him being the mad doctor.

They had to film things on the cheap, but that added to the charm of it all. Jeremy Borash helped them direct and create an entire "Broken Universe" of crazy characters. This led to a crazy new push for cinematic-style wrestling from the fans and the whole wrestling world. They wanted more.

These cinematic matches were brilliant. I could only explain them as being a mix of wrestling, horror flicks, and/or even mini movies – ones that the wrestling world had never seen before. This push for different content immediately put TNA back on the map. I naturally was brought for these broken appearances because I, too, was different.

The Hardys became TNA's top names. They brought new life to the promotion. Entire episodes of *IMPACT Wrestling* came from his home in Cameron, North Carolina. One, for example, was called *Total Nonstop Deletion*; it was an open invitational tag team tournament to wrestlers from any promotion, anywhere. The Hardys were hot everywhere. They dipped into their own pockets to provide content for TNA as they found it was mutual for both of them.

Eventually, legal issues between Billy Corgan and the company went down. Corgan apparently was not getting his cut of whatever deal was promised to him, and he refused to be worked like a money mark. When Billy Corgan left, he was upset with unkept promises from the lovely Miss Dixie Carter. He was done dumping money into something without being able to see any returns. It became evident that he was an investor in their eyes, not a "part-owner" as they might have said. Eventually, however, more money was needed to keep the company afloat and that is when Anthem Sports & Entertainment stepped in.

Early 2017, Anthem acquired majority stake and essentially bought TNA, renaming the promotion "Impact Wrestling" after its flagship show. The new owner didn't like the idea that Hardys were taking other gigs doing their broken thing without getting a cut of what Anthem felt was their intellectual property. The problem was they felt the Broken Hardys were part of their investment, but the Hardys contract allowed them to work elsewhere.

The Hardys began their big "Expedition of Gold" storyline where they would teleport (with the worst ever special effects) to different promotions everywhere just to win that promotion's tag team championship gold. This is when it hit Anthem that the fans liked the Hardys and not specifically TNA. Small independent promotions that were never heard of were getting plugs everywhere with little hype for TNA. TNA tried to reel them back in but to no avail.

Eventually, Matt and Jeff saw it was more lucrative to work elsewhere and left TNA. Then, there was a legal battle over the gimmick. After Matt and Jeff left, Matt's wife, Reby Sky, went on a social media tirade in which she repeatedly slammed TNA, the company's new management, and the way contract renegotiations had been conducted. Anthem got pissed. Many in the locker room felt TNA should just let the boys do their thing, as they were the ones who put in the hard work. However, Anthem started mailing cease and desist letters to any promotion where the Hardys were being booked. They refused to let the brothers even acknowledge the existence of Broken Matt and Brother Nero. This was despite the fact that the Hardys came up with the gimmick on their own and the fact that other wrestlers were allowed to keep their gimmicks upon exit. Their argument was that the gimmick was created on company time, so it belonged to the company.

See, back when the Hardys were in TNA, they had full creative control over the broken gimmick and told they owned it which is why they put lots of their own money into it. They were so invested in the whole idea that they even filmed their own segments using their own money just to air them on TNA programming. (I know this because I was on some of them and saw it first-hand.) We would go to their house and film with no Carter, no Corgan, no TNA people there at all. Therefore, the Hardy family argued that they were off the clock and the owners of the broken gimmick.

With the Hardys gone, newly-appointed Impact Wrestling President, Ed Nordholm, continued on with the broken world without the Hardys for a short time. To revisit an analogy, this was like the TV network changing the name of Roseanne Barr's show after she was gone and just calling it, *The Conners*, hoping to find the same success. In this new

Hardy-less universe, that shit flopped. It just wasn't happening without the Hardys. Eventually, most of the guys in TNA (like Borash and Abyss) moved over to WWE. New deals were made. The legal battle officially concluded. Matt legally acquired ownership of all trademarks related to the gimmick including Broken Matt, Brother Nero, Broken Brilliance and their robot/drone Vanguard1 (whom I had the pleasure of motor-boating on one episode.)

    Around the time they were moving on, I was moving away from TNA and wrestling altogether. I also saw money opportunies elsewhere and started a transformation of my own. I got a professional wrap done on my Airstream to advertise my new food service brand. Then, I was ready to experience a journey of my own brilliance.

CHAPTER 13 – THE FOOD TRUCK

The bartending and barbecue sauce selling continued. Come 2017, Jimmy Hart got wind of my aspirations and called me. Like me, Hart was in and out of TNA quite a bit and knew me well from our time together there.

"Hey baby," he said in that familiar trademark voice that isn't a work.

"Hey, Jimmy," I said.

"Is it true you are bartending?"

"Yes."

"And you are selling your own sauces and all?"

"Yes."

"That's great, baby!" he said. "That's perfect!"

It wasn't long before I was leaving Nashville and off to Daytona Beach to work for Jimmy!

Jimmy had just opened his own wrestling-themed bar. Jimmy already had a manager named Paulie who looked like an older version of Hulk Hogan. They were both kind of carnie at times, believing that big things were always coming. Bringing me in might have been just the bit of grounded realism they needed to help get things going.

Jimmy was cool. He knew fans would appreciate me and booked me out as an attraction more than just a bartender. He put me up right on the beach in a nice apartment with a balcony view for two months as I got ready for what seemed to be a bit of a future there.

As far as the bar itself was concerned, he did it right and made the place look awesome to a wrestling fan. Jimmy also planned to be there himself as much as totally possible. The idea was that we were going to play off of the wrestling connection even harder than The Lil' Bar did back in Minnesota – a wrestling bar with actual wrestling names in it.

Before you even walked in, there was a custom Cadillac with Jimmy Hart art painted all over it. Since my Airstream also had my ODB Whiskey Sauce logo on it as well, we parked that out front, too. That got the word out quickly and left fans of wrestling with no mistakes in their minds as to where to go.

Inside, the bar was decorated from the floor to the ceiling in memorabilia. There were ring-worn jackets of Hart's as well as all kinds of other rarities he picked up from various wrestlers that he had worked with over the years. There were action figures. There were signed 8x10s. The walls of this place looked like a wrestling museum.

Wrestling wasn't the only thing, however. The Rock 'n' Wrestling connection was also showcased. Since Jimmy was also a legit musician before wrestling, he also had a spotlighted little section of various memorabilia from his music career. His group, The Gentrys, was also there on display.

A lot of people don't really know Jimmy Hart's music background. The Gentrys were a rock band from Memphis, Tennessee, originally called The Gents. The original members were Larry Raspberry (guitar/lead vocals), Bruce Bowles (vocals), & Jimmy Hart (vocals), Bobby Fisher (saxophone/keyboards), Jimmy Johnson (trumpet), Pat Neal (bass), Larry Butler (keyboards) and Larry Wall (drums).

The Gentrys got their start playing high school dances and signed their first record deal after winning a local Battle of the Bands contest. Their debut single "Keep on Dancing" was picked by MGM Records and ended up selling a million copies and peaking at #4 on the *Billboard* pop charts in 1965. The group toured with The Beach Boys and Sonny & Cher. The Gentrys two follow-up singles failed to make the Top 40. After that, they broke up in 1966.

Four years later, Hart relaunched a new version of The Gentrys with new members. They found continued success recording covers of hit songs like "Cinnamon Girl" and "Wild World." Under the Sun label, they also released some original tracks like "He'll Never Love You" and "Why Should I Cry," before ultimately shutting down in 1974. Soon after that, Hart transitioned his act into becoming the loud, professional wrestling manager that everyone came to know as "The Mouth of the South."

Fun fact: the late "Hurricane" JJ Maguire successfully auditioned for The Gentrys when the group was looking for a new drummer. Maguire and Hart would then go on to co-create many memorable WWE and WCW pro wrestling entrance themes together.

Incidentally, being a music man helped make Jimmy Hart success in the wrestling world. Then his knowledge of wrestling helped turn him into a legitimate business man.

The bar as one of his plan B's was a no-brainer.

For me, the bar was a really neat gig. I was given the title of "featured bartender." Maybe you could look at it as being like a resident booking at a Vegas casino, or like when a big name chick shows up as a "featured dancer" at a dance club. I don't know. We were making it up as we went along. No matter how you looked at it, however, I would soon learn that my "featured bartender" role was more than just being a bartender and/or an attraction.

Essentially, I was about to be the most famous wrestling manager's manager.

"How much should we charge for this drink?" I asked on my very first day on the job.

"I don't know, baby," he would say. "Whatever you think."

"How much booze do we want to give away? Like which size glass should I use for the mixed drinks?"

"I don't know, baby," he would say again. "Whatever you think."

After a handful of the same type of questions and answers, I learned quickly that he was leaving all that stuff up to me.

I was making money moves. I wasn't just the guest bartender anymore; I was also the uncredited bar manager.

Jimmy put me in charge, and I could charge whatever I wanted. It was a little scary, but it was awesome.

Now, I never had that type of power role before. I will admit, I had to do some on-the-fly training and essentially build the airplane while we were already up in the air. But I didn't mind it. I actually liked it. I could be creative. It was interesting to see what worked and what didn't.

I made up all these gimmicky wrestling-related items for the menu. We had "Steve-wiser" drink specials, and Bob Backlund Crossface Chicken Wing Specials, you name it.

The place quickly became a tourist attraction, but that wasn't all. The locals came in, too. The regulars are the bread and butter of any establishment, and we had 'em. They would come every Monday night like clockwork to watch *Monday Night RAW* on a big screen TV.

Now, Jimmy wanted to take the show on the road, but he didn't know how that was going to happen. He had this really nice tiki bar outside all set up, but no plans on how to use it. With all the people who walked by his place, I figured it was definitely a missed opportunity to rake some people in.

"Why aren't you using the tiki?" I asked him candidly one day.

"I know baby, I know," he said as I pointed out a possible shortcoming.

"No, you don't know," I suggested as cutely as I could. "Hire anyone to stand behind it, and you will likely pull in people who don't want to invest time coming in. You might reach a whole other group of customers!"

"You know, Jess, you are right," he said. "It's time. We have to do that next, and I will set it up next week."

Jimmy always had a million things going on, however. Therefore, next week, of course, never came.

Eventually, I just took matters into my own hands. One night, on a weekday, I just set up outside. I set up a table and set up shop. I wasn't on the clock, so I decided to do some kind of on-the-fly food deal. I set up five Crockpots to sell the easiest stuff I could think of. I had two kinds of chili, meatballs, pulled pork, and macaroni and cheese. I practiced preparing the food, and figured out my own best recipes for all of it.

I kept Jimmy updated on the tiki bar drills I did. During some of our business talks, he told me that his long-term goal was also to figure out how to get a food truck so that he could drive our gig out to the even hotter social spots along the beach, and "bring the bar to them." For the first few weeks, that is all we talked about.

I worked there for a number of months and didn't see any movement in that area. We continued to talk a big talk of what the mobile bar would look like in various inclinations. He also talked about a delivery service. He talked about an expansion to another location. He talked about offering his chain as a franchise. A lot of this, however, was like the wrestling industry. There was always talk of a big TV deal, or a big tour somewhere, but without the mark-money investor these things never happened. The same seemed to be happening with Hart's ideas for the bar.

It was always, "we got this going on, and we got that going on." All the big plans Jimmy had for sure, but the plans never took off. It seemed either they all fell through, or he just had so much going on he didn't have time. I don't know. We butted heads a little on this, but I still think everything happens for a reason. My time there was truly invaluable.

Jimmy's food truck idea lingered with me. While I knew a food truck was never going to happen for Jimmy Hart's place, I thought about ways that maybe something like that could for me.

WHAT'S BEST FOR BUSINESS

One night, my good friend Mickie James asked me to come over to her place to hang out and talk some business.

For those of you who don't already know, Mickie is married to wrestler/entrepreneur Nick Aldis. Now, Aldis knows how to work. As far as having a business mindset goes, he really is the man. Aldis has a whole line of supplements, suits, and all kinds of things for sale.

When I showed up for dinner, they knew I was dabbling in the food industry. Eventually, they too were kicking around the idea of bringing the show on the road.

Mickie and Nick liked my idea and were seriously thinking about buying a food truck to also push their wrestling merch sales.

This idea was not at all unlike what Jimmy Hart was going to do. Going a step further, however, they had already bought a box truck trailer that had been customized with the intent to offer food at big events. The trailer was much like what you would see at perhaps a fair or carnival, and still very mobile in nature.

Their plan was to offer barbeque fare being doled out by me with my custom sauce, along with whatever wrestling merch we wanted to sell and a wrestler meet-and-greet experience for the customers at the same time.

The idea of the Meat & Greet Food Truck was born.

It seemed like we were going to do good business together, but there were some different viewpoints on how everything would work. In the end, we decided to not partner up so that it wouldn't hurt our friendship. Then, they were super cool and I just bought the trailer off of them.

Once I had that in hand, I could see my future after wrestling.

ODB's Meat & Greet.

Before taking my truck out for business, I did my homework. I sat in my kitchen, toying with various recipes and dishes to feature my sauce with. I had to figure out what would both taste the best, as well as what would be the easiest dishes to prep and sell out of a tight space. Once I was set with my menu, I was ready and able to go to any old place to open shop.

I got a permit and started setting up shop and selling stuff. My first thought was to make it like a diner on wheels, offering all kinds of stuff – a little something for everyone. I quickly learned however, I was offering way too much and it was very easy to get in over my head.

I had deep fryers and a flat top grill. I had smoothies. I had an oven. Eventually, I knew I had more than I needed in there and something had to change.

That is when I called Tilly.

Tilly used to be backstage at TNA. He was friends with Dusty Rhodes and used to manage the gorilla position. He also ran a number of restaurants in Florida and I knew he would have some valuable insight for me.

"It's great to have a lot of options," he said, sitting down with me at a coffee shop near the beach. "But you have to figure, the more stuff you keep on hand that doesn't get used, the more that goes to waste."

I listened.

"Also, if you specialize a little, you will get your following and you will make things easier on yourself. You can also buy in bulk and then save money that way, too."

He sat me down and taught me how to keep it simple. Since I had my own barbeque sauce and hot sauce, it only made sense to run a barbeque food truck.

"You don't have to offer everything. Pick a few proteins you can use with a few side dishes and that's it."

Duh! Why didn't I think of that?

It all sounded so simple, so I did just that. I simplified the food truck's menu, and I was off and running.

CHAPTER 13 – The Food Truck   261

After that, everything fell right into place. If a customer came up to the window, I knew they wanted one of only a handful of options. Then, I would just go right into make mode and not have to reinvent my countertop to make it happen every time.

It was almost like the idea of not expanding too fast in business. When you have too much going on, it takes away from the one place that is working. I needed to establish that one place first and make it work, before I could add other stuff to it. Learning to listen is the key to success. I can't stress this enough. That is how ODB's Meet & Greet was becoming a success.

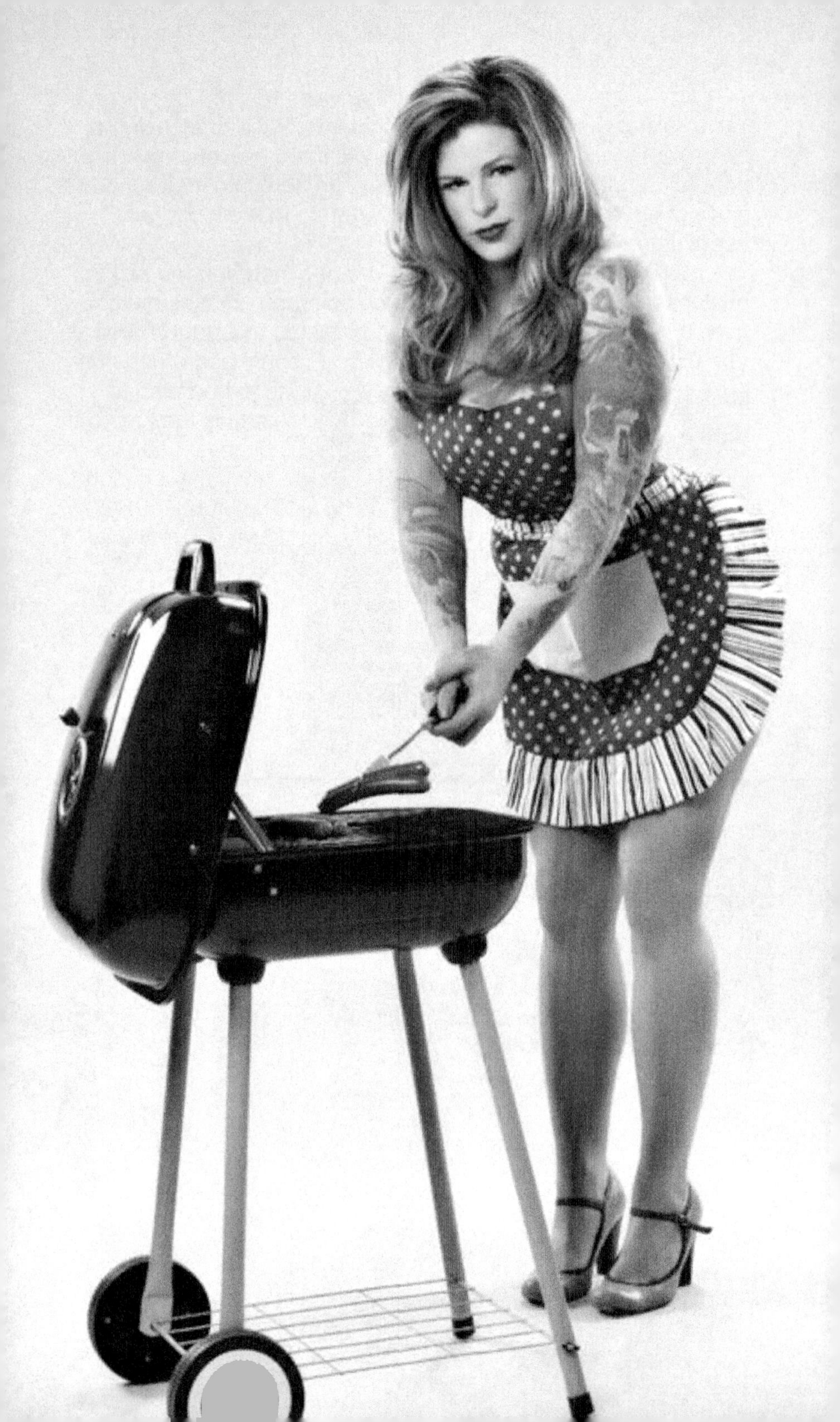

CHAPTER 14 - THE SAUSAGE PARTY

Every wrestling book has to have a debauchery story, right? A lot of my time in wrestling was in TNA where wrestlers showed up after already having had their wild, partying days, for the most part. Because of this, I didn't see a whole lot of nonsense. The funny thing is, my best tale o' filth happened after I left the business.

Back in 2017, I was contacted by the self-proclaimed nephew of Gary Busey, Mike Busey. The best way I can describe this guy is to call him a hillbilly Hugh Hefner. He kind of looks like a cross between Guy Fieri and Steve-O. Mike Busey was a huge wrestling fan. I had met him a few times at wrestling shows. I had heard some stories about him before, but no real details other than he threw the biggest parties ever. He eventually took my business card.

When he finally called to book me to cater one of his big events, I was psyched. He started off by saying everything I wanted to hear... It was a big bash. It was a benefit for military veterans. It was going to have hundreds of hungry people. It was going to be paid upfront in cash.

I was excited at the idea. It was these types of events where you could really shine, network, and get your name out there while still doing something good. I was excited, that is… until I heard the final last part of the details.

"So, what should I know about the event?"

"It's called The Sausage Festival for a reason," he said laughing a little with just a tad of pervert in his voice. "That, and it all takes place at The Sausage Caste."

I've heard laughs like this before. This could definitely be a red flag.

"Sausage Festival," I repeated needing clarification and trying to clean up a conversation that could be heading for the gutter. "Cool. Is this like say Boston's Chowder-Fest, with different sausages to try from different vendors?"

"Not really. It would just be you for all the food."

"Umm, I'd love to cater, but sausages aren't really my deal. I mean, I could do it, but it's not my regular thing. I don't handle them."

"Oh, you don't need to worry about handling the sausages," he laughed again. "We have experienced girls for that."

What in the actual fuck?

I laughed but didn't want to. I didn't like where this was going. "I mean… I do barbecue food usually."

"Oh, no big deal. Yeah, that is what we want. Would you come and also cook other stuff? We will pay for and provide all the other food, too. The stuff you don't carry."

Ok, everything is cool, I think?

"It's not a big deal. I can get sausages and work it in. I just don't make them and all or carry them usually."

"The emphasis on sausage at the Sausage Festival doesn't really mean food," he clarified. "It's more like saying it's a sausage party."

"Oh boy."

Then Mike went on to explain how much of a patriot he was and how everything was on the up-and-up.

"Okay, so you see, once a year," he laughed, "we throw these huge parties to give back to the vets to thank them for their service. A lot of the boys are hard on their luck after giving up so much for their country. They deserve it. Some of them even lost limbs, or can't walk."

"That's sad," I said, wanting to believe his plight.

"What we do is we give them one night where we treat them like kings. We pay for everything out of pocket to give back to them one night a year to look forward to."

"That's nice of you," I admitted, but waiting for a bomb of some sort to drop.

"We feed the veterans," he said.

"Cool."

"We also book live music for the veterans."

"Cool."

"And of course, we give free blowjobs to the veterans."

"Wait, what?" I laughed. "WHAT?"

There it was. The mic drop. The raw sausage meat hit the floor.

"You heard me, right?"

"Oh boy," I said. "Well, I think you might have me confused for someone else. THAT is not a service we offer."

"No, no," Mike said, as I was about to hang up.

I interrupted him again. I was pissed and wanted him to know. "The ODB Meet & Greet does not offer what you are looking for. The character I played on TV wouldn't do that, and even so, that was just a character."

"I KNOW," he said. "I know. No disrespect. We have a specialist for that part of the evening. You have nothing to do with that in any way. I assure you."

"A specialist? Free blowjobs?" I asked again.

"Yes. Free blowjobs, but I assure you, that part of the event has nothing to do with you," he smirked, "There are some girls here, however, who would eat your asshole though if you wanted," he joked.

"Thanks, but I'll pass."

"We want you for the food, period. Some of the guests have been disfigured or have medical issues that make things difficult for them with the ladies. It is a cruel world out there, so we try to even the playing grounds and give them something else besides the food to look forward to."

"Okay, but free blowjobs?"

"Free blowjobs."

"You are a real humanitarian."

I was new to the food business and wanted to get into doing big events, but hearing that was just so fucked up.

How do they say it? FUBAR?

"Fucked Up Beyond All Repair." Anyhow, just like a newbie in wrestling who was willing to work anywhere for little of anything, I felt like I had to do it. I made Mike promise that I had nothing to do with any sort of sex stuff. He promised. He swore to it, so I agreed, despite my instincts and better judgment. (Hey, I wanted the payday!)

Busey asked me to be there the night before to set up and get everything right. He made it out like it was a freaking wedding with all his attention to fine detail, but, I was in. After I hung up with him, I decided to do a little research.

Okay. Let's see what a Google search finds for me.

Come to find out, the Sausage Castle was a real place with a real history. Very real.

I went to a site called VICE that said, "There's a place in central Florida where all your dreams come true. The weirder ones, anyway… Sexual fantasies, the ones where you're wandering through a party that never ends, or launching eggs into a 500-pound man's asshole, or fucking a girl while simultaneously taking a shit in a shower."

"Oh boy," I said. "What am I getting myself into?"

I continued on like looking at a train wreck. The place called The Sausage Castle is legendary to some. It is out of Osceola County which is a redneck region about an hour from Disney World – another place ironically where you can make your dreams come true. "The Castle" itself is a super nice house but in a the middle of a swampy, feces-infested pond called Alligator Lake. There, I read, were some of the wildest parties in the world. It looked like a human zoo.

The Sausage Castle is like the sinful gluttony of Pleasure Island from *Pinocchio* with the freaks of Misfit Toy Island from *Rudolph*. During their famous all-night shindigs, it's normal to see open sex, drugs, and rock 'n roll all go down with all walks of life, including celebrities.

ICP. Glam Rockers. Rappers. Jackass. GWAR.

It sounded like a foul mixture of something I did not want to swallow. Google pulled no punches on Mike Busey. I learned that over only a couple of years, his name quickly became legend in central Florida. One newspaper even named him Florida's 51st most famous person.

YouTube had a video of Busey in action at the ICP's Gathering hosting The Freak Show. He had an outdoor strip club going on with all these harlots hanging on him who he called The Busey Beauties. His girls were giving disabled guys water lap dances in a shady looking hot tub that made Walmart toilets look more appealing.

I'm not known for making the best life decisions. Despite my better judgement and seeing some pretty questionable Busey content on the internet, I didn't think about cancelling. I still agreed to Busey's booking.

I guess you could say curiosity killed the cat.

When Sausage Day finally came, I put a bat under my seat. I braved the boonies of Orlando, and cautiously pulled up to a huge Graceland-looking gate outside Busey's lair.

The Sausage Castle is before me.

I punched in the secret code (69) that he gave me on his security console. There was a little beep.

I hesitated as the gates to Hell opened.

CHAPTER 14 – The Sausage Party

When I got to the mansion, the front door was wide open. I mean legit open, like nobody had bothered to close it. I stuck my head in and called for Mike, with no answer.

A naked girl finally walked by pulling something in tow. She had a leash on a critter that looked like a ferret.

"Mike's over there in the den," she directed.

"Oh my God," I said looking around. "Thank you."

Outside, the castle was totally classy and beautiful! It had gorgeous landscaping. It had a sparkling swimming pool. It had a volleyball court. It was like the mansion of a millionaire! But when you took just one step into the place, that was a whole different story.

Inside wasn't classy at all. Weiner World looked like some dickhead designer went out of his way to make the place obscenely tacky. It was like a giant X-rated version of *Pee-Wee's Playhouse*... Shag rugs. Tacky furniture. An animal print skee-ball alley. Weird paintings. Naked art. Stripper poles. Purple paper-maché penis statues.

I walked in a little further and saw one of those arcade claw machines that you put a quarter in and try to lift a teddy bear from. However, this was no ordinary claw machine. This one was completely filled with dildos.

What in the hell? Of course, right?!

Busey came out wearing some bullshit zebra skin Hugh Hefner smoking jacket that looked like a poorly-made Halloween pimp costume. My first impression of him was that he seemed like a Juggalo version of Willy Wonka and The Doctor of Style, Slick.

Busey hugged and dismissed one of his degenerate babes in a shady She-Ra costume who was tailing him. She apparently was one of the live-in "Busey Beauties."

"Hey! ODB!"

"Hey," I said.

"So?" he said waving his arms all around him. "What do you think of The Sausage Castle?"

"It's very nice. Very nice," I said, noticing one of those shitty leg lamps from *A Christmas Story* on an end table that looked like a giant Rubik's Cube. I tried to take everything in for the complete effect, then looked back at the man claiming to be Gary Busey's nephew.

He was rough. He looked like he had been up all night doing strippers and blow.

"So, are you actually part of the Insane Clown Posse?" I asked, not fully getting the connection and wanting to know exactly how this sausage was made.

"Well, I guess, but the sausage guys, we are more like a subgenre of the Juggalos," he said. "I totally fit into the Juggalo community because I'm a broke piece of shit who used to live in a trailer. But I'm non-exclusive."

Busey saw me cringe a little and recognized that I looked uncomfortable. He decided to tell me what he had hoped would be the relatable story of his messed up life.

As a teenager, I guess he was pretty religious and had a relationship to God. So eventually he went to some super strict Christian college to be a preacher. There he polished his public speaking skills, but then said "bullshit started to open his eyes." He eventually decided to drop out. "Eventually, I recognized the hypocrisy. They collected money promising to help people but the only people they helped were themselves."

Busey left the church, but had no direction in his life anymore and soon became depressed. To break his depression, however, he decided to move in with some friends who threw crazy parties. Then, he started to throw crazy parties himself. However, not to be out-done, Busey took "crazy" to the next level. First, he took out loans to secure the fanciest place he could. Then, he rented out rooms to veterans. Next, he bussed in "bored Disney interns for parties" to pay a cover charge and help him pay the bills.

"Hey," I said. "I was one of those interns once."

"Well, it's a small world after all then," he joked.

He was sick but smart, I guess. There was a market for a less G-rated college party place spring and he discovered it. The filthier he made his events, the more they would draw. He also charged people for subscriptions online where he would livestream his live-in strippers doing outlandish stuff in his Sausage House. He had "Rockstar Weekends" where rich people would pay a few thousand dollars to act out any of their sexual fantasies. I don't know. The dude had all kinds of nasty money-making shit going on!

"Alright, alright," I said hearing his life story. "I'm just here for the food stuff though."

"Ok, my bad," he said, "Let me bring you to the kitchen." He continued the small talk as he gave me a tour.

He said he spent like $50,000 transforming the original beat-up house he bought into the luxurious Sausage Castle. I believed him. Even the walls looked crazy. They were all different and customized. He flew top-name artists in to paint murals everywhere featuring pop culture figures like Michael Jackson, Luke Skywalker, and Fred Flintstone. There were also giant paintings of orgies, but they weren't just paintings; they were actually interactive works of art. You see, actual sex toys were built into the carnal collages! There were paintings of naked chicks with sex toy flesh-lights strategically embedded into the sheetrock so you could walk right up and fuck the wall.

Yes! FUCK THE WALL, I said. Legit.

Busey also had humpable hallways for the hoochies and gay dudes respectively. As a gay right advocate, he had dildos and buttholes installed into paintings of naked dudes. That way, LGBTQ partiers could bum blast the dining room wall if they wanted to. Yes, he thought of everything.

Once we made it to the living room, I saw a giant television, but it was dwarfed in size by a fully operational strip club stage. Instead of individual lapdance accessible chairs like you would see in a titty bar, the dance stage had church pews that were covered with vintage porno pictures lacquered onto the surface.

Hanging from the wall was yet another masterpiece. This work of art consisted of a framed, impressive memento: *the very first condom Busey used to end his virginity.*

Nostalgic and beautiful. He saved that shit.

Off to one side, there was a big Vegas-style roulette wheel complete with the wildest sexual positions/instructions you could ever think of. This wheel of debauchery was there ready and waiting so you could spin the wheel and make a deal to inspire any guest to take part in the foulest of all activities.

"The kitchen is right down there," he said.

As we headed to my final destination, the kitchen, we passed a few massive fish tanks with large rubber dicks protruding out of the rocks and upwards from the sea floor.

"That's Dildo Atlantis," he said.

"God damn," I shook my head. "Dildo Atlantis?"

"Yes."

"Oh boy."

The kitchen was great, but much different than any kitchen I had ever seen. From the ceiling, there was a fan slowly spinning with panties hanging on it that girls had given to him. The microwave was gone, but in its place was a box covered in cheetah-print fabric, housing a live snake. And on the fridge, he had photos of all his friends, featuring Z-list celebrities like Wee Man, and Poison's Bret Michaels.

Yes, wrestling often makes a connection between people who aren't typically connected, and Busey in this case also related to me. He invited me to stay with him and his gang of misfit toys for the weekend. He promised to give me my own private room where nobody would bother me. While I did feel less and less threatened by him after taking the tour and hearing his origin story, still, something seemed really off. Staying in the castle seemed Scooby Doo risky.

All I kept thinking is, "Even if nobody creeped on me, I bet there would be a camera over my bed or in the shower."

"Thanks, I'm good though," I finally said out loud. "I'll start digging through all these boxes and get everything ready for tomorrow. I'll hit you up if I need anything."

"Sounds good!" he said. He bowed and disappeared down a hall after one of his buxom Busey Beauties. "Just text me then if you need anything."

I was a big girl. I got everything together on my own. I never texted him. Once I had everything prepped for the party, I was beat. I looked over at a checkered couch, and thought about crashing. Then, I looked over at Dildo Atlantis again and shook my head.

I went outside and slept in my truck.

The next morning, I got all the food together and got my smoker up and running. I set up shop just outside the kitchen door, by my truck and waited in what I had anticipated to be the quiet before the storm.

CHAPTER 14 – The Sausage Party

Come a little after noon, the storm hit, just as I had thought. However, when it hit, it hit harder than I had ever imagined. The skies turned dark. Three big Busey busses unloaded. Loads of landlubbers rained down on me. They didn't trickle in, they poured down on my unsuspecting truck. Waves of hungry people came forth in droves, each with their own dish requests.

Despite the chaos, I was happy.

The more the merrier.

Accumulation was more than I had predicted and this was good. I watched my tip jar grow and grow and grow.

The sausage goers were of all walks of life. They went in and complimented the strange decor that made The Sausage Castle special. They came to party with Busey for all kinds of reasons, and he was right: most of the veterans had been socially outcasted from their families and the world. They were appreciative and I saw this in gratuities.

They were loving everything. A live band played some funk song somewhere on the other side of the house. People were swimming in the pool behind me. There was some kind of game going on in the court beyond the trees.

Lots of people were naked, however. Old dudes with their sweet saggy nutsacks were chasing strippers around.

I served food for a good three hours before the demand dropped off. I had to pee. I went inside to use the facilities in the massive bro-pad. I stumbled my way through what looked like one of those massive parties you would see college kids having in the movies back in the eighties. It was so big, it seemed unrealistic. Right before my eyes, it looked like a scene plucked right out of a John Hughes movie, only maybe the knockoff porno version perhaps.

I made my way to the girls' bathroom. It was painted all in purple and pink. On the shelves by the sink, they had some interesting reading material; vintage issues of *Playboy* of course. Across from the toilet, there was a giant hand-painted sign that read: "Family, Friends, Forever."

I made my way back to my post. Come the dinner rush, I heard an announcement come from a dude hanging out of a window shouting into a Jimmy Hart-style megaphone.

"Ladies and gentlemen, friends and family, and now to pleasure your sausages, Jenna Jizz will be performing (fellatio) in the entertainment room," he said in his best ringmaster voice. "And don't worry about COMING right now, she will be in there all night!"

Everyone cheered and ran into the house like footage from a Black Friday sale. They reminded me of bloodthirsty fans at a Roman Gladiator event, only this time they were thirsting for other bodily fluids and functions.

The floodgates were lifted. The remaining few people waiting in line for dinner bowed out as everyone poured into The Sausage Castle. When the dust had settled, I looked out and there was one very small, frail old man waiting in line. He was still standing before me holding a paper plate.

"What was that all about?" he said, adjusting his hearing aid.

Jesus, now do I have to tell grandpa that he is missing out on the sex? Can he even still get it up?

"Um, did you want something to eat?" I asked.

"Eat. Yes," he said. "But what was that announcement, honey? I can't hear a blasted thing."

"Um, well sir," I said, imagining that the old man wasn't medically cleared for sexual activity and probably couldn't even perform if he was. "The man said free blowjobs for veterans."

The old man stopped and scratched his head. "I'll have a barbecue sandwich," he said putting his plate up on the counter in front of me.

"Okay, sounds good sweetie," I said.

"...And a blow job, I guess," he laughed.

I shook my head and put a sandwich in front of him with a handful of chips.

"Well," he said waiting.

"Well?" I said laughing at the sexual harassment of the dirty old man before me who looked about 70 pounds probably, soaking wet with a brick in his pocket. "Well, lunch is all I can help you with."

"I am a veteran," he specified.

"Well, thank you for your service," I said saluting him. "That's inside. From Mike, he's a real humanitarian."

"He's a real American," he corrected me. "But Mike isn't providing that service, is he?"

"Um, no," I said. "Some chicky... Jenna Jizz."

"Good," he said grabbing his plate. "Now which way are the hummers again?"

The last man left after my directions. I shook my head and laughed. "Good for him," I thought. "Grandpa is going to get him some." I looked around. Not a soul in sight.

It's sausage time, after all. What did you expect?

My push was over. It was totally dead – just as I had incorrectly diagnosed Grandpa's sex life, apparently. My competition inside was just too good. I figured it was as good a time as any to go get some more supplies.

The kitchen door was locked, so I had to go right in through the front and journey into the eye of the storm. It looked like a *Revenge of the Nerds* Tri-Lambda frat party just after they passed out the wonder joints. I heard music. I smelled the drinking and drugs in the air. I parted the sea of horny humanity and swam my way into the refuge of the kitchen.

I immediately shut the door behind me. I grabbed a cardboard box and started filling it with some buns. I heard all kinds of commotion so I peeked through the crack in the door expecting to see more buns, but of a different variety.

All I could see was a wall full of people. I could only imagine what was going on. I quickly closed and locked the inside kitchen door as to contain the carnal activities to the game room.

As I filled my box, I became more and more intrigued at the loud sex sounds coming from the human zoo. The merriment was coming from the other side of what was more like a divider than an actual wall. It had a long, open space at the top and didn't connect all the way to the ceiling.

I looked up, surveying the long opening and did some math. With something to stand on, I was just tall enough. I pulled over a chair and I stood up on the counter. I peered over the top like *Home Improvement*'s, Wilson.

It was the best seat in the house. A bunch of people had gathered around to watch some girl squirt chocolate out of her vagina, before blowing a veteran.

When she was done, she grabbed the megaphone.

"Who's next?" she announced like Goldberg, wiping groin gravy off of her chin.

Then, one dick became two… two dicks became four… five became six…all graciously offering their menacing meatsticks up for public marination.

In no time at all, we had a baker's dozen of volunteering vets (thank you for your service) being called to duty. They walked up to the front of the line and stood in a circle inside of a circle of on looking fans, and Jenna Jizz pushed in an office chair to the very center.

Then, she spun around and around in that rotating chair, blowing each and every one of them. *WTF!*

"God damn!" I said. My eyes bugged out of my head. I jumped down from my perch like I had just witnessed a crime. "I need another beer."

I unlocked the kitchen door and ran outside laughing my ass off. "What a story this is going to be for the girls!"

I headed over to my trailer feeling dirty like I needed a wash. I rubbed the sin out of my virginal eyes. It was still dead around my food truck. I reached into an ice bucket and drank a beer to numb my mind from the live sex show I just saw to try to unburn the image from my brain. Thirty minutes dragged. I drank another beer to pass the time, and then curiosity killed the cat again. I got enough liquid courage to go back into the kitchen to watch some more of the show.

I came back in, locked the door behind me, then jumped up on my counter again. I peered around the circle of strokers. Guys had their pants down to their ankles and were masturbating furiously with no shame.

Right in the middle was Jenna Jizz in all her girly glory. She was bent over showing everyone her leather Cheerio. Full debauchery. After the act, there was no time out. She just flicked some vaginal filth off of her posterior and assumed the position again for the next comer.

"That's it," I said. I tapped out.

I went outside to close up shop.

Busey came by as I was packing up. "Yeah, they probably aren't going to eat anymore – food that is," he laughed. "Want to come in and hang out?"

"Yep, um," I laughed. "No. I'm good. I gotta go."

I thanked Busey and bailed. I fired up the flux capacitor and sped out of the Sausage Compound doing at least 88. I never planned to go back in the future.

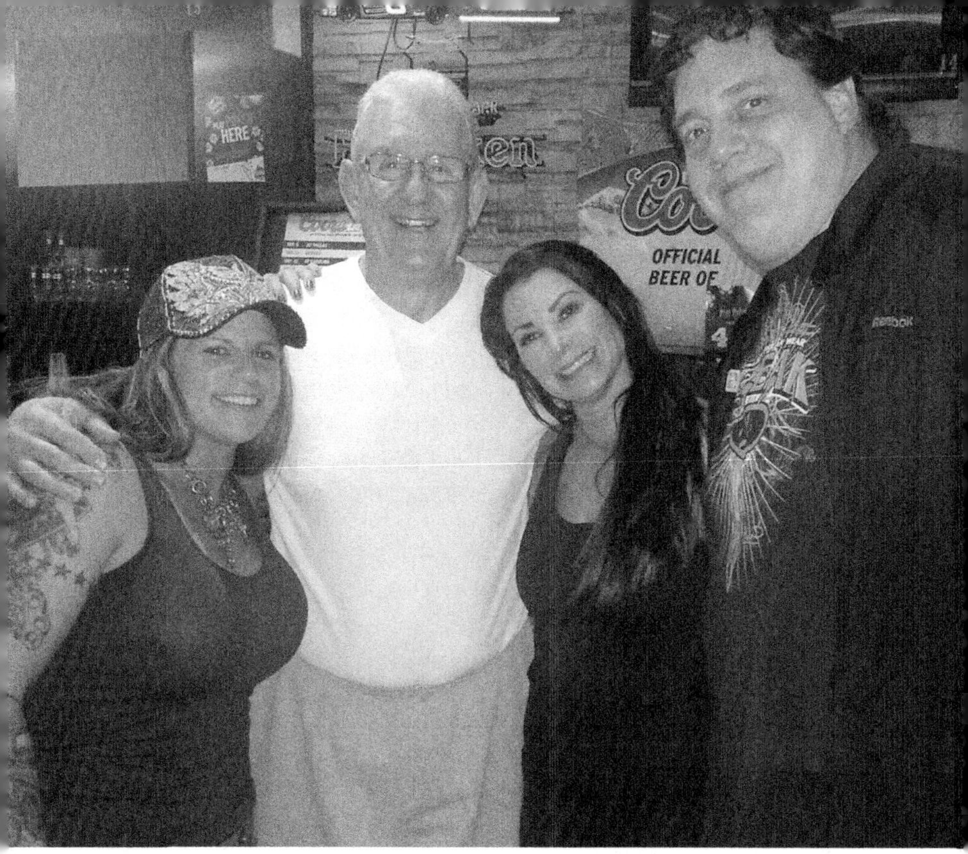
HERE
OFFICIAL
BEER OF

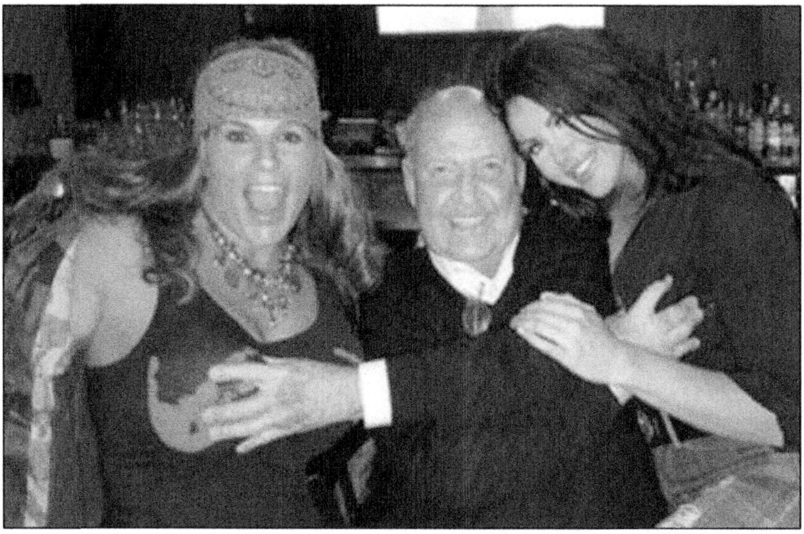

CHAPTER 15 - BURNT ENDS

To take things to the next level and reach my potential with my new food truck, I knew I had to set up shop outside a major wrestling event, then I would be hitting the optimal target demographic. I was banking that they would all want to buy food from a wrestler over anyone else if they could, just because it was a wrestler. The whole idea after all was you got the experience as well as the food.

The timing was perfect. I set things up with some friends to be at that first All Elite Wrestling (AEW) show when *Starrcast III* was in Chicago.

Now, I was legit booked for the 21-Women Casino Battle Royale during *AEW All Out: The Buy In* pre-show. But I asked to be a surprise so I could also work it in my truck.

Before the show had even started, I had made bank. I was right. I had a line down the street all day and more business than I had ever seen my truck make before. That type of turnout was like my Black Friday. I sold more shit than I could even carry.

It was pretty damn cool! I was there with my food truck and everyone was rolling up on me, ODB. I wasn't just some wrestler selling food to them like many of my customers were. The gimmick worked perfectly. It was wrestling fans who wanted food and also wanted to meet someone they admired from television.

"ODB!" they would say before placing their order. "Big fan!"

I had been off TV for a bit trying to get my food stuff together, but wrestling fans are among the most loyal fans in the world. None of them forgot about me.

"Will you be in the girls' battle royal?" many of them would ask.

"Nah, I'm just here with my food truck," I would say kayfabing the surprise.

"Come on ODB," a fan would say as I handed them a big cone of pulled pork with some of the most scrumptious sauce you have ever had. "What if like Angelina Love or someone gets in your face or something?"

"Well, I always bring my gear with me!" I said, playing along. "I mean, I could fight in my jeans if I have to. But, if any of those bitches wants to challenge my ass, I'm ready!"

Then, the show started. When I finally came out, all of those super loyal fans were like, "Holy Crap!"

It felt pretty damn good hearing 15,000 people chanting ODB again!

Wrestling is an addiction.

I want to do this again! I want to keep doing this again!

When it was all over, I rushed outside after the show and sold even more. The fans didn't want it to end, and to be honest, neither did I.

ODB ON FIRE

After *Starrcast* was done, Labor Day weekend was coming quick. I figured that I would continue to do good business better up in Minnesota, relying on the devil that I knew. It was already starting to get cold there, but I knew the natives would be out and about enjoying the last warm days as much as they could. And what better to do so than with a little barbecue action in hand, no? So, I left Chicago and went back home to Minnesota with plans to crash with my parents.

Part of the whole food truck thing is making sure you had a vendor permit if one was needed, and finding a place to set up shop. In this case, neither was a problem. I had my permit, and I had my place.

I parked the Meat & Greet at a bar called The Maple Tavern. It was owned by a friend of mine named Chad who was always a big supporter of mine. Chad was on vacation, but always happy to lend a hand. I had free reign to do whatever I wanted in his lot, short of bodyslamming anyone of course.

I parked at my buddy's bar in the far end of the parking lot by the road as planned, and just as I thought, I had picked well. As they always say, the three most important things about a business are location, location, location. I did a pretty good job there and was doing a lot of business. Everything was going great.

After one day's hard work, I retired to my parents' house to spend the night. The sun had already set, and I was in bed. I was dozing off with some dumb rerun on TV in my old bedroom.

Over at The Maple Tavern, it was business as usual. People were having a good old time at one of their favorite watering holes, and all was good in life.

The Maple millers were milling about and drinking when all of a sudden, a guy came running in.

"I think that wrestler girl's truck is on fire," he said to the bartender.

"What?"

"I smelled like rubber burning or something," he explained. "When I went over to see what was going on, I could see black smoke coming out of the doors and window frames."

A handful of guests rushed to the window. A few looked out puzzled and then headed to the door. One returned.

"Hey man, he's right!"

Now, the bartender wasn't Chad and so he had no idea how to get a hold of me. First, he called the fire department, then Chad. Chad didn't answer.

"I have no idea how to reach her," he said.

A couple of people I knew from The Lil' Bar, Holly and Ryan, were also there coincidentally playing darts. They had dropped everything and looked outside. Fortunately for me, Holly heard what was going on and stumbled to find her phone. "Oh my God. Oh my God."

My phone woke me up. It was late, and I had to get up early to prep for the day.

What the hell?

I picked up the phone.

"Uh, hello?" I said, half expecting it to be some dumb wrestling rib or something. I was pissed knowing I had to get up early in the morning.

"Your food truck is on fire!" I heard from the voice on the line.

What is this bullshit?

I thought someone was just busting my ass at first. You know how wrestlers like their pranks. However, once I realized it wasn't a joke, everything changed.

"What the f...."

"Seriously, Jess!" the familiar voice said. "This is Holly from The Lil' Bar. There's all this black smoke, and it looks like flames inside! Quick! Get over here!"

I don't remember what I said after that. All I remember was throwing on some clothes. I dashed right the fuck out of my room like a bat out of hell and out to the front door.

Please no. Let this actually be a joke.

A jumped in my car. I didn't even worry one second about speeding or anything. I figured this was as good of an excuse as any in the event that I were to be pulled over.

I took off. As I swung around a corner, I saw some fire trucks.

Shit.

I shook my head and hit the gas. I rode behind them for a minute or so, realizing that the odds were that the trucks in front of me were actually for me. I actually ended up eventually passing the fire trucks on the way there.

I left them in my dust.

I drove like a maniac and beat the firemen by a long shot to the scene.

All the while, I was hoping that it would all just be a little mess inside that I was going to have to clean. Maybe something a little paint could fix, but immediately I saw that wasn't the case.

I don't know why I rushed, though. When I finally got there and saw the burning mess, I wanted to be anywhere but there.

I wanted to throw up.

Holly and Ryan from over at The Lil' Bar were waiting for me. The bartender was also there standing helpless in the lot with a handful of other onlookers. He was shaking his head.

"I'm sorry," he rushed into saying. "It went so fast."

My face was hot.

There was a giant flame that looked like a demon's hand clawing over my trailer. In the darkness of the night, this evil red palm was pitching light on us. The fist was as big as a wagon wheel and it had punched its way out of a side of the box truck.

There was no window where the hand was coming from. There was no door. The fiery fingers were finding an exit where there shouldn't have been one. They were making an exit.

The fiery hand with its burning fingers was there trying to take away my career after wrestling. It felt like some force, some thing, was trying to tell me this life was "not the life for me."

The fire trucks still weren't there. Just as the bartender said, "it was all happening so fast." However, at the same time, each moment felt like an eternity to me.

My first impulse was to fix the problem myself.

I needed to find water.

I looked around for a bucket. I looked for a garbage can. There was only a blue dumpster in the alley. I thought about running into the bar and filling something, then realized from my camping days, nothing was going to cut it. I was maybe 50 feet away. Running back and forth with whatever I was going to carry to put it out was useless. A bucket of water wasn't going to do shit to that monster campfire in front of me.

Where are the fire trucks?

I pulled my phone out and punched in 9-1-1.

"My trailer's on fire! Aaaargh!" I screamed into the phone. "Fire! Fire!"

"Calm down, ma'am," the voice replied.

"Hurry!"

"Ma'am. Where are you?"

"Hurry!" I growled. My voice probably sounded like a death metal singer by now.

"Where are you?"

After that, I didn't say anything. I knew where I was, but I couldn't find the words. Every breath I took, more and more of my breath was being taken away from me.

"Um, sir," the man said, confused at the animal sounds coming from my mouth. "Please, slow down and explain where you are."

"Fuck!" I yelled. "Fire! Aargh!"

"They already called," an interrupting voice in the distance interjected.

"Called who? Who called?"

Over the crackle of bubbling paint, I finally heard the sirens bouncing off a building. I hung up and pushed the phone back into my hoodie.

My call didn't matter. They already knew. Either someone else had the foresight of calling the fire department before me, or the growing bonfire before me had tipped them off. (It felt like forever, but it wasn't. To the fire department's credit, they probably showed up maybe a minute or less after I did.)

Before I could act, I felt a buzz on my side. I pulled my phone out again. It was my parents calling.

"Aaargh! It's on fire! Everything's burning!"

"Jessie, are you okay?"

After that, I had another hysterical conversation spill from me, with me trying to explain exactly where I was and exactly what was going on. I don't know what I said, but it was probably not in English.

Click.

I don't think I said goodbye. Courtesies were out the window, right along with all that fire pushing its way out of my box truck. That must have been one restless late-night call for my parents.

As the firemen rushed to their target, I realized that the flames had doubled.

The hot hand of fire wind clocked me.

It was the real deal.

I was dazed. Under the stars, time froze for a moment as I took it all in. I finally had a life after wrestling within my reach, but then I saw it all melting before my very eyes. Reality hit. My new life was being pulled away from me. Ripped away from me.

All my hard work, all of my time...

It was a giant smack in the face to watch my hard work literally going up in smoke.

"Oh my God," I said. "Please. Please."

I took two hesitant steps then ran right towards the arms of the fiery devil himself. But just before I got there, I felt somebody else's arms stop me. They were the yellow sleeves of a fireman.

"Hey, hey," he said. "Back up!"

"You don't understand. That's my..."

He cut me off. He didn't say anything, but just shook his head.

"My... my whole business," I said sucking back a sob.

Everything seemed surreal. It looked like a scene out of a movie.

Here I was, a big tough fighter, but I was in a battle I couldn't win. I had to let them fight for me. I had no choice. There was nothing I could do. I had to let them do their job.

I turned to find sanctuary in familiar faces. I reluctantly walked back to Holly who frowned and put her arm around my shoulders. I tilted my head a little. Then, I watched helplessly as the firemen went to work.

Another pair of firemen pulled the hoses from the side of the truck. Water immediately filled the flat tubing and then jetted its contents onto the fiery center.

Hush... Shhh...

The same fireman who stopped me from running right into the inferno was on safety duty. I watched as he backed up the sidewalkers who were gathering at 2 a.m. to see what the hell was going on. He ushered the pile of people backwards towards us into the parking area, and I pushed my way back to the front of the crowd to reclaim my front row seats to hell.

The firemen swayed from side to side under the pressure. The blue stream of water traded blows with the bright red flames.

It burned. The box truck ached in pain, until the weird orange glowing hand of light flickered. It lowered in intensity as the beams of liquid touched down on them. First the claws disappeared, then the fingers, one by one. Black smog filled the empty space and drifted into the air.

The fire hand was finally out cold.

Once the firefighting was over, I was told to go home. They knew I was exhausted and in total shock. I was no good to anybody in the shape that I was in. My directions were to leave, get some sleep, then figure everything out in the morning.

It was the last hours of the worst night of my life, and I just wanted it all over then, but I listened. I had no strength left in me.

There is nothing left.

I hugged Holly and Ryan goodbye and thanked them. Then, I took the first few slow steps in my walk of shame towards my car.

Chin up. You are a fighter.

I had lost, but I tried to look positive as I left. I tried to think positive.

Somebody's words echoed in my head: "At least nobody got hurt." That much was true. However, my mind did not stay in the positive zone.

"Nobody got hurt," I retold myself, hoping to convince myself that was all that mattered. I headed back to my parents' house to try to sleep, but somehow, I knew that just wasn't happening.

My parents met me in the doorway. I gave them the Cliff Notes version of what had happened and promised to tell them more in the morning. I repeated somebody's words on auto-play to my mother.

They both hugged me goodnight, and repeated back to me, "At least nobody got hurt."

I looked in the mirror. Runny mascara had left my eyes completely black. I had a handprint of soot on my face. My hair was a mess. I shook my head not knowing what to do.

I shut off the light and tried to get at least an hour or two of sleep.

"At least nobody got hurt," I told myself.

But I was hurting.

THE MORNING AFTER

It wasn't long before I was right back at that parking lot, ready to see the charred mess in the daylight.

I didn't cry that night, but the next morning, I broke down. I mean, that box truck was my everything. It had been my life for the past three years, and it was what I was banking on for the next three years of my life!

I cried at what was left standing before me. I cried for my past. I cried for my future.

I busted my ass building this business.

I looked at the smoky mess hoping and wondering if any bit of it could be fixed, and I knew the answer. That shit was gone.

Nothing was salvageable.

Now, there had been no explosion. There was no propane on hand. Everything I used in the food truck was electric. As I stared off into the collapsed structure, I just couldn't figure out what had happened.

All I had left was an empty carcass, and an empty heart.

I picked through the mess. A few fans took some pictures for a dirt sheet. One offered to send me some of them, and I took him up on that.

A kid came up to me after and offered condolences, like it was a funeral.

"Will insurance cover it?"

My parents had asked me this the night before. I said something like "of course," but in reality, I didn't know how much.

My next move, was certainly going to be the fun part. I had to call to see what I could retain.

I made the call, and you guessed it; insurance companies suck.

My insurance company wanted to give me like a thousand or two, but they were easily $60,000 off.

I didn't even say anything at first on that initial phone call. We were so far off that I didn't see how they would ever even come close.

"Okay," I said after feeling the drizzling dogshit splatters that they were dropping on me. "I don't see how this is going to work."

I hung up.

Because it wasn't "damage to an actual vehicle part" of a truck, the insurance decided they were going to "cheap out." You see, a box trailer by itself was only worth a few grand, and mine was used. They took nothing else into consideration.

There was no way a few grand would cover what I needed to replace it. A few grand wasn't going to pay for everything inside of it that burned and all the custom work that had been made to the structure itself. Box trucks don't come stock with windows, custom paint jobs, and all the serving amenities needed to be a food truck.

Keep your chin up.

After that, I didn't call the insurance company back. They were going to be of no help to me anytime soon. Instead, I decided to shift focus.

& GREET
FOOD
TRUCK CO.

We are going to get through this.

As I have said before, "wrestling fans are the most loyal fans in the world." I decided to put my misfortune into their hands and believe. I posted some of the fan's pictures on social media not knowing what to expect.

TheODBbam: *Woke up to my food truck on fire. Still in shock... nobody was hurt. I'm stayin positive and it will be one helluva Meat & Greet coming soon!!!! #hookinupwithodb #foodtrucks #foodtruck*

I had hoped that some loyal wrestling fan with a law background would see the mess and give me some advice on what I needed do to save my business.

I was right. People came out of the woodwork wanting to help. Wrestling fans and wrestlers from all walks of life were there showing support.

I can't tell you how many people lifted my spirits that day. I can't tell you how much I needed it. All I can tell you is that so many people came through for me when I needed it most. Thank you for that. I really appreciate it.

It is then that I realized the power of being grateful. Being humble and being thankful was all I had left, and it was the best weapon I could have ever had.

Rather than giving up and walking away defeated, I listened. I heard how other people in my shoes dealt with similar situations and thanked anybody I could for their insight.

EVERYTHING HAPPENS FOR A REASON

After that, Diamond Dallas Page (DDP) reached out to me. "O-M-G!" my fellow wrestler said to me on the phone, spelling out each one of the letters individually. "You just got that truck, too?"

"Yep," I said dejected.

"That's terrible."

Just like all the wrestlers had got to see my food truck at that AEW event, DDP realized it was my new baby and it was gone. These days, for those of you who may have been living under a rock, DDP has become a savior to many.

Therefore, it was great to hear from him and no surprise when he extended a hand immediately without a second thought.

"I really want to help, what can we do?"

Soon after that, I was flying out to the *DDY YOGA* Performance Center in Smyrna, Georgia.

Did I mention that DDP is the man?

Back in the day if you had asked the locker room, nobody could have predicted that DDP would have put together a health craze like DDP YOGA that would help people all over the world. Hell, when it was first introduced, people were skeptical.

Knowing DDP was a wrestler, many people figured that it was all probably some gimmick to make a couple of dollars after his time in the ring was drying up. Nobody realized that his plan B would arguably surpass his plan A, and change people's lives forever.

DDP was kind of a man's man in the locker room. He was someone who nobody expected would be doing yoga in the gym, or as a workout back then. However, in the twilight of his in-ring career, things needed to change.

DDP ruptured the L4 and L5 discs in his back, and he was messed up.

Out of desperation, he tried anything to help and nothing worked, until he started mixing Yoga with aerobics and a healthy diet.

It worked.

With such great results, he decided others needed to hear about it, so he paid it forward. His plan immediately helped people with unhealthy lives who had struggled with weight loss their whole lives.

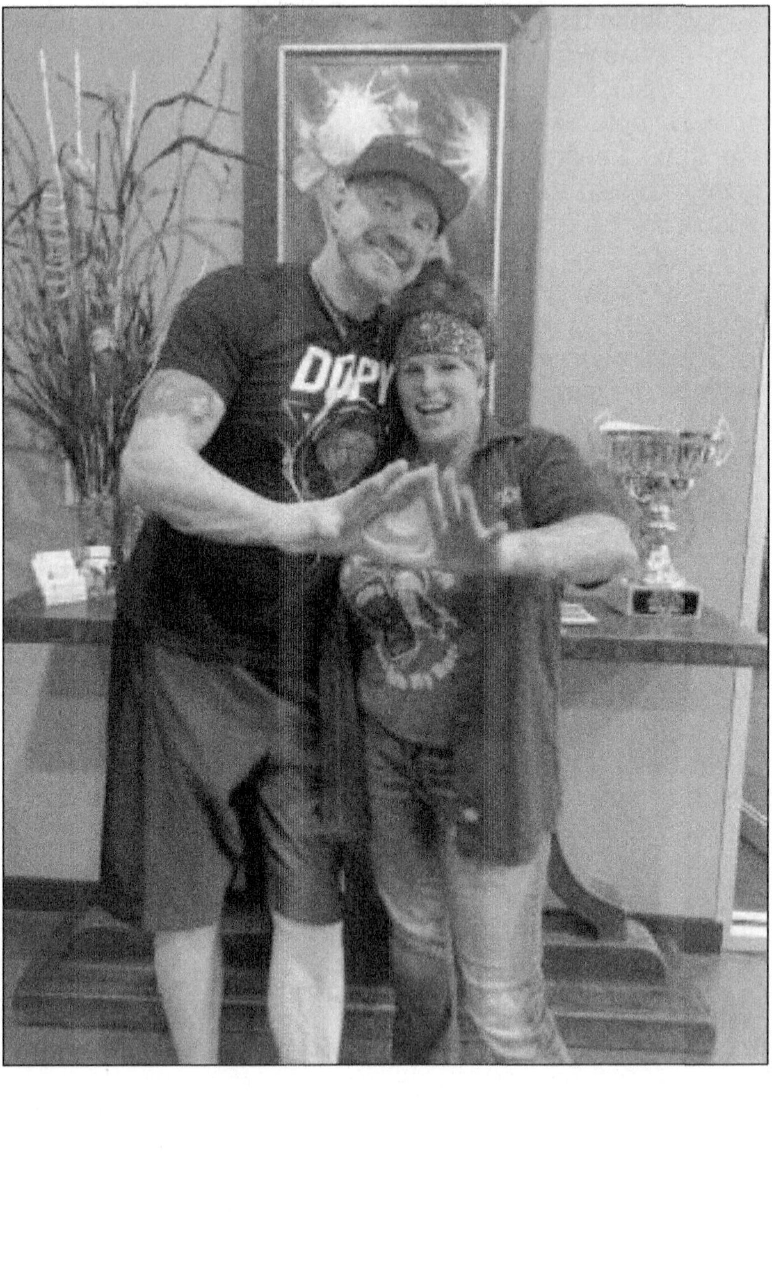

"Weight loss just happens to be a really awesome side effect of DDP Yoga," he says.

I keep preaching this whole plan B thing, but a piece of the puzzle I left out of the equation is passion. DDP found passion in what he was doing and it created a new direction for where he wanted to go for the rest of his life after wrestling.

He also recognized the passion I was developing in this new chapter of my life, and how the carpet was ripped out from under me. He put together a DDP YOGA event and quickly raised money for me. He started a fund for truck replacement, to the tune of $25,000.

"Holy shit!" I said to the other wrestler with three letters for a name. "Thank you so much."

And that wasn't all.

I still talked to a lot of guys in the wrestling business, so when Tommy Dreamer reached out to me, I figured it was just to see how things were going. That wasn't the case. After his call, Scott D'Amore reached out to me and then, Josh Mathews.

What the hell? Holy crap! I was NOT expecting this!

The boys at Impact Wrestling booked me and paid me to appear for what they were calling *ODB Appreciation Night*. When I showed up, I found out that *ODB Appreciation Night* also meant that they were donating 100 percent of the proceeds from their NYC TV tapings to my food truck cause.

Ever notice how in wrestling everybody calls each other "brother"? It's because we are family. They, too, just like DDP, were more than happy to present me with a hefty check – all because of our wrestling family connection.

TNA has always been my home, and it felt pretty damn good to know they still loved me. We've always had a pretty good relationship. They have been good to me and still continue to bring me in from time to time. I'm always excited to go back and see what TNA has in store for ODB.

And after that, I found out that wasn't all.

After that, I was home again, back on the phone with the insurance company. I had no intentions of pocketing any money. I wanted to stay persistent and true to my dream. I called the insurance over and over again, every day. That didn't really work right away, but after talking about my situation on social media in front of the world, I finally got a call back. As they say, "airing a grievance on Twitter sometimes helps," and for me – it did.

The insurance finally gave me what I needed to replace the whole trailer, including customizations for food services, with a new one.

But wait, there's more.

Before I could even start shopping, soon after that, "The Hardcore Legend" himself, Mick Foley, called. Soon after that, I was both having a nice day and having a nice flight.

Foley has a phenomenal one-man show that he does at comedy clubs around the world for his plan B... his "life after wrestling." (If you haven't seen it, you should! Let me tell you, he is an excellent storyteller and very funny!) He called to tell me he wanted me on his show. He was out on the west coast and wanted to fly me in as his guest.

So just after my TNA appreciation appearance, I was off doing yet another ODB Appreciation on Sunday, November 10th, but this time in San Jose, California.

Like me and Traci Brooks, Mick was legendary for being cheap on the road, but that night, you would never know it. Not only did I get booked to appear on his show for a super generous booking fee, but Mick also donated all of the ticket money to my food truck cause.

"We raised almost $15,000 in one night for ODB," Mick said recently, "...and that was one of the highlights of the entire tour. The crowd was good and they really wanted to support ODB and get her cooking again on her food truck!"

Mick was right. I could not believe the love from everyone in the wrestling community. Money came in from everywhere.

In the end, on top of the insurance payout, I had collected $41,000. The wrestling world had blessed me with more than double what the box trailer was worth to replace. The donations were perfect for me to upgrade.

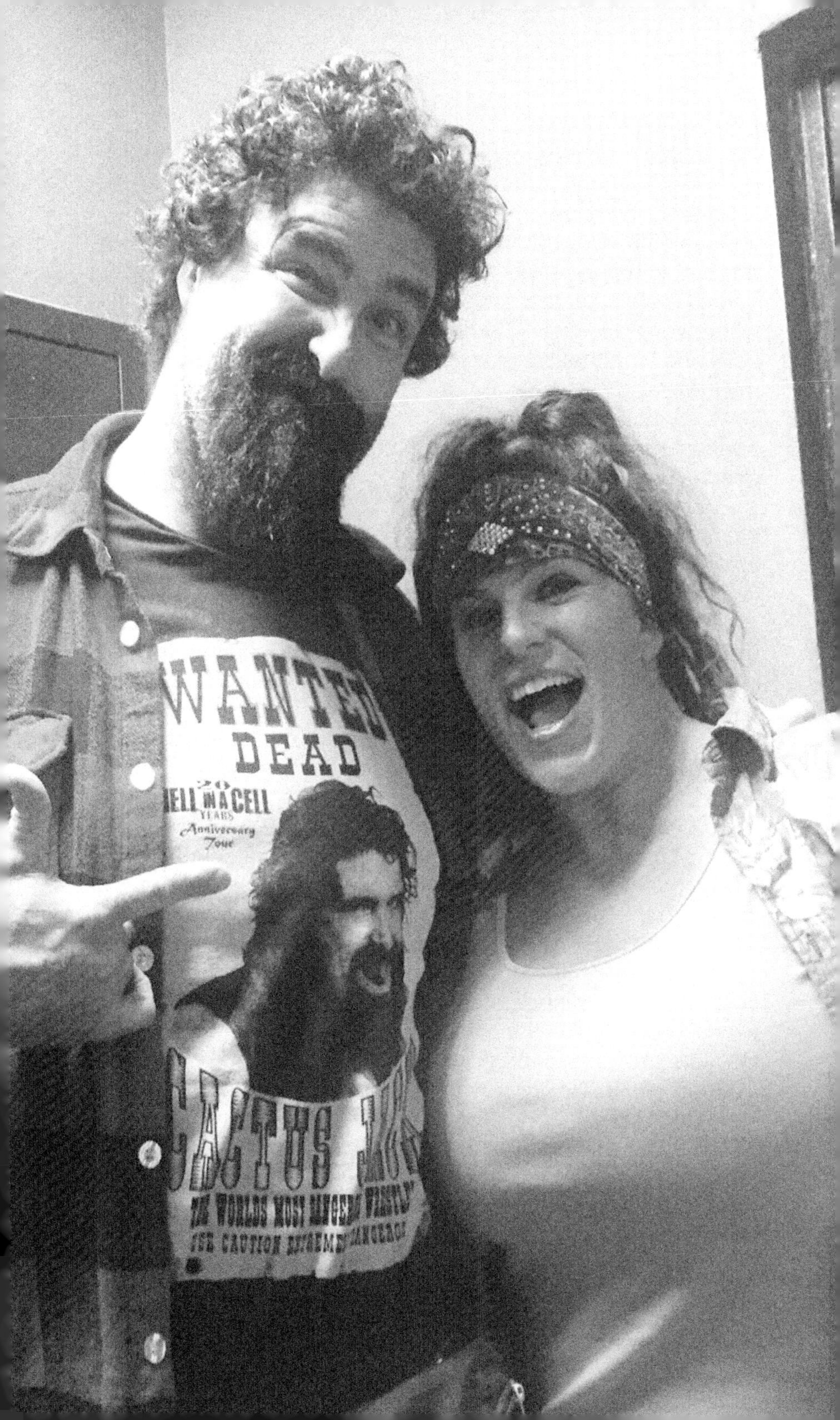
DEAD
Anniversary

LIFE AFTER DEATH

Now, I am probably considered a grizzled ring vet. I'm not going to name names, but I am sure that a number of wrestlers who have had GoFundMe campaigns and also various other crowd-sourcing fundraisers in their names could and would have just pocketed that money. After all, wrestling has its roots in the carnival. Wrestling itself is a big work where we make our living off of working our fans into believing stuff that is not true. However, I could not do that to my people.

I took all of that money and put it into the biggest, baddest, best version of a food tuck that the world has ever seen.

No longer was ODB's Meat & Greet going to be a pull-along trailer, but this upgrade was going to give the food truck its own motor.

Yep, you guys brought my food truck to life.

My truck had fried and died. What was once my dream had turned into a nightmare. I had no idea that the resurrection was going to be even possible when I saw the charred remains of the next chapter of my life before me. But then, only a few short months after all that mess, my plan B came back, better than ever, flying like a phoenix out of the ashes.

Then there was life.

I took that money and bought the equivalent of a UPS delivery vehicle. I had it customized with all the trimmings.

In the end, it was, to me, the mack daddy of all food trucks – my real dream come true.

My new baby is a 30-foot drivable beast. It is a custom-made stainless steel gift from the gods. It has just what I needed, plus the extra bonus of having the barbecue smokers built-in inside.

I can do anything with this new truck. Cater an inside event, or serve delicious food right out of the side window.

Now I have a massive, professional grade Rec Tec Smoker, which is a smoker that does 30 pork butts all at the same time. I can feed an army with that thing. Since then, no more working for tips at The Sausage Castle for me.

In recent days, I have been working hard. I have found success at big wrestling events serving the hungry fans, but that is not all. I have also found that setting up my truck around big concerts in the music world also work great!

Plan B is a success! Onward and upward for plan C.

The food truck business is great. I am happy to report that I have been doing well for myself. You shouldn't be surprised if you head out to a show to see Kid Rock, Luke Bryan, or even Lizzo and see the ODB food truck outside serving my peeps. *Yes, even Lizzo!*

She too is another tough cookie who isn't afraid of breaking the cookie cutter. Incidentally, I remember when I first got the food gig for one of her shows, I thought to myself, "What is Lizzo going to be like? Will it be a bunch of young kids with no money?"

Nope.

It was hungry housewives and dads with daughters, who all bought a ton of food from the brand new truck my wrestling family gave back to me. Thank you for that!

Everything happens for a reason.

FINAL NOTE TO FANS

To my fans who have supported me over the years:

Thank you so much for going on this journey with me. Oh, the life I've lived as a rolling stone. I've traveled the country and the world because of you, doing what I do best – kickin' ass. You gave me all that energy and adrenaline when you chanted in the arena, "ODB! ODB!" That was just crazy. It is a feeling I'll have with me forever.

But in the end of the night when that curtain closes, I put all of that away. I'm just Jessie, a girl who loves to live. I've lived my life all these years doing things my way, my rules; I've always had no strings attached and no commitments being this rolling stone never settling down until now.

I knew one day when I was ready it would be all worth it… That time is now. Looks like sometime next year, I'll be getting together one more time with all my girls, but not to fight – only love. This time, I'll be getting married for real.

Thanks for everything!
Jessie

CREDITS

AUTHOR:
Jessie "The ODB" Kresa

CO-AUTHOR:
Kenny Casanova

EDITOR:
Jamie Hemmings

LEGAL STUFF:
Marty Carbone

RESEARCH WORK:
"Timeline Master" Jim Ruehrwein
Rob Rosen
Mike Johnson

BEHIND THE SCENES:
Maria Bevan, Kerri Bevan

QUOTES & CONTENT:
Mick Foley (Foreword)
Al Snow (Back Cover)
Traci Brooks
Lisa Marie Varon
Jimmy Hart
DDP
Bob Evans
Ed Hellier
Carmine DeSpirito

PUBLISHING INFO:
Check out WOHW.com for more books like this including:
Kamala Speaks, Brutus Beefcake, Mr. X ~Dangerous Danny Davis, Vader Time, TAG, Sabu: Scars, Silence, & Superglue, Tito Santana: Don't Call Me Chico and Just a Dream to... Justin Credible.

PHOTO COLLECTION CONTRIBUTIONS:
Mary-Kate Anthony (Cover)
Scott McGregor (Cover design)
The Kresa Family
Jill A. McKee
Wayne McCarty
Catherine Riccio
George Tahinos
Dr. Mike Lano

HELPFUL RESOURCES:
odbsmeatngreet.com
KennyCasanova.com
WOHW.com

VERY SPECIAL THANKS FROM KENNY CASANOVA:
"I dedicate my work to my badass wife Maria for the countless hours spent on this project! ...To Marty EAD! ...And to you the reader for supporting wrestling books and keeping the legends alive!"

Kenny Casanova is a pro wrestling manager, a wedding DJ, an author, English teacher, and also a Fulbright Scholar. As the organizer of this project and other ones like it, his recent mission of late has been helping professional wrestlers get their stories out for the appreciation of future generations.

Email questions or promotional inquiries to Kenny Casanova at **ken@kennycasanova.com**, or find him on all social media platforms.

Printed in Great Britain
by Amazon